SILENT VOICES

SILENT VOICES

PUBLIC OPINION AND
POLITICAL PARTICIPATION
IN AMERICA

Adam J. Berinsky

PRINCETON UNIVERSITY PRESS

PRINCETON AND OXFORD

SECOND PRINTING, AND FIRST PAPERBACK PRINTING, 2006

PAPERBACK ISBN-13: 978-0-691-12378-3

PAPERBACK ISBN-10: 0-691-12378-0

THE LIBRARY OF CONGRESS HAS CATALOGED THE CLOTH EDITION

OF THIS BOOK AS FOLLOWS

BERINSKY, ADAM J., 1970–

SILENT VOICES : PUBLIC OPINION AND POLITICAL PARTICIPATION

IN AMERICA / ADAM J. BERINSKY.

P.   CM.

INCLUDES BIBLIOGRAPHICAL REFERENCES AND INDEX.

ISBN 0-691-11587-7 (ALK. PAPER)

1. PUBLIC OPINION—UNITED STATES. 2. PUBLIC OPINION POLLS. 3. POLITICAL

PARTICIPATION—UNITED STATES. 4. REPRESENTATION GOVERNMENT AND

REPRESENTATION—UNITED STATES. 5. UNITED STATES—RACE RELATIONS—

GOVERNMENT POLICY—PUBLIC OPINION. 6. PUBLIC WELFARE—UNITED STATES—

PUBLIC OPINION. 7. VIETNAMESE CONFLICT, 1961–1975—PUBLIC OPINION. I. TITLE.

HN90.P8B47 2004

303.3'8—DC21   2003056326

BRITISH LIBRARY CATALOGING-IN-PUBLICATION DATA IS AVAILABLE

THIS BOOK HAS BEEN COMPOSED IN PALATINO

PRINTED ON ACID-FREE PAPER. ∞

PUP.PRINCETON.EDU

PRINTED IN THE UNITED STATES OF AMERICA

P

IN MEMORY OF MY FATHER,

Burton T. Berinsky

1931–1991

CONTENTS

FIGURES

TABLES

ACKNOWLEDGMENTS

THESE WORDS—the last of this book that I write—are the sweetest. They are sweet not only because they signal the end of this long project, but also because they give me the opportunity to thank those individuals and organizations that made this book possible. Over the last five years, interactions with numerous scholars have caused me to change my thinking on the technical and normative issues addressed in this book many times over. Sometimes, I ended up back where I started. But more often, the comments and criticisms raised by my colleagues made the final product better than it would have been had I been left to my own devices. Any remaining errors are here despite the best efforts of my friends and colleagues in the profession. So if the acknowledgments that follow seem overly effusive, it is only because I have accumulated a series of debts to which it is difficult to do justice.

First and foremost, I would like to thank my undergraduate advisors at Wesleyan University, Richard Boyd and Martha Crenshaw. Over the last twelve years, they have been my teachers, my advisors, and my friends. They encouraged me to pursue a career that I had never considered, but one that is far more fulfilling than the life as a corporate attorney I had envisioned for myself.

Next, I would like to thank the members of my doctoral committee at Michigan: Nancy Burns, John Jackson, Don Kinder, Ken Kollman, and Mike Traugott. I am especially indebted to my co-chairs Don and Nancy. I came to Michigan with the hopes of working with Don. Meeting Nancy in my second year at Michigan was the most pleasant surprise of my graduate career. Without their support, their patience when listening to my sometimes incoherent and often neurotic rambling, and their thoughtful feedback, this book would not have been possible. They asked the tough questions that I did not always want to hear, but in the process, they made me a better scholar.

I was also fortunate to have an amazing number of colleagues at Michigan and—in time—at Princeton and other departments with whom to discuss the ideas that developed into this book. Conversations and correspondence with Chris Achen, Scott Allard, Mike Alvarez, Gary Bass, Lewis Bateman, John Brehm, Gregory Caldaria, Kathy Cramer, Fred Cutler, Stanley Feldman, Paul Freedman, Marty Gilens, Fred Greenstein, Paul Gronke, Kim Gross, Vincent Hutchings, Cindy Kam, Jeffery Lewis, Eric Oliver, Vincent Price, Anne Sartori, Ken Schultz, Norbert Schwarz, Joshua Tucker, Cara Wong, several anonymous reviewers, and—in particular—Larry Bartels were all extremely valuable. I would also like to single out several individuals for special (heroic?) mention: Jake Bowers, Jamie Druckman, Tali Mendelberg, and Nick Winter. They have read at one point or another—and in some cases at many points—nearly every word in this book. The ideas presented here have been profoundly shaped by our interactions, and I am eternally grateful to them. In more formal settings, seminars at Columbia University, Harvard University, the Massachusetts Institute of Technology, New York University, Northwestern University, Princeton University, the University of Chicago, the University of Michigan, the University of Minnesota, the University of North Carolina at Chapel Hill, and Yale University were valuable as I brought this project to completion over the last several years. Finally, Chuck Myers at Princeton University Press was an enthusiastic supporter of this manuscript from its beginning and provided a great deal of guidance and advice over the last couple years.

I am also grateful to a cadre of research assistants. Alison Franklin, Chris Karpowitz, Jonathan Ladd, Gabriel Lenz, James McGhee, Paul Gerber, Ellie Powell, Alice Savage, and Elizabeth Suhay all provided outstanding assistance. For financial support, I thank the University of Michigan and Princeton University. And I thank the University of Wisconsin Press for permission to reprint materials originally published in "The Two Faces of Public Opinion," *American Journal of Political Science* 43 (October 1999): 1209–1230, and "Silent Voices: Social Welfare Policy Opinions and Political Equality in America," *American Journal of Political Science* 46 (April 2002): 276–287, as well as Blackwell Publishers for permission to reprint materials originally published in "Political Context and the Survey Response: The Dynamics of Racial Policy Opinion," *The Journal of Politics* 64 (May 2002): 567–584.

Above all I would like to thank Deirdre Logan, for everything. She came into my life around the same time as the ideas that developed into this project. Then, she was my friend. Now, she is my wife. I am happy that this book is finally finished. But I am happier that my life with Deirdre is just beginning.

SILENT VOICES

INTRODUCTION

REPRESENTATION, PUBLIC OPINION,

AND THE VOICE OF THE PEOPLE

THROUGHOUT his eight years as president, the recurrent image of Bill Clinton was that of a weather vane, constantly shifting to and fro in response to the fickle political winds of opinion polls. "Clinton's legacy is in many ways a story about polls," writes John F. Harris of the *Washington Post*, capturing a prominent view of Clinton. "It is true that no previous president read public opinion surveys with the same hypnotic intensity. And no predecessor has integrated his pollster so thoroughly into the policymaking operation of his White House" (Harris 2000). Some of Clinton's own staffers have taken the view that he was too reliant on polls. As Harris notes, former Clinton aid George Stephanopoulos and former Labor Secretary Robert Reich both wrote memoirs that recalled bitterly Clinton's reliance on consultants and polling.

Given the derisive tone of such portrayals, one might think that George W. Bush, Clinton's Republican successor in the White House, would carefully avoid such a shallow appearance. Not surprisingly, during the 2000 campaign, Bush repeatedly claimed "we take stands without having to run polls and focus groups to tell us where we stand" (Carney and Dickerson 2000). As president, Bush publicly sought to distance himself from a Clintonesque reliance on polls. During a press conference concerning tax reform in May 2001, for example, Bush argued, "I'm not really that concerned about standing in polls. I am doing what I think is the right thing to do. And the right thing to do is to have proposed a tax relief package that is an integral part of a fiscal policy that makes sense."[1]

Although Bush may have claimed not to care about polls, he funded a polling apparatus comparable in scope to that of the Clinton administration. In the 2000 campaign, the Bush administration was kept abreast of public opinion through polls and focus groups paid for by the Republican National Committee and conducted by Bush's campaign pollster, Matthew Dowd (Hall 2001). Through the first two years

---

[1] Quoted in "Excerpts from Bush News Conference on Tax Relief, McVeigh and Energy," *New York Times*, May 12, 2001.

of his presidency, Bush continued to rely on polls—especially those conducted by his principal pollster, Jan van Lohuizen. All told, in 2001, Bush spent almost a million dollars on operations to gauge the public reaction to Social Security reform and his energy plan. Though this figure is approximately half the amount Clinton spent during his first year in office, it represents a substantial sum of money (Green 2002).

Such developments should not surprise those who follow American politics. Though it may be an open question as to whether politicians pander to opinion polls or use those polls to craft support for their preferred policies (Jacobs and Shapiro 2000), what is not in dispute is that polls lay at the center of American politics. Polls provide the most obvious and ongoing link between citizens and their leaders. Regardless of one's views of the polling enterprise, the fact remains that surveys have become a critical mechanism for the communication of information between the mass public and political elites. In addition, unlike other forms of political participation, polls do not require citizens to make a significant investment of time or resources to make their voice heard. Thus polls have the potential to ensure that all citizens are heard by politicians and policymakers. Understanding the information carried in polls—how well polls measure the underlying preferences and perspectives of individuals in society—is therefore a critical political question.

In this book, I cast a critical eye on public opinion polls in the United States. I demonstrate that opinion polls may fail to equally represent the preferences of all Americans with regard to some of the most important issues of our time: racial policy, the scope of the social welfare state, and attitudes toward war. This misrepresentation arises from what I term "exclusion bias"—the exclusion of the preferences of the sometimes sizable portion of the public who say they "don't know" where they stand on the issues of the day, due either to an absence of those resources that would allow them to form a coherent opinion or to a fear of expressing sentiments that might paint them in an unfavorable light. The political voice of these abstainers is, in certain cases, systematically different from the voice of those who respond to poll questions. The existence of these "silent voices" must lead us to question whether polls truly are representative of the underlying sentiments of the entire mass public. Thus, to understand public opinion in America, we must carefully consider the political interests and values of the politically silent. In this way, we can see what information we capture with opinion polls, and—more importantly—what information we leave behind.

Public Opinion, Political Participation, and the Voice of the People

Given that democracy cannot function without some form of mass input into the political process, how should we best gauge public opinion? To make the compromises and tradeoffs essential to the functioning of a political system, we need information about both the direction and the intensity of the public will. When considering the place of public opinion in the government process, then, it is important to strike a balance that enables the broad expression of political views and recognizes that some preferences are more intensely held than others (see, for example, Dahl 1956).

Direct political participation facilitates the transmission of intense preferences and perspectives to political elites. If citizens care enough about a particular issue, they may convey their particular desires to the government in a variety of ways. They may contact government officials, donate money to political causes, or become involved in electoral campaigns (Bauer, Pool, and Dexter 1963; Herbst 1993, 1998; Kingdon 1973; Verba, Schlozman, and Brady 1995). Because the civic sphere in the United States is relatively permeable and citizens are free to voice matters of concern to them, traditional forms of participation do a fair job of ensuring that intense interests are heard in the political process.[2]

Though participation may represent adequately some intense interests, it does a poor job of guaranteeing political equality. Political activists, after all, do not come to the political world by chance. Instead, they are drawn disproportionately from those groups more advantaged in the resources that aid participation, such as education and disposable income. Activists therefore differ in politically consequential ways from those who do not engage in politics. As Verba, Schlozman, and Brady conclude, "the voice of the people as expressed through participation comes from a limited and unrepresentative set of citizens" (1995, 2; see also Schattschneider 1960; Verba and Nie

---

[2] Of course, this is not true for *all* issues. The two party system in the United States undoubtedly serves to restrict certain issues from reaching the policymaking table altogether (Bachrach and Baratz 1963; Schattschneider 1960). But the point here is a relative, not an absolute, comparison. No form of political participation perfectly represents the interests of the mass public. Thus, we need to consider the advantages and disadvantages of different forms of participation in relation to each other. Here, then, I speak of the *relative* benefits and shortcomings of direct forms participation, such as contacting officials.

1972). Some interests might be muted, not because citizens lack concerns relevant to a particular controversy, but instead because they have difficulty making themselves heard on the political stage. For example, those citizens who benefit from direct government aid programs, such as welfare, by and large lack the economic and civic resources necessary to contribute to political candidates or effectively petition their representatives on their own behalf (see Verba, Schlozman, and Brady 1995).

But many observers believe that where traditional forms of participation fail, opinion polls or surveys may succeed. Over the course of the twentieth century, polls have emerged as an important tool to measure the public will. Surveys have become a major component of political reporting, and—as the discussion of the polling operations of Bush and Clinton above demonstrates—politicians are willing to expend large sums to conduct surveys (Brehm 1993; Frankovic 1992; Ladd and Benson 1992; Warren 2001).[3] But polls are not merely pervasive in modern politics. More important for present purposes, they seem to ensure that the full spectrum of political interests in the political system is heard. The reason is straightforward: Surveys, if executed correctly, are conducted through random sampling. Under this system, every citizen has an equal chance of being selected for a poll, regardless of his or her personal circumstance. Furthermore, by underwriting the direct costs of participation, opinion polls ensure that disparities in politically relevant

[3] A great deal of evidence exists concerning the pervasiveness of polls. By way of illustration, a 1989 Roper study found that over 80 percent of American newspapers were directly involved in some form of opinion polling. And much of this polling concerns the public's preferences. While many media-sponsored polls measure candidate support in forthcoming elections, not all media polls are "horse race polls" of this sort. In fact, a large number of polls—40 percent in election years and 70 percent in off years—do not deal with horse races (Ladd and Benson 1992). Thus the media are concerned not only with who is ahead in a given election, but also with the public's views on current political controversies. Candidates too are extremely interested in polls. One study, for example, found that the amount of money spent each year on opinion polling by politicians grew from $6 million in 1964 to $40 million in 1984 (Crespi 1989). A study in the late 1990s estimated that candidates spent well over $100 million combined during each campaign season (Warren 2001). Journalistic accounts of the relationship between politicians and political consultants suggest that politicians are extremely reliant on their pollsters (see Moore 1992; Morris 1997). Moreover, a poll of policy leaders conducted in 2001 by the Henry J. Kaiser Foundation in collaboration with Public Perspective found that a large plurality (46 percent) of those leaders believed that polls were the "best way for officials to learn what the majority of people in our country think about important issues." (The policy leader sample was interviewed December 21, 2000, through March 30, 2001, and included three hundred senior executive branch officials, senior congressional staff members, think tank scholars, lobbyists, trade association executives, and two members of Congress).

resources will not discourage the expression of politically relevant values and interests. Survey organizations, after all, contact respondents, not the other way around. In short, polls hold special appeal as a form of gauging the public's will because they appear to be free of the resource-based bias that plagues traditional forms of participation.

This conception of opinion polls as broadly representative of public sentiment has long pervaded academic and popular discussions of polls. Polling pioneer George Gallup advanced the virtues of surveys as a means for political elites to assess the collective "mandate of the people." If properly designed and conducted, Gallup argued, polls would act as a "sampling referendum" and provide a more accurate measure of popular opinion than more traditional methods, such as reading mail from constituents and attending to newspapers (Gallup and Rae 1940).[4] More recently, in his presidential address at the 1996 American Political Science Association Meeting, Sidney Verba argued, "sample surveys provide the closest approximation to an unbiased representation of the public because participation in a survey requires no resources and because surveys eliminate the bias inherent in the fact that participants in politics are self-selected. . . . Surveys produce just what democracy is supposed to produce—equal representation of all citizens" (1996, 3; see also Geer 1996).

Even critics of the survey research enterprise have adopted the populist conception embodied in the work of Gallup and Verba. Polling critic Susan Herbst writes, "Modern survey techniques enable the pollster to draw a representative sample of Americans. . . . The public expression techniques of the past—such as coffeehouses, salons, and petitions—did not allow for such comprehensive representation of the entire public's views" (1993, 166). Benjamin Ginsberg offers further criticisms of polls precisely because they are *too* inclusive of popular sentiment. Surveys, he argues in his 1986 book, *The Captive Public*, dilute the intensity of those political actors who choose to make their voices heard on the public stage. As Ginsberg writes, "polls underwrite or subsidize the costs of eliciting, organizing, and publicly expressing opinion. . . . As a result, the beliefs of those who care relatively little or even hardly at all are as likely to be publicized as the opinions of those who care a great deal about the matter in question" (1986, 64).

---

[4] In the early days of opinion polling, some researchers advocated using opinion surveys as a measure of the public will in other forums as well. Waterbury (1953) advocated the use of opinion surveys in some civil litigation cases. Waterbury suggests, for example, that an opinion poll could be used to justify a manufacturer's claim that it engaged in truth in advertising. If the majority of consumers agreed that that the product in question was not worse than advertised, the judge could use that as a basis to uphold the company's claim.

What Gallup and Verba see as a virtue, Ginsberg labels a vice, but these differences are largely normative.[5] At an empirical level, there is a general agreement on one point among academics and professionals, be they proponents or opponents of the polling enterprise: opinion polls are broadly representative of popular sentiment. Whatever their limitations, surveys appear to provide a requisite egalitarian complement to traditional forms of political participation. They seem to balance the biased voice of traditional forms of participation by enabling the broad expression of political interests and thereby allowing *all* citizens to communicate their preferences and perspectives to those responsible for legislating and implementing public policy. Polls can provide—at least in theory—a clear picture of the public's will, which can then be used both to aid political elites in the decision-making process and to gauge the adequacy of political representation in the course of policy formation. Through opinion polls, the voice of the people may be heard.

Or so the story goes. In the pages that follow, I make the case that this view of polling is incorrect. The very process of collecting information concerning the public's preferences through surveys may exclude particular interests from the political stage. In the course of the survey, the interaction between the individual citizen and the larger social and political context of American society may foster bias in polls. Thus, the first principle of opinion polls—that they allow all citizens to make their political voice heard, regardless of their interests and values—may be faulty.

The Argument in Brief

For polls to meet their egalitarian promise, a set of fairly strong individual-level assumptions about the way in which citizens approach being interviewed by pollsters must be met.[6] We must first assume that

[5] There may be important empirical differences between the authors as well. Ginsberg believes that the overrepresentation of uninterested, uninformed voices results in bad public policies. This could be an empirically demonstrable point, although identifying "bad" public policies seems largely to be a measure of personal preference. In any event, Ginsberg does not provide such evidence.

[6] Of course difficulties may arise before interviewing even begins. Prior to measuring public opinion through a poll, a researcher must select a group of individuals to serve as potential respondents. So, for example, if a researcher is interested in studying members of the voting-age public, he or she must collect a list of *all* members of that public. This process is known as drawing a sampling frame. Drawing a sampling frame can be difficult, especially if a researcher wants to represent the entire mass public. Some individuals may inadvertently—or even advertently—be excluded from a poll's frame, meaning that they have no chance of being selected to participate in the survey. For

all individuals will, given the chance, express their views to the interviewer.[7] Second, we must assume that the answers that individuals express (or do not express) in opinion surveys are a fair representation of their underlying individual wants, needs, and desires.[8]

These assumptions, until tested, remain just that—assumptions. And while reasonable, they may or may not hold in practice. During

---

example, about 5 percent of American households do not have telephones. Individuals living in these households, therefore, have no chance of being included in telephone surveys. Such people tend to be poorer and older than those individuals who live in households with telephones. Thus, in practice, personal resources might play a role in determining whose voice is heard in an opinion poll and whose voice is lost. Of course, not all sampling is done by drawing a simple random sample from a list of the target population (e.g., the population of interest for study) (Kalton 1983). However, the central point here remains true of any sampling undertaking. If the target population cannot be defined as the survey population—the population of potentially contactable respondents—then some individuals of interest will be excluded from an opinion poll before a single call is even made. In theory, however, if a sampling frame for the full population of interest—here the American public—can be constructed, every individual has an equal chance of being selected to participate in the poll.

[7] Some individuals may choose not to express *any* sentiment to the interviewer. In any survey, some respondents refuse to participate in the poll altogether. This type of nonresponse—where we have no information about the selected respondent—is known as *unit* nonresponse. Such nonresponse is distinct from *item* nonresponse, where we have some information about the respondent, but we are missing data for the variable of interest. The empirical analyses presented in this book are concerned with correcting for item nonresponse. But the phenomenon of survey nonresponse has become an increasingly serious problem over the last forty years. Surveys by academic organizations, such as the National Election Study and the General Social Survey, have nonresponse rates between 25 and 30 percent, up from 15 to 20 percent in the 1950s (Brehm 1993; Luevano 1994). Non-response rates at the commercial polling houses that produce the majority of polling information in circulation in the political world, though not well documented, are often even higher. These relatively high rates of nonresponse are potentially problematic to the representativeness of opinion polls. As Verba himself concedes, those individuals who respond to polls are not perfectly representative of the mass public. In the National Elections Study (NES), for example, nonrespondents are more likely to be black and female, and are more likely to live in rural areas than those who respond to surveys (Brehm 1993). Thus, the very process of contacting individuals could threaten the egalitarian promise of opinion polls. However, and somewhat surprisingly, the existence of significant differences between respondents and nonrespondents does not seem to undermine the representativeness of polls. While it is no simple matter to determine the effects of nonresponse on survey estimates of public opinion, the existing work on this topic suggests that it may not, in practice, affect estimates of the public's will (see, for example, Brehm 1993). In sum, while the failure of certain individuals to respond to surveys should, in theory, prove damaging to the ability of opinion polls to accurately measure the public's will, in practice it appears that the threat may not be serious.

[8] Throughout this book, I use the term "wants, needs, and desires" to refer to the underlying politically relevant interests of an individual or a group of individuals. Alternatively, I use "sentiment" and "interests and values" to refer to the same concept. These "wants, needs, and desires" can be thought of as the building blocks of opinions; with-

the question-answering process, individual respondents might vanish from our estimates of the public will in a way that undermines the representativeness of opinion polls. Opinion surveys are long affairs consisting of many, sometimes scores of, questions. Some respondents who agree to participate in a survey do not answer particular questions on that survey. Depending on the topic, anywhere from a handful of individuals to large portions of the respondents fail to answer questions. By volunteering a *don't know* response, segments of the population are effectively removing themselves from measures of the collective will of the public—their political voice is simply not heard. If random, these withdrawals are inconsequential to the flow of information regarding the preferences and perspectives of the mass public. However, if abstention from a survey question follows predictable and systematic patterns across individuals due to the particular social and political context of a given issue, public opinion, as read in polls, may suffer from what I call in this book "exclusion bias."

Exclusion bias—alternatively termed "compositional bias"—is the bias that results in measures of public opinion when particular types of political interests are not represented in opinion polls. Such bias could threaten the representational relationships central to the functioning of a democracy. Representatives seeking information concerning the full spectrum of the public's preferences may, in fact, be missing the sentiments of individuals who speak in a different political voice—the "silent voices." It is critical, then, to ascertain the nature of information lost through individuals' decisions to say they *don't know* where they stand on given controversies. On some questions, only a handful of respondents choose to abstain. But on other questions—as the chapters that follow demonstrate—a third or more of the population fails to give an answer. Perhaps these *don't know*s originate from a genuinely uncertain portion of the citizenry. Or perhaps more systematic processes grounded in the social and political context in which the survey takes place are at work. Maybe those left out of opinion polls have different views from those who are included. Without a careful examination of those respondents who abstain from survey questions, we cannot know the preferences of the silent voices.

---

out these underlying feelings and ideas, political cognition is not possible. The concept I am interested in is similar to the "considerations" discussed by Zaller (1992), but I take a more expansive view of the term. From my perspective, any personal characteristic or value of a citizen that has relevance to a given political controversy is a "politically relevant want, need, or desire" regardless of whether the citizen is aware of the link. Thus "interests and values," or "wants, needs, and desires," can be conscious self-interested political drives, mere ephemeral values, or simply undifferentiated needs that could be addressed by government action.

Outline of Chapters

In the next two chapters, I explore how exclusion bias might arise in measures of public opinion, and how we can measure the extent of such biases. I consider how to conceptualize the opinions on issues of concern to government expressed through public opinion polls. Do these opinions reflect the voice of some but not others? Who are these silent voices? Under what circumstances might polls fail to represent the opinions of segments of the mass public?

I start down this path in chapter 1 by examining how it is that citizens approach the survey interview. If we wish to draw information about public opinion from individual-level survey data, we need to begin by understanding the behavior of those individuals. My analyses therefore begin with a discussion of how individuals come first to form and then to express opinions on political matters. I draw upon theories of attitude formation from recent literature at the intersection of cognitive and social psychology and sociolinguistic models of interpersonal relations. Together, this literature allows me to explore the effects of the cognitive processes of the respondent and social interactions of the survey setting on the opinions individuals express (and do not express) to the interviewer.

I then explore the implications of these theories of the survey process for the construction of public opinion. Political scientists and professional pollsters have typically viewed *don't know* responses as a nuisance—an expression of "nonattitudes." But *don't know* responses are important for the consideration of mass input into democratic politics. By volunteering a *don't know* response, segments of the population are effectively removing themselves from measures of public opinion. These withdrawals are inconsequential for our understanding of the voice of the people to the extent that such decisions are random. But, as I argue in chapter 1, *don't know* responses typically arise because respondents must pay costs—albeit small—to form and express their views in a survey. If the decision to abstain from survey questions follows predictable and systematic patterns either in the process of opinion formation or in the process of opinion expression, then polls may misrepresent the political sentiments of segments of the public.

In chapter 2, I move to an explicitly political framework and identify those conditions where public opinion polls might foster opinion distortions. Certainly, the gap between survey results and the public's underlying wants, needs, and desires is greater for some issues than it is for others. To identify those areas, I move from an examination of individual political cognition to a discussion of the social and political context in which the survey interview takes place. I examine the effects of the larger context in determining the types of issues where distortions are possible, if not likely. In those cases where the costs of opinion formation and expression are higher for some groups than for others, exclusion bias may develop. To identify such cases, I outline a two-dimensional typology of issue difficulty.

Carmines and Stimson (1980) have argued that particular issues may be "hard" if they require careful consideration of technically difficult choices. "Easy" issues, on the other hand, are those familiar to large portions of the mass public and may be structured by gut responses. These issues are simple and straightforward for even those citizens who pay little attention to the political world. This cognitive aspect of an issue—the cognitive complexity of an issue—defines the first dimension of my typology. The second dimension captures the ease with which respondents report their beliefs to the survey interviewer on particular political topics. The measurement of public sentiment concerning sensitive topics may be hindered by some respondents' attempts to avoid violating the social norms that govern everyday conversations. Put simply, issues may be easy and hard not only in the cognitive sense described by Carmines and Stimson, but also in a social sense. This two-dimensional conception of issue difficulty leads to specific predictions concerning the presence of exclusion bias in measures of public opinion. As issues become more difficult—in both a cognitive and a social sense—for certain groups of individuals, the potential for the exclusion of particular interests increases because those individuals who find it more difficult to answer survey questions will be more likely to abstain from those questions and, as a result, will be lost from collective measures of public opinion.

In the second portion of chapter 2, I lay out the analytic strategy I will use in the rest of the book to measure the nature and direction of exclusion bias in public opinion. The key to this empirical enterprise is to ascribe opinions to people who do not provide answers to survey questions. These opinions can then be compared to the picture of the public will gleaned from surveys, and the differences between the two groups can be assessed.

To begin this process, we need to take a close look at the determinants of individual opinion and see how the factors that influence the direction of response are related to the factors that influence whether the respondents will offer an opinion on a given question. Insofar as these two sets of factors are closely related, the potential for the creation of misrepresentative public opinion is great. For example, as I discuss later, I find that the politically relevant resources—such as education and income—that facilitate the formation of coherent and consistent opinions on social welfare policies also predispose citizens to oppose the maintenance and expansion of welfare state programs. Thus, opinion polls on social welfare policy controversies give disproportionate weight to respondents opposed to expanding the government's role in the economy.

We can then use what we know about the opinions of the question-answerers to characterize the opinions of those individuals who declined to answer the question. In effect, we can estimate what the non-answerers would have said if they were willing and able to give voice to their underlying politically relevant interests and values. This done, we can compare the unexpressed political voice of these citizens to that of those individuals who answer survey questions. We can then determine what opinion polls reveal, and, more importantly, what they conceal. However, this strategy is not in itself complete. Given that I assess the difference between these two groups, in part, by ascribing interests to individuals who opted out of answering survey questions, a healthy degree of skepticism is understandable. Where possible, then, I look for external confirmation of my results.

The next three chapters of the book examine the development of bias in opinion polls within specific policy areas. I examine public opinion across three diverse issue areas—race, social welfare policy, and war. By considering the measurement of public opinion across a range of important political topics, I identify the ways in which those who abstain from survey questions differ from those who answer such questions and trace out the political implications of these differences.

In chapter 3, I explicitly take up the effects of the social dynamics of the survey interview on public opinion by examining the consequences of social desirability concerns. I present analysis of NES data from the early 1990s that show that public opinion polls overstate support for government efforts to integrate schools. My analyses demonstrate that some individuals who harbor anti-integrationist sentiments are likely to mask their socially unacceptable opinions by abstaining from questions concerning those issues. Such actions ensure that a racially conservative base of opinion remains unheard through opinion polls. I also find similar effects in opinion concerning support for government intervention to guarantee jobs. I then validate these findings by demonstrating that the same methods that predict that opinion polls understate opposition to government involvement in race policy also allow me to predict the final results of biracial elections—specifically the 1989 New York City mayoral election—more accurately than the marginals of the pre-election polls taken in the weeks leading to the election. Finally, I use data from the early 1970s to show that the strong social desirability effects found in the 1990s do not characterize opinion in the earlier era. All told, these results suggest that surveys concerning government intervention to ensure racial equality—and more generally questions on racial attitudes—may provide an inaccurate picture of underlying public sentiment, depending on the larger social context in which the survey interview takes place.

In chapter 4, I consider equality of political voice in the realm of social welfare policy. This analysis indicates that expressed public opinion on matters of the overall distribution of economic resources is not entirely representative of the views of the public writ large. Using data over the last thirty years concerning opinions on economic redistribution, I find that public opinion on these matters holds a conservative bias. For individuals who tend to the liberal side of the social welfare policy spectrum, questions of redistribution are cognitively hard. I demonstrate that inequalities in politically relevant resources and the larger political culture surrounding social welfare policy issues disadvantage those groups who would be natural supporters of the welfare state. These groups—the economically disadvantaged and those who support principles of political equality—are less easily able to form coherent and consistent opinions on such policies than those well endowed with politically relevant resources. Those naturally predisposed to champion the maintenance and expansion of welfare state programs are, as a result, less likely to articulate opinions on surveys. In short, the voice of those who abstain from the social welfare policy questions is different from the voice of those who respond to such items. This result has serious consequences for the measure of public opinion because the bias mirrors the patterns of inequality found in traditional forms of political participation.

Finally, in chapter 5, I turn to the question of public sentiment concerning war in the context of the Vietnam War. I demonstrate that the imbalance in political rhetoric surrounding Vietnam in the early years of the war disadvantaged those groups who were the inherent opponents of the war. When pro-intervention rhetoric dominated elite discussion of the war in the period from 1964 to 1967, the process of collecting opinion on Vietnam excluded a dovish segment of the population from collective opinion. However, as anti-intervention messages became more common in the public sphere and the Vietnam issue became less cognitively complex for those citizens with anti-intervention views, this bias receded. So while there may indeed have been untapped sentiment concerning Vietnam, President Nixon's claim of a "silent majority" aside, it was a group of citizens that were, on balance, less supportive of the war effort.

All told, this book sounds a note of warning to those who seek to assess the voice of the people through surveys. The weaknesses of opinion polls are well known. As the critics of polls note, surveys do not do a very good job of conveying detailed information concerning the underlying intensity of responses. But opinion polls are typically hailed—by supporters and critics alike—as the most egalitarian of means of collecting the public's views on the issues of the day. In this book, I argue that while opinion surveys may indeed be more egalitarian than other forms of participation, polls too may suffer from systematic inequalities of voice.

Opinion polls, then, like any measure of public preference, are imperfect. This book should not, however, be viewed as an indictment of the survey enterprise, or of attempts to collect individuals' opinions on the issues of the day. Instead, it is a call to understand and account for biases that arise in the collection of public opinion. To measure the public's will more accurately, we should pay closer attention to just what it is that we are measuring—the interaction between individuals' underlying sentiment and the social and political context of an issue. By integrating our knowledge of the political and social forces at work in the larger world into an understanding of the individual-level question-answering process, opinion polls may better serve the egalitarian purpose envisioned by scholars, pollsters, and political elites.

ONE

OPINION POLLING AND THE SILENCING

OF POLITICAL VOICE

THIS CHAPTER begins with a discussion of how citizens decide what to say when interviewed by pollsters. I describe the cognitive and social processes at work in the survey interview. I argue that respondents answer survey questions in two stages. In the first stage—attitude formation—respondents form a private attitude by evaluating whatever program, policy, or person they are asked to judge. In the second stage—attitude expression—they communicate that attitude publicly to a survey interviewer. Depending on the social context of the interaction, this expressed attitude may or may not be an accurate reflection of their private views.

Later in the chapter, I consider the construction and meaning of the *don't know* response. Responding to surveys is an action that brings little direct benefit to citizens. It is therefore important to consider the cognitive and social costs associated with answering particular questions. Any costs, no matter how small, may lead individuals to abstain from particular questions. *Don't know* responses may arise at either the opinion formation or the expression stage. *Don't know*s arising at the opinion formation stage may represent uncertainty, ambivalence, or confusion. *Don't know*s at the opinion expression stage, on the other hand, arise because of the fear of punishment—be it physical threat or social sanctions. Understanding these two paths is important because the two classes of *don't know* responses have different implications for the nature of information communicated by polls.

In the final section of this chapter, I explicitly consider the implications of this process for measures of public opinion. If, as recent research indicates, respondents do not necessarily reveal coherent or candid answers, the possibility exists that the attitudes they do reveal may reflect poorly their underlying political wants, needs, and desires. To the extent that revealed preferences are disconnected from these underlying predilections, the individual's survey response can be considered a "distortion" of his or her fundamental preferences over political ends and means. Attention to such deviations is especially important when considering *don't know* responses, because if a respondent does not answer a particular question in the course of a survey on account of the cognitive or social costs associated with that action, his or her voice disappears from the public's voice altogether, potentially undermining the egalitarian promise of opinion polls.[1]

The "New Look" Models of the Survey Response

Conventional theories of public opinion have treated responses to survey questions as the product of individuals' attempts to reveal their fixed preference on a given policy issue. Recently, however, a more fluid view of the survey response has emerged, based in part on theories of preference construction developed in cognitive psychology (see, for example, Fischoff 1991; Slovic 1995). This view, advanced most forcibly by Zaller and Feldman, argues that "individuals do not typically possess 'true attitudes' on issues, as conventional theorizing assumes, but a series of partially independent and often inconsistent ones" (Zaller 1992, 93; see also Chong 1993, 1996; Feldman 1989; Iyengar and Kinder 1987; Tourangeau, Rips, and Rasinski 2000; Zaller and Feldman 1992). According to this line of public opinion research, a survey response is not necessarily a revealed preference. Instead, answers to survey questions can be considered a random draw from an individual's underlying response distribution, which itself is an aggregation across one's potentially diverse feelings and ideas concerning political issues.

Zaller's Reception-Acceptance-Sampling (RAS) model, for example, argues that individuals answer survey questions "off the top of their head" by "averaging across the considerations that are immediately salient or accessible to them" at the time of the survey interview (p. 49). Survey answers, then, are a summary judgment of the mass of con-

---

[1] My concern regarding the effects of deviations or distortions here is akin to the compositional bias concerns raised by Verba, Schlozman, and Brady (1995) in the realm of political participation. In their case, distortions emerge in the participatory arena because participants differ from nonparticipants in their demographic attributes, their economic needs, and the government benefits they receive. I argue here that distortions and the resulting biases can emerge in public opinion polls because those whose preferences and needs become visible to policymakers through public opinion polls—like the voices heard through the participatory acts of Verba, Schlozman, and Brady—may be unrepresentative of those who are quiescent in potentially significant ways. The use of the term "bias," then, should not be read as a deviation from the truth. Instead, as it does for Verba, Schlozman, and Brady, "bias" refers to a compositional bias. A measure of public opinion is biased if specific interests are systematically excluded from that measure. Depending on the circumstances, polls may compound and exacerbate the socioeconomic biases of traditional forms of participation, or they could introduce new sets of biases altogether.

siderations—reasons for favoring one side of an issue rather than another—that happen to be on their mind when they answer a particular question. The types of information encountered about politics in daily life, and even the wording of survey questions, can bring about systematic changes in the base of available considerations. Because different considerations may be salient at different times, the response obtained from the same person may change from interview to interview. Thus, according to Zaller, survey answers are "opinion statements"; they do not reveal a single true attitude but instead reflect a *sample* of the types of concerns and predispositions people bring to bear when considering issues in the realm of politics. How well predispositions are integrated into a survey answer depends in part on a respondent's level of engagement with the political world and his or her willingness to expend the mental energy required to form an answer (Zaller 1992; Krosnick 1991, 2002).

A second body of literature has advanced this model by thinking about the survey as a form of political conversation and considering the effects arising from the *social* nature of the survey interview. This step is extremely important. Ignoring the social context omits a key factor from consideration. The interview, after all, is a "conversation at random" (Converse and Schuman 1974), a form of *social* interaction between two individuals—the interviewer and the respondent. Thus, as Sudman, Bradburn, and Schwarz note, the survey interview is "best considered as an ongoing conversation in which respondents conduct their own share of thinking and question answering in a specific social and conversational context. Hence, conceptualizations of the question answering process in survey interviews need to consider conversational as well as cognitive processes and pay close attention to the complex interplay of social communication and individual thought processes" (1996, 55). Thus the environment of the survey setting may have potentially significant effects on the nature of the opinions individuals express when voicing their political views (for early work on this question, see Hyman 1954).[2]

---

[2] The preoccupation with the social realm here is somewhat different from the social concerns advanced by scholars critical of the "atomistic" tradition of opinion collection and analysis. Beginning with Blumer (1948), a number of scholars have argued that public opinion is formed through the *interaction* of individuals and groups of individuals. These authors argue that care must be paid to the social context of the individual. Otherwise, as Blumer notes, opinion research will fail to capture opinions as they are organized and operate in a functioning society. This line of work continues to the present day, most recently and persuasively by Huckfeldt and Sprague (1995). In a similar vein, Mutz (1998) has examined the effect of "impersonal influence"—individual perceptions of the views of mass collectives—on public opinion. While these lines of work are ex-

This social dimension of the survey response process has received little systematic attention in political science. As Green has written, "Notwithstanding recent efforts to devise unobtrusive measures of attitudes, the bulk of survey research operates on the premise that respondents furnish truthful answers when asked questions" (1996, 335). Such a premise may be problematic. This is not to say that many respondents lie when answering questions, but the social nature of the survey interview may affect the views some citizens express in that interview.

Like everyday social interactions, the survey interview is constrained by "the logic of conversation" (Grice 1975; Schwarz 1996)—the presumption that both the respondent and the interviewer will make relevant statements and avoid ambiguity. For example, the interviewer and the respondent will presume (and presume that the other presumes) that each will make statements that are relevant to the ongoing exchange of the survey interview.[3] So, if the interviewer is asking about the budget deficit, the respondent will not bring his or her views on gun control to bear on the topic. Perhaps more importantly, the social nature of the survey interview introduces concerns relating to politeness—the desire to preserve the public self-image of both the interviewer and the respondent.[4] When individuals answer survey questions, they reveal something about themselves to the interviewer. Even in a situation where free speech is permitted and encouraged, that

---

tremely promising, I argue that a concern for the effect of the broader social context of society must not come at the expense of a rigorous examination of the social context of the interview. Specifically, we must pay attention not only to the effects of social networks on the transmission of information, but also to the effects of social relationships on the nature of attitude expression.

[3] This presumption is known as Grice's Maxim of Relation, one of the four maxims—or tacit assumptions—that Grice claims governs conversational exchange. Grice's other three maxims are: (1) the Maxim of Manner, which asks speakers to make their conversational contributions such that they can be easily understood by their audience, for example, by being brief and avoiding ambiguity; (2) the Maxim of Quantity, which requires that speakers make their contribution as informative as required—providing all information that is relevant to the conversation, but not *more* information than required (e.g., not repeating information that their conversational partner already has); and (3) the Maxim of Quality, which enjoins speakers to be truthful—to not say anything that is false or for which they lack evidence. Together, these four maxims express the General Cooperative Principle of Conversation (Schwarz 1996, following Levinson 1983).

[4] Under certain circumstances, there could be more tangible costs to free expression. In countries where free speech is dangerous or forbidden, for example, people might experience sanctions for freely speaking their mind. These individuals would have good reason not to answer survey questions in a straightforward manner. For example, respondents in the former Soviet Union who were used to keeping criticisms of the state to themselves had real incentives to reserve political judgments for fear of reprisal.

speech might come with a price. One source of such costs is concern about appearing to violate social norms relating to sensitive topics.

In everyday conversation, individuals can engage these concerns in a variety of ways. Most simply, they may choose to ignore the norms and the resulting social costs altogether to speak in a forthright manner. While such a course of action may offend others and result in personal embarrassment, a person who follows this path will make his or her interests and values clearly understandable (Grice 1975). But, not everyone so flippantly dismisses the costs arising from violating norms. As sociolinguists Penelope Brown and Stephen Levinson (1987) note, people care about more than simply being relevant and succinct. They also often seek to reduce social friction with others. Individuals can follow such secondary goals because they do not have to say everything that comes to mind when talking to others. In fact, they have a variety of conversational strategies from which to choose when communicating in everyday conversation.

Brown and Levinson (1987, 61) argue that when choosing a particular conversational strategy, an individual will select the strategy that best preserves the "face"—the "public self image that every member [of society] wants to claim for himself"—of himself and his conversation partner.[5] There may, therefore, be times when individuals intentionally violate the principles governing the straightforward communication of information in conversation to pursue a subsidiary goal, such as "saving face" (Levinson 1983; Grice 1975; Schwarz 1996). Individuals may draw upon a variety of strategies to do so. When two acquaintances speak, for example, one individual may choose to hedge his or her opinions, using terms such as "sort of" and "kind of," to be intentionally vague about his or her desires and not to seem to violate particular norms of proper conduct.

In a survey interview, however, such strategies are rarely available. Respondents are highly constrained by the standardized format of the interview. A survey is, after all, not exactly like a conversation. It is highly constrained by the survey researcher's desire to standardize the

[5] Brown and Levinson argue that "face" consists of two related aspects: negative face and positive face. Negative face is "the basic claim to territories, personal preserves, rights to non-distraction"—essentially the freedom to act as one wishes without the imposition of others. Positive face, on the other hand, is the "positive consistent self-image" of the speaker and the address (61). Put another way, negative face is the individual's desire that "his actions be unimpeded by others," while positive face is the individual's wish "that his wants be desirable to at least some others ... the desire to be ratified, understood, approved of, or admired" (62). Here, my interest lies primarily in the notion of positive face because in the context of the ongoing survey interview—once the respondent's cooperation has been obtained—concerns relating to positive face are most relevant.

interaction between the interviewer and the respondent in the interest of obtaining reliable data (Suchman and Jordan 1990, 1992). Interviewers are instructed not to explicate the meaning of ambiguous statements; respondents are forced to choose one of several preexisting response categories and are not permitted to add caveats and qualifications to their statements. Respondents are therefore not able to draw upon all the face-saving strategies described by Brown and Levinson. Respondents cannot, for example, assert common ground with the survey interviewer by presupposing shared knowledge or values. Given such constraints on the face-saving conversational tactics familiar to them, respondents may shade or hide those opinions that run against prevailing norms for fear of the social sanctions that may be levied upon them should they violate those norms.

Thus, while it is the social nature of the interaction between the survey interviewer and the respondent that may lead individuals to attend to social norms, it is the way in which surveys *differ* from everyday conversation that may lead respondents to misrepresent their wants, needs, and desires on particular issues rather than give statements that run contrary to prevailing social norms. In this way, opinion surveys may fail to measure accurately the conscious will of individuals who are uncomfortable expressing opinions that are socially undesirable.

Of course, not everyone is equally concerned with how they are viewed by others. Individuals almost certainly vary in the degree to which they engage in the "self-monitoring," or regulation, of their public behavior (Snyder 1983, 1987).[6] Some individuals will be more sensitive to social concerns than others: What is a face-threatening act for one individual is not for another. We should, therefore, expect differential patterns of nonresponse on sensitive questions across different groups. Furthermore, what might be considered unacceptable behavior may vary across different social contexts. Norms against speaking freely on specific issues may be strong in one social or geographic location, but weak in others.[7] However, even given this variation in sensi-

---

[6] Self-monitoring is a concept similar to other measures of social sensitivity but, as Snyder's (1987) review of the relevant literature demonstrates, self-monitoring is more than extraversion or a simple need for approval. A high self-monitor, according to Snyder (14), is "particularly sensitive to cues to the situational appropriateness of his or her social behavior" and uses these cues as guides for behavior. A low self-monitor, on the other hand, is "less attentive to social information about the situational appropriate self-presentation" and uses "inner attitudes, dispositions, and values to determine their behavior." Terkildsen (1993) demonstrates the importance of these differences in the survey research setting, finding that levels of self-monitoring determine, in part, the opinions respondents will express concerning minority candidates for elected office.

[7] For example, a 1942 National Opinion Research Center (NORC) study of attitudes toward World War II among blacks in Memphis, Tennessee found that white interview-

tivity to social concerns, social desirability effects may affect the shape of public opinion if some survey respondents attend to such concerns in certain circumstances. Empirically, this appears to be the case. Singer, Von Thurn, and Miller (1995) find, in a broad review of the literature, that the balance of experimental evidence indicates that significantly different responses are often obtained on sensitive questions— such as questions relating to sexual attitudes or criminal behavior—as the privacy of the response process is increased (see also Tourangeau and Smith 1996).[8] These results suggest that a sizable group of respondents may not faithfully report to the interviewer the opinions they have constructed at the attitude formation stage.[9] Thus, social concerns may lead to individual reticence, or even silence, on potentially embarrassing matters for large portions of the population.[10]

Many authors in the survey research literature argue that these social effects are mediated through the specific conditions of the survey interview—in particular, in the relationship between a specific interviewer and a particular respondent. Some scholars find that respondents are sensitive to group-specific social cues in an interview, such as the perceived social class (Hyman 1954), race (Anderson, Silver, and Abramson 1988; Davis 1997; Finkel, Guterbock, and Borg 1991; Kinder and Sanders 1996; Schuman and Converse 1971), and gender (Huddy et al. 1997) of the interviewer.[11]

---

ers obtained significantly higher portions of responses indicating acquiescence to the existing Jim Crow system than did black interviewers. Black respondents were, for instance, more reluctant to express dissatisfaction with discriminatory hiring practices to white interviewers than they were to black interviewers. However, the same questionnaire administered to blacks in New York City did not show such interviewer effects. As Hyman's (1954) discussion of this study concludes, the difference in the cultural norms surrounding black-white relations in the two cities appeared to affect respondents' willingness to speak freely to the survey interviewer.

[8] By "significant" I mean here statistically significant.

[9] This phenomenon appears to be especially prevalent in questions concerning racial matters. For example, Dovidio and Fazio (1992) find that open expressions of racism increase as respondents believe the truthfulness of their statements is being monitored. Similarly, Hurley (1997) finds that experimental measures that unobtrusively measure racial prejudice reveal racism to be far more prevalent than do traditional measures of racism, which are presumably influenced by the respondents' efforts to give socially desirable answers (see also Krysan 1998; Kuklinski and Cobb 1998).

[10] This concern with social desirability, broadly defined, has even been extended to the study of preferences in an economic framework. Kuran (1995) argues that seeking to maximize one's reputational utility—the payoff people receive from public responses to their private preferences—could, and sometime does, lead individuals to take public positions at odds with their private beliefs.

[11] Even more subtle cues regarding the interviewer's group affiliation may affect the respondent's answer. For example, Hyman (1954) reports a NORC study that found that respondents were more willing to reveal anti-Semitic beliefs to non-Jewish interviewers

While the literature concerning interviewer effects is interesting in its own right, it is important to recognize that in addition to these interviewer-specific effects, social effects may arise from the very nature of the social interaction of the survey setting, regardless of who is asking the question. The norms that govern everyday social interactions, after all, are not checked at the door to the survey interview. Concerns relating to norms that transcend the particular social transaction between the interviewer and the respondent could also alter the nature of the survey response. For example, Schuman et al. (1997, 95) find that "at least some white respondents feel pressure in an interview situation to appear more racially liberal than they would indicate under conditions of greater privacy," even when the interviewer is also white. Social desirability effects may, in part, depend on who is asking the question, but pressures to hide attitudes that might paint the respondent in an unfavorable light may not be simply a function of interviewer effects. To use the example above, it is not the case that whites will adjust their attitude reports when speaking to black interviewers but speak in a completely forthright manner when conversing with white interviewers. Social desirability effects may arise from concerns relating to the broader political and social norms in which the survey conversation takes place.[12]

In the end, these results all lead to the same conclusion. Regardless of the source of social effects, it is plausible that under circumstances where respondents fear that they might be censured or socially shunned for their attitudes—either by society or by the interviewer—they might mask their attitudes when reporting them to the interviewer.[13] Thus, the opinion constructed by the respondent is not neces-

---

than they were to Jewish interviewers. The perceived political and cultural affiliation of the interviewer may also affect the interviewee's response. For example, in the mid-to-late 1940s, the Information Control Division of the U.S. Office of Military Government conducted a series of surveys in occupied Germany. Using a split sample survey, researchers found that significantly different answers were obtained by interviewers who claimed to represent the military government against those who claimed to represent the (fictitious) "German Public Opinion Institute," especially on questions concerning American prestige, militarism, and Nazism (Merritt and Merritt 1970).

[12] While we might not know the precise mechanism by which social norms affect the answers people give on survey questions, as noted above, experimental evidence has revealed that interviewer effects—and mode effects—are strong and consistent across a variety of measures. Perhaps respondents do not believe that their responses will remain anonymous. Perhaps the respondents do not wish to admit openly to opinions they believe are "racist" or otherwise undesirable. In any event, regardless of the precise mechanism, the social factors at work in the survey interview are potentially powerful and should be accounted for.

[13] A word of caution is in order here. When discussing social effects, many researchers mention only the factors that might prevent individuals from speaking what is on their

sarily the same as the opinion expressed by that respondent. Under many circumstances, it is safe to presume that respondents will communicate their attitudes in a straightforward manner. That is, subjects will often reveal the opinions they have formed. However, the social nature of the interaction between the respondent and the interviewer might thwart such a candid conveyance of a respondent's beliefs.

In sum, the lesson of recent literature concerning survey responses is simple. The answers citizens give when making their political voices heard depend on the cognitive and social processes at play in the survey interview. While the lesson is simple, it makes the task of understanding what it is that we collect through opinion polls more difficult. We must acknowledge that surveys are complex processes; both opinion formation and opinion expression play a role in determining why individuals choose the survey responses they do.

Getting to Know the *Don't Knows*

The conception of the survey response advanced here has important implications for how we view respondents who fail to answer particular questions on a survey. Answers to questions may or may not reflect citizens' underlying predispositions. In a variety of circumstances, a *don't know* answer may conceal important information concerning the underlying wants, needs, and desires of a significant segment of the mass public. The important question is for which segment is the voice lost?

When thinking about who offers a *don't know* response, it is useful to consider what factors might affect the decision to offer an opinion. Just as not all individuals choose to participate in a survey when contacted (Brehm 1993), some individuals might choose to abstain from the questions they are asked on surveys. Like scholars who study the causes and consequences of political participation (Aldrich 1993; Rosenstone and Hansen 1993; Verba, Schlozman, and Brady 1995), public

---

mind. While it is important to consider the social costs of opinion expression, it is also critical to consider the benefits a person receives from revealing his or her underlying sentiments on a particular political matter. Not all individuals are equally attentive to social concerns (Snyder 1983, 1987). In fact, some individuals might incur personal costs by *not* expressing their private preferences. Kuran (1995) posits that individuals might seek to maximize not only their reputational utility (as described above), but also their expressive utility. Expressive utility, he writes, is the satisfaction individuals receive by supporting publicly their private beliefs. Though personally I do not find the Kuran argument persuasive, we need to attend to interindividual variation in the social costs and benefits to different individuals. A social cost, like reputational utility, that might be too burdensome for one person might be insignificant for another, particularly if he or she will obtain expressive utility for speaking freely.

opinion researchers should therefore consider the decision to answer particular opinion questions as a function of the costs and benefits to the individual of that act.

One of the most obvious properties of the sample survey is its low cost to the subject of the interview. Respondents do not, after all, contact pollsters. Instead, they simply answer the questions put before them. Thus, pollsters and their media and political sponsors assume the costs of participation by contacting poll respondents and mobilizing them into this limited form of political action (Ginsberg 1986; Verba 1996). However, while authors such as Ginsberg and Verba have addressed the low material costs of survey participation, there has been little research into other potential costs to the individual of answering specific questions.

Such concerns should loom especially large in the survey setting because, unlike other forms of participation, the benefits of the participatory act are not immediately clear. Similar to Aldrich's (1993) conceptualization of the decision to vote in an election, answering polls is not only a low-cost activity, but also a low-benefit activity. Respondents, after all, are no better off materially at the end of the interview than they are at the beginning, regardless of the answers they give.[14] Any psychic benefit they receive from participating in the survey—such as the fulfillment of the need for self-expression or personal understanding—is achieved in the survey interview by answering the first few questions (Krosnick 1991). Given the apparent minimal benefits associated with surveys, any costs—even those at the margin—should tip the balance against offering a response. These costs could be the mental effort required to bring together diverse predispositions into a coherent opinion, or they could be the social costs of offending others. The central point here is that given the low benefits of surveys, we must closely examine the costs associated with answering survey questions and consider whether those costs might cause particular types of interests to be excluded from the political stage.

Figure 1.1 presents an overview of how costs related to the formation and expression of opinion might lead to question abstention.[15] In this

---

[14] Kuran (1995) might disagree with this statement, however.

[15] Figure 1.1 presents a useful mental model of the question-answering process but, like all models, it is a simplification of the real world. In practice, opinion formation and opinion expression need not literally be in sequence. As Tourangeau and Rasinski (1988) note, the question-answering process may proceed through different stages in a nonlinear manner. For example, work by Davis (1997) and Sanders (1999) on race of interviewer effects suggests that respondents think in fundamentally different ways when interviewed by a white interviewer as compared to a black interviewer. In this case, what one is "allowed" to say may influence not simply the expression of opinion, but also the process of forming an opinion.

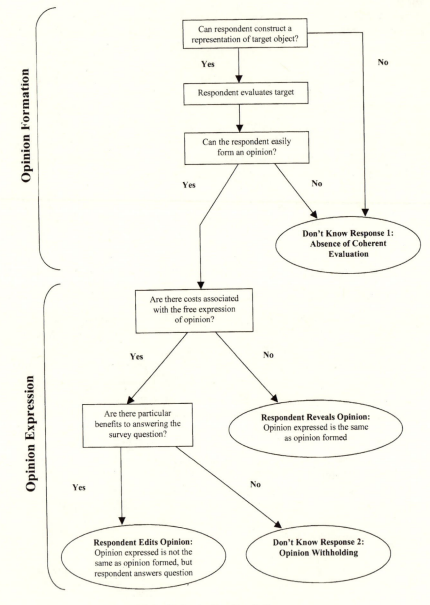

FIGURE 1.1. Paths to the *Don't Know* response.

model, individuals may come to a *don't know* answer by two very different but still plausible routes: either after they first attempt to form an opinion about a particular political controversy or when—if successful in coming to a judgment—they express their answer to the survey interviewer. In the first case, the respondent fails to answer the question because of cognitive costs; in the second case, question abstention results from social costs. Though the outcomes of these pathways are the same, the political consequences are different. In one case, individuals are saying that they truly don't know how they feel about a political issue; in the other, they are implicitly saying, "I think I know, but I don't want to tell you." In order to sort through these different processes and trace out the implications of an individual's decision to abstain from a survey question, I discuss each of these paths in turn below.

Attitude Formation and the Don't Know *Response: Uncertainty and Ambivalence*

Traditionally, scholars of public opinion have viewed *don't know* responses as advantageous devices—a way to prevent "nonattitudes" from contaminating measures of public opinion. There are, however, several reasons to believe that *don't know* responses arising at the attitude formation stage may conceal real underlying interests and values of citizens. These reasons relate to the nature of the question-answering process, the prevalence of elite discourse, and the nature of the survey interview. In all these cases, the costs paid in cognitive effort—no matter how small—may cause certain groups of individuals to abstain from survey questions.

THE QUESTION-ANSWERING PROCESS

If we accept Converse's grouping of individuals into those who hold attitudes and those who have nonattitudes, then we should seek to remove people who hold nonattitudes. But if attitudes are fluid constructions—temporally changing and subject to contextual cues—then the line between answering and abstaining from a question should be fluid as well. Under these circumstances, drawing a single, stark line between citizens with "attitudes" and citizens with "nonattitudes" is an impossible enterprise. Responses to survey items are formed by drawing on whatever happens to be on the top of a citizen's mind at the time of the survey interview. From this perspective, individuals might arrive at a *don't know* answer when trying to form an opinion because they cannot draw upon a coherent base of politically relevant predispositions. Such a response does not necessarily indicate that the respondents do not possess politically relevant wants, needs, and desires. Instead, respondents might not wish to put the effort into answering the question because they have low "need for cognition" (Bizer et al. 2000, Cacioppo and Petty 1982).[16] Or respondents may simply have poorly developed connections between their predispositions and the political controversy addressed in the survey question. A *don't know* response does not therefore indicate the lack of articulated political concerns or political thought, but rather the lack of political thought structured enough to easily form a summary evaluation in response to the survey question.[17]

Put another way, some people may have difficulty linking their personal situation to the world of politics because of uncertainty, ambivalence, or both. In an interesting and promising line of research, Alvarez and Brehm (1995, 1996, 1997, 2002) have attempted to peel uncertainty apart from ambivalence in opinion responses. While the inferential approach adopted by these authors is useful for their purposes, it is difficult to employ their method to question abstention and to distinguish among confusion, uncertainty, and ambivalence. In any event, for the purposes of this book, such a distinction is not critical. It is enough to note that if question abstainers are similar in the types of wants, needs, and desires they bring to the survey interview, the end result—their removal from the opinion signal through a *don't know* response—will have the same political implications for the creation of bias in public opinion.[18]

Given additional time and motivation to explore the matter, respondents may be able to draw on many politically relevant predispositions. For example, in-depth, open-ended interviews on the subjects of rights and liberties (Chong 1993), social welfare policy (Hochschild 1981), and equality and freedom (Lane 1962) reveal that, given the opportunity, individuals—even those whom we would expect to be reticent in such situations—will expound at length about a given political

[16] The analyses in this book do not incorporate measures of need for cognition because these items have only been recently introduced to the world of survey research (see Bizer et al. 2000). However, a pilot study of these items by the NES in 1998 found that need for cognition is predicted by many of the same variables that proxy for politically relevant resources, such as education and political knowledge. Thus, the arguments I make about resource inequalities and receptiveness to elite discourse are still valid, regardless of the direct power of need for cognition measures. Future work should, however, explore the power and effects of this interesting concept (see, for example, Krosnick 2002).

[17] See Krosnick (2002, 94–95) for a nice short summary of empirical work on *no opinion* responses and ambivalence.

[18] To underscore the difficulty in distinguishing between uncertainty and ambivalence, Alvarez and Brehm (2002) note that political scientists have used several, sometimes conflicting, definitions of ambivalence (see especially chap. 3).

controversy, though there may be only modest organization and so-phistication to that discourse (Lane 1962).

Elite Discourse

We also need to pay attention to the help and hindrances that citizens have when attempting to make their voice heard on the political stage. To be precise, we need to be aware of the tenor and tone of elite dis-course. Kinder and Nelson (1998) find that reminding individuals about relevant predispositions through question-wording frames in-creases the proportion of respondents who offer opinions on survey questions. Moreover, they find that these additional opinions are not "flimsy fabrications created by the momentary presence of persuasive-sounding frames" (11) but are instead the expression of real, poten-tially relevant political voices. Similarly, Zaller (1990) notes that opin-ion questions framed using the language of elite discourse yield fewer question abstentions than unframed items. Like Kinder and Nelson, he concludes that these additional answers come without any loss in the quality of response because the answers obtained using the framed and unframed forms are equally stable over time.

These results underscore the importance of attending to elite dis-course when investigating *don't know* responses. Most often, the hard work of defining what an issue is about is done by those who have the largest stake in getting the public to view an issue their way. Political elites therefore constantly attempt to define, or frame, issues in a way that makes it seem that their concerns—the particular values and inter-ests they support—are central to understanding ongoing political con-troversies. Elite discourse, in other words, provides recipes of sorts; it enables ordinary citizens to combine their many, and potentially con-flicting, predispositions into coherent attitudes.

Elite discourse is not, however, magical; it cannot simply create po-litical opinions for citizens. Particular ways of understanding the polit-ical world appeal to particular individuals because they resonate with the underlying interests and values of those individuals. In *The Respon-sible Electorate*, V. O. Key (1966) pointed to the importance of the elite portion of this relationship: "The voice of the people is but an echo. The output of an echo chamber bears an inevitable and invariable rela-tion to the input. As candidates and parties clamor for attention and vie for popular support, the people's verdict can be no more than a selective reflection from among the alternatives and outlooks pre-sented to them." However, the public also plays an important role, through their underlying distribution of predispositions. Elite rhetoric may indeed echo from the public, but only after reaching individuals whose predispositions are consistent with that rhetoric. For example, elites who advocate health reform programs because they expand the scope of medical coverage will find supporters among those citizens who believe that equality of results is an important value. Thus, even if mass opinion depends on the information and analyses carried in elite discourse (Zaller 1992), the underlying balance of predispositions in the mass public shapes public opinion. These predispositions—the wants, needs, and desires of individuals—are the building blocks of opinions. Without these underlying feelings and ideas, political cognition, much less the construction of political opinions, is not possible. In sum, elite discourse may guide mass opinion, but it cannot conjure that opinion out of thin air.

The top-down process of public opinion observed by Key and Zaller can be thought of as akin to radar. Through discourse, elites send out "signals" concerning how the political world can be organized and related to human concerns. When that discourse reaches individuals with predispositions that are in harmony with that discourse, those individuals adopt the recipes championed by elites. When answering survey questions on relevant topics, these individuals will respond with opinions consistent with the elite discourse. They do so not because they have been brainwashed or because they are parroting back whatever they last heard in the news. Rather, they will respond with opinions consistent with elite discourse because that discourse resonates with their underlying values. In sum, elite rhetoric does facilitate the expression of the mass public's underlying wants, needs, and desires, but not necessarily by means of persuasion. Instead elite rhetoric can guide opinion by helping people find a political voice for their underlying predispositions.[19]

But this process can cut both ways: what elite discourse gives, it can also take away. The absence of elite discourse could hinder the expression of certain predispositions. If particular arguments are not championed in political discourse, individuals with those predispositions might not see how a particular political controversy affects their interests. Consequently, these individuals may incur disproportionate cognitive costs and not offer opinions in opinion surveys. The balance of the volume and salience of elite discourse on a particular issue can greatly influence the ability of citizens to form coherent judgments on political matters. Where elite rhetoric gives strong expression to interpretations on all sides of a given controversy, no particular set of pre-

---

[19] By delineating the social norms that govern political conversation, elites discourse can also affect the types of opinions that people express. I return to a consideration of this process in chapter 5.

dispositions will be advantaged over any other. Every political viewpoint will have the recipes that enable individuals to link their personal concerns to the world of politics. But if certain types of interests are not promoted in elite discourse, those interests will be disadvantaged on the rhetorical stage. To return to Key's metaphor of the echo chamber, if one side of a particular controversy is not discussed by political elites, that silence will echo from the mass public.

THE NATURE OF THE SURVEY INTERVIEW

Finally, it could be that the specific context of the survey interview encourages *don't know* responses, even among those respondents who have a sense of where they might stand on a given political controversy. The survey interview is a sometimes difficult and often tedious affair. Given these demands, it might be easier for respondents to give a *don't know* response and move on to the next question if they have difficulty readily forming a political judgment. To use the words of Krosnick (1991), respondents may engage in "satisficing" behavior—they may pick the *no opinion* response rather than engage in effortful cognitive behavior. Thus, some respondents may offer a *don't know* response because they do not feel they have sufficiently strong views to meet the demands of the question being asked or because they do not want to pay the mental costs associated with fashioning such views. This behavior may be exacerbated by the structure of the information conveyed from the interviewer to the respondent. The use of a "full filter"—where respondents are first asked if they have an opinion on a particular issue and are then asked their opinion—or a "quasi-filter"—where the *don't know* option is presented explicitly—may serve as an implicit (if unintentional) signal that the question-answering task ahead of them is especially difficult. As Schwarz notes, full and quasi-filters imply that the forthcoming questions will ask "for a careful assessment of the issue, based on considerable knowledge of the facts" (1996, 59; see also Krosnick 2002). The very process of asking the survey question may encourage satisficing behavior.

However, simply because people may satisfice when they answer a survey question with a *no opinion* filter does not mean they are without thought on the question. Hippler and Schwarz (1989), for example, find that those respondents who decline to answer strongly filtered questions are willing to provide substantive responses at a more general level of evaluation. In such cases, the decision to give a *don't know* response may be more a function of the specific survey instrument—such as an opinion filter—than of the particular political predispositions of the respondent.

Regardless of the specific pathway to the *don't know* response in the attitude formation stage, what is important for the present purposes is that some individuals might find it difficult to answer closed-ended survey questions, even if they have politically relevant wants, needs, and desires and engage in political thought (albeit loosely structured thought). Simply because respondents are unwilling or unable to pay the mental costs to translate their thoughts and feelings into a summary judgment does not mean that those concerns are irrelevant to those who are interested in how the mass public regards the goings-on of the political world.

Opinion Expression and the Don't Know *Response*

Having considered the first type of *don't know* response presented in figure 1.1, I now move to an examination of the second type—the "opinion withholding" *don't know*—arising at the opinion expression stage.[20] It is helpful here to return to the notions of costs and benefits discussed earlier in this chapter. Just because an individual can easily construct an opinion on a political matter does not mean he or she will necessarily express that opinion in the political world. Opinion, as psychologists and political scientists have long known, is not necessarily commensurate with action. This fact is seen most clearly in studies of an individual's decision to engage in participatory acts, such as contacting government officials or donating money to campaigns (Rosenstone and Hansen 1993; Verba and Nie 1972; Verba, Schlozman, and Brady 1995). The translation of opinion to action in these cases is directly related to the costs of the act; as the costs of participation increase, the probability of participation decreases.

Studies of public opinion must also consider the mechanics of the translation of opinion into action. Opinion polls, after all, are a form of political action (Brehm 1993). The process by which individuals translate their private constructed judgment about a political matter into a survey response, therefore, is an important subject in its own right. As noted above, the cost/benefit calculation regarding the decision to answer any particular question leans heavily on the cost side of the balance sheet. The answer to the question of whether the subject receives particular benefits for answering a given survey item—posed

---

[20] The withholding of an opinion through item nonresponse is the communication of information about the wants, needs, and desires of the individual. A *no opinion* response may, therefore, be considered a form of opinion expression even though, to be precise, the respondent has not directly transmitted information about himself or herself to the survey interviewer.

in figure 1.1—is almost always "no."[21] It is important, then, to attend to those environmental factors that could incur additional costs to individuals when reporting their constructed judgment to the survey researcher. The most obvious source of these costs is in the opinion formation stage—those instances where individuals experience tangible costs for the opinions they express.

To return to the discussion earlier in this chapter, some respondents may choose to navigate awkward or embarrassing questions in a survey interview by abstaining from those questions altogether. Such a strategy brings clear benefits. Rather than putting oneself in a socially difficult position or lying to the interviewer, a respondent can simply pass on a particular question. Even if respondents do not fear direct punishment for expressing their views, the fear of social sanctions might preclude them from speaking. Indeed, Johanson, Gips, and Rich (1993) find across a variety of experiments that the propensity to give a *don't know* response when evaluating others is related to negative evaluations of the target, as revealed in responses to other questions. In other words, some respondents seem to follow the maxim "when you don't have anything nice to say, don't say anything at all." Moreover, to the extent the question is formatted to give respondents an explicit option to say they don't know where they stand on a controversy—thereby signaling that a *no opinion* answer is an acceptable response to the question—we would expect respondents to gravitate increasingly to that answer. Thus, the use of full or quasi–*no opinion* filters on opinion questions can serve as an implicit invitation for citizens to opt out of the question-answering process at an early stage and avoid a socially uncomfortable response.

We cannot, therefore, say that social pressures will necessarily dictate the relation—or nonrelation—of attitude construction to attitude expression. Rather, it is the interaction among (1) particular social norms—the labeling of certain actions and attitudes as undesirable—in a specific context, (2) the degree to which specific respondents care about those norms, and (3) the underlying needs and values of those individuals that determines which types of attitudes are freely expressed in the survey and which are censored at the stage of opinion expression. If an individual holds a view that is contrary to the prevailing social climate and censors that view because of a personal distaste for violating social norms, then the attitude expressed will not accu-

---

[21] The opinion expression branch of figure 1.1 bears some similarity to Kuklinski and Cobb's schematic of how Southerners converse about race. While this similarity is coincidental, it does point to the importance of considering the effects of the social dynamics of the survey interview on opinion polling across a number of contexts.

rately reflect the individual's underlying wants, needs, and, desires. These attitudes, then, may properly be considered opinion distortions. Indeed, the limited empirical work that has been done on the subject indicates that this might be the case. For example, Ying (1989) found that older Chinese American women were more likely to decline to answer specific questions on a depression scale than younger and male respondents. Ying postulates that while these older respondents might find being questioned by a stranger about their mood foreign and intrusive, they are unlikely to refuse directly to participate in the survey, especially after the interviewer has identified herself as Chinese and spoken in the respondent's primary language. To refuse in such an instance, Ying argues, is to not "give face" to the interviewer. On the other hand, agreeing to be interviewed but responding to specific questions with a *don't know* is a more culturally acceptable means of refusal.

Silent Voices and Opinion Polls: The Question of Democratic Worthiness

This view of the *don't know* response has important implications for the representativeness of opinion polls. When individuals fail to answer survey questions, they in effect silence their political voice. If there is no systematic explanation for the decision to abstain from survey questions, the traditional view of polling advanced by Gallup and Verba is correct: surveys are a broadly representative measure of the public will. On the other hand, if there is a systematic process to the decision to offer a *don't know* response, and if the same factors determine the direction of opinion as well, particular interests will be removed from collective opinion, thereby creating exclusion bias. We must, therefore, look at the cognitive and social costs that lead a respondent to abstain from an opinion question as well as those factors that determine the respondent's position on that question.[22]

A wide range of interindividual variation in politically relevant resources and sensitivity to social norms exists in the population. Some individuals carefully attend to ongoing political controversies and will easily link their personal values and concerns to specific issues ad-

---

[22] The most obvious form of exclusion bias is where the determinants of opinion position and opinion direction overlap significantly. But exclusion bias may affect expressed opinion in more subtle ways. For example, if respondents who hold a particular view or similarly situated points of view on a given question are more likely to abstain from questions than the rest of the population, the voice of the people may be distorted. So, for example, if extremist views on a particular topic of controversy are socially undesirable, extreme positions on both ends of the political spectrum will be truncated.

dressed in the survey interview when forming opinions. Other individuals will shy from the political world—because they have neither the time for nor the interest in political matters—and will be unable to draw such clear links in the context of the survey interview. Some individuals will freely state their opinion at the opinion expression stage, no matter the nature of the topic under consideration. Others will hold their tongue on certain topics rather than risk violating social conventions with their political views. If these individuals are of a given political temperament, bias may develop. The message here, then, is simple: the very process of measuring and collecting individual attitudes through opinion surveys may foster biases. We must therefore be attentive to precisely which groups of individuals pay disproportionate (albeit small) costs to answer such questions. It is these individuals whose voices will be silenced in opinion polls.

That the egalitarian promise of opinion polls may not be realized in the political world is not, in and of itself, necessarily problematic. It could be argued that the distortions in public opinion discussed above serve a democratic political system well. Under some formulations, it may be acceptable, or even normatively desirable, to remove from public opinion the voices of those individuals who choose to remain silent when asked their views on the political matters of the day.

The notion that some opinions should matter more than others in the political process has a long tradition in political thought. Even the more egalitarian versions of traditional liberal democracy demand that some interests be weighted more heavily than others. In *Representative Government*, John Stuart Mill (1861) argued that a system of plural voting was required to give more voice to "those whose opinion is entitled to greater weight" by virtue of their superior intelligence or ability. Under Mill's view, as Macpherson (1977, 58) notes, some individuals are "not only better than others, but better in ways directly relevant to the political process." Some early scholars of public opinion appropriated Mill's proposed solution. For example, Lowell (1926) argued that public opinion must be more than a simple exercise in counting the opinions of individuals. Individual differences in political knowledge and intensity, he maintained, must also be taken into account when determining the proper role of the public in the process of government.[23]

An opinion collection process that deliberately weights individuals by their willingness to express their views in a public forum, their

---

[23] Certainly, intensity is an important component of representation. But, as noted in the introduction, other forms of participation—such as direct contact with officials and community engagement—do a fairly good job of ensuring that intense interests are heard in the political system. Here, however, I am primarily concerned with the egalitarian properties of public opinion.

knowledge, or a similar measure of democratic worthiness could, then, yield a measure of the public opinion that is a better guide for the actions of policy elites than a more inclusive measure. Perhaps a more restricted view of public opinion, one that screens "nonattitudes" from "attitudes" (Converse 1970), could be beneficial to democratic society. Put simply, perhaps it is a good thing that some individuals choose the *don't know* response.

There are problems with such a view at empirical and normative levels. As noted in the introduction, public opinion polls are commonly viewed as a balm that, while imperfect, complements the more restricted and biased forms of participation, such as contacting government officials or participating in campaigns. If polls are viewed as a component of participation—one measure of the public's will, among many—the critical stand taken by Mill and Lowell loses some of its power. While poll results may include the sentiments of the ill informed, or those who hold weak views, traditional forms of participation compensate for such shortcomings by representing the views of those who hold their opinions more intensely.

Even if polls are to stand on their own merit as a form of political representation, the elitist view adopted by those authors is problematic. The belief that only the "best" attitudes should be heard in public opinion might be acceptable if we were to trust that the attitude—or the absence of an attitude—expressed in an opinion survey is an entirely reliable measure of a respondent's desires, wants, and needs concerning a particular political issue. But, as noted above, the more fluid constructionist approach embodied in the recent public opinion research suggests that an attitude is a summary judgment based on the considerations that come to mind when answering a particular opinion question. To the extent that the individual-level process of answering survey questions is compounded to an unrepresentative view of the preferences of citizens, surveys will exclude a particular type of interest from the political stage.

Thus, even if one believes that we should shed the uninformed, disengaged, and reticent segments of the citizenry from public opinion, it is important to identify those concerns we are setting aside. As scholars have noted in critiquing the pluralist view of the political process (Bachrach and Baratz 1962, 1963; Gaventa 1980; Schattschneider 1960), the study of politics must focus not only on who gets what from whom, when, and how, but also on who gets left out and—most importantly—how these are interrelated. In this way, we can determine what it is that we hear, and what it is that we leave behind.

Conclusion

This chapter described the intellectual tools I use in the remainder of the book. First, I presented an integrated conception of the survey response that describes the manner in which individuals construct and communicate their political preferences through surveys. This model provides an account of the cognitive process by which individuals evaluate the political world and incorporates response effects that arise from the fact that the communication of this evaluation is mediated through the social interaction of the survey interview. Individuals may choose survey answers because, on balance, they prefer particular alternatives. They may also choose answers because they do not want to violate social conventions and norms.

I next discussed the implications of this conception of the survey response for the meaning of the *don't know* response on surveys. I focused on the cognitive and social costs that might lead individuals to respond *don't know* to questions in the survey interview. Individuals may abstain from survey questions because they are uncertain, ambivalent, or just confused about a particular political controversy. Or they may select the *don't know* response because they wish to conceal those opinions they fear might paint them in a poor light. In both cases, the selection of the *don't know* response does not mean that individuals are lacking in politically relevant interests and values. Indeed, citizens who decline to answer specific questions may have several predispositions relevant to those questions. By understanding the two paths to the *don't know* response, we may better understand what interests are expressed in opinion polls, what interests are concealed, and how they differ.

TWO

THE SEARCH FOR THE VOICE OF THE PEOPLE:

CONSIDERING THE UNSPOKEN

IN THE PREVIOUS chapter, I described the social and psychological factors that determine the opinions individuals give when asked their views on the issues of the day, paying particular attention to the *don't know* response. In this chapter, I move to an explicitly political context and identify those conditions where public opinion polls might foster opinion distortions. The term "distortion" is used here to refer to compositional biases in public opinion, or "exclusion bias." As stated previously, I consider a measure of public opinion to be biased if the sentiments of nonrespondents are systematically different from those of respondents.

To identify those instances where we should expect surveys to foster biases, I examine the social and political context in which the survey interview takes place. First, I develop a twofold notion of issue difficulty that describes differences in the cognitive and social complexity of issues in the political world. Some issues may foster distortions in polls because they are technically complicated, making it difficult for the whole of the mass public to connect their politically relevant wants, needs, and desires to the political options on the table. Other issues might contribute to the development of distortions because the prevalence of social norms stifles free expression of certain sentiments.

In the second part of this chapter, I move to a discussion of methods, laying out the analytic strategy I will use in the rest of the book to measure the nature and direction of biases in public opinion. The key to this empirical enterprise is to ascribe interests to people who do not provide answers to survey questions. These interests can then be compared with the picture of the public will gleaned in opinion polls. I can then assess differences in the opinions of these two groups. In this way, we can see just whose voice is heard in opinion polls, and whose voice is lost.

Cognitive and Social Complexity:
The Two Faces of Public Opinion

To this point, I have argued that the very process of collecting the opinions of individuals may create politically consequential biases in mea-

sures of opinion. These biases, in turn, have potentially serious implications for how we conceive of political representation in the United
States. This is not to say that public opinion polls always foster opinion
distortions. Certainly, the gap between opinion surveys and the underlying interests and values of the mass public is greater for some issues
than for others.

The political world may often seem, as Walter Lippmann put it, to
be a "swarming confusion of problems" (1925, 24). But not everything
is always confusing. Some controversies are easier to understand than
others. Some issues are affected by the norms that govern discourse in
particular societies; others are untouched by these norms. The issues
that lie at the heart of the political world are a heterogeneous bunch.
That said, it is reasonable to parse the plethora of political issues into
coherent groupings. In fact, such a task is necessary for the current
enterprise. In this section, I propose a twofold classification of cognitive and expressive difficulty to capture the ease with which people
may first form and then express opinions on political matters.

The first dimension to consider when assessing polls is the cognitive
complexity—or "hard" versus "easy" issue—dimension identified by
Carmines and Stimson (1980). Those authors argue that some issues
are "hard" in the sense that they require careful consideration of technically difficult choices relating to the means by which government
should respond to (often) novel problems on the policy agenda. "Easy"
issues, on the other hand, involve symbolic concerns relating to the
ends of public policies long in the public's eye.

Though the authors developed this typology in the context of issue
voting, it has important implications for the study of public opinion
more generally. Structured attitudes on hard issues—such as the Vietnam War, to use Carmines and Stimson's model case—are limited to
those individuals who have the conceptual skills and knowledge of the
political world necessary to come to grips with difficult controversies
in a consistent manner. These people, after all, are easily able to pay the
cognitive costs associated with opinion formation. In addition, certain
groups of individuals are aided in opinion formation by elite discourse
that resonates with their underlying wants, needs, and desires, as discussed in the last chapter. But if other citizens are not blessed with
political skills and appropriate elite discourse, indecision and uncertainty might remove their voice from measures of collective opinion.[1]

---

[1] Put another way, as Bartels (1998) notes, the complexity of an individual's opinion on
a given question depends on the number of variables, or factors, that are logically related
to that question. Issue areas that invoke a great number of considerations will be more
difficult to contend with than areas that involve simple tradeoffs among a limited number
of considerations. The issues of public policy I consider in this book are likely to evoke

In short, hard issues incur greater cognitive costs for certain segments of the population, regardless of their underlying interests. As a result, it might be possible to accurately measure the sentiment of only a limited segment of the mass public on cognitively difficult issues.

For example, the realm of tax policy is a difficult issue, requiring a great deal of specialized and technical knowledge. It could be difficult for any but the best informed and most attentive individuals to discern the links between specific policies and their particular interests. This is not to say that respondents who have failed to elaborate such strong links lack relevant sentiment on that matter. They too have concerns that come into play in the formation of tax policy. But if they are not able to match their interests to policy proposals, they may declare they have no opinion on the question.

On the other hand, easy issues involve minimal cognitive costs. These issues have been ingrained in the political culture over such a long period of time that they can be easily structured by "gut responses" for both well-informed and ill-informed citizens alike (Carmines and Stimson 1980). Meaningful and well-formed attitudes should therefore be widely distributed throughout the public, regardless of individual variation in cognitive sophistication. Carmines and Stimson argue that racial desegregation is a prototypically easy issue. The legacy of the civil rights movement and the resulting developments of the last forty years have placed desegregation firmly on the policy agenda. Elite discourse on both sides of the issue is well defined. We would, therefore, expect that even the least-informed segments of the population would respond meaningfully to questions of desegregation (Carmines and Stimson 1980). In other words, the vast majority of the public should easily be able to form coherent and well-grounded opinions on the subject of desegregation. Thus, while gauging broad public sentiment on hard issues might be difficult, Carmines and Stimson's work suggests that public opinion surveys should provide accurate reports of the public mood concerning easy issues.

It is useful, therefore, to conceive of issues ranging across a continuum of difficulty in attitude formation—what I will call cognitive complexity or cognitive difficulty. Cognitive difficulty may range from (1) those issues where broad classes of individuals are able to form accurate reports of their underlying preferences to (2) those issues where only a limited segment of the mass public—that segment advantaged by political skills and/or elite discourse—is able systematically to tie their interests and values to their political attitudes.

---

multifaceted responses, but some issues—the cognitively hard issues—are more complex than others.

While the dimension of cognitive complexity is important, it is also important to pay attention to a second dimension of hardness: the ease of attitude elicitation at the opinion expression stage. The work described in the last chapter implies that respondents' attempts to avoid statements that run contrary to the norms of the day may hinder the measurement of attitudes concerning sensitive topics.[2] As the social costs associated with expressing certain types of sentiment increase, it grows increasingly likely that such sentiment will be muffled. So opinion polls on sensitive issues—questions concerning racial polices in the modern era, for example—may accurately reflect only the underlying preferences of those individuals who are unaware of social norms, have preferences that are consistent with those norms, or are not concerned with the public face they present.[3]

Sensitive issues are socially hard because it is only possible to accurately gauge the sentiment of a particular segment of the population who are able to form an opinion on that issue. Issues that do not activate relevant norms—for example, questions of economic policy—should be unaffected by social concerns. We should be able to accurately measure the sentiment of all respondents who are able to form an opinion. Thus, issues may be hard and easy not only in the cognitive sense identified by Carmines and Stimson, but also from a social standpoint.

This two-dimensional conception of issue difficulty, presented in figure 2.1, leads to specific predictions concerning the potential for compositional biases in opinion polls. As issues increase along the dimension of cognitive complexity, those individuals who have difficulty linking their wants, needs, and desires to the goings-on of the political world will be more likely to offer a *don't know* response. Similarly, those individuals who have difficulty resolving multiple predispositions or contrary arguments into a single summary statement—those respondents with a high degree of ambivalence—will also abstain from the question. Thus, as cognitive "hardness" increases, public opinion as measured in polls will increasingly reflect the views of those individuals who have the ability to answer easily the closed-ended opinion

---

[2] In certain situations, the effective measurement of public opinion may also be hampered by the fear of physical sanctions. The mechanics of the process of opinion withholding at the stage of opinion expression should, however, be the same as the questions described in this book. It is, after all, not merely the social nature of the sanctions that makes an issue socially difficult. Rather, it is the costs involved with revealing an opinion in a *public* setting, no matter what those costs might be.

[3] Social norms, it is important to note, are not necessarily static. As the social and political world changes, the norms governing public behavior will change as well (see chapter 3).

Cognitive Complexity

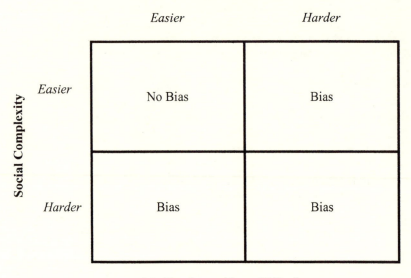

FIGURE 2.1. Typology of Issue Difficulty.

questions. That is, it will reflect the opinions of those respondents for whom the hard question is relatively simpler.[4]

Question abstention on cognitively hard questions is not itself a problem. It becomes politically consequential to the extent that the factors that make it difficult to answer survey questions overlap significantly with factors that produce opinion of a particular stripe. If abstention from a survey question follows predictable and systematic patterns across individuals, the full spectrum of the public's preferences will not be heard.

To illustrate this proposition with a concrete example, consider a (simplified) scenario in which opinion concerning the capital gains tax

---

[4] As this discussion indicates, the two-dimensional conception of issue hardness as it relates to opinion polls is somewhat more complicated than portrayed in figure 2.1. Issues that are "hard" are, in fact, hard for only a portion of the population. On the cognitive side, issues are hard for those individuals who (1) are disadvantaged by the balance of elite discourse, (2) possess few politically relevant resources, and (3) are prone to ambivalence on account of the political culture surrounding an issue (see chapter 4). On the social side, an issue is hard for those who are sensitive to particular social norms and hold views in opposition to those norms. For the rest of the population, that issue is easy. Thus, issues that are equally hard for all members of the population will not foster the kind of bias I discuss in this book. Though this relativistic notion of issue hardness complicates the analysis somewhat, it is critical to understand bias in opinion polls.

is perfectly predicted by one's income level. Say high-income respondents are more likely than lower-income respondents to oppose a capital gains tax and, simultaneously, are more certain in their opinions regarding that issue. Here, the potential for an antitax bias in public opinion as measured in polls is great because the supporters of such a tax are likely to get washed out of public opinion due to their higher levels of uncertainty and, consequently, proportionately higher rates of item nonresponse.[5] Conversely, if income level affects the direction of opinion on the capital gains issue, but not the level of uncertainty, then the supporters of the capital gain tax are no more likely than the opponents of the tax to be removed from the sample of respondents. Under these circumstances, where item nonresponse is unrelated to opinion direction, the threat of bias is eliminated.

Similarly, as issues increase along the dimension of expressive complexity, those individuals who are aware of relevant social norms, do not wish to appear to violate the norms, and have values and needs that run counter to the norms will gravitate to the *don't know* response. Opinion polls concerning issues of increasing social hardness, then, will exclude the interests of those individuals who oppose a particular policy but are concerned about the social ramifications of presenting those views. So, for example, say that some individuals who oppose laws protecting homosexuals from discrimination do not reveal their preferences because they fear they will be shunned for their attitudes. Public opinion on this issue will be composed of the attitudes of (1) individuals who support the laws, (2) individuals who oppose the laws and are not aware of norms opposing discrimination against homosexuals, and (3) individuals who oppose the laws, are aware of the norms, but are willing publicly to express sentiment that runs counter to the norms. Thus, all of the supporters of the law may speak their mind, but only some of the opponents might reveal their underlying preferences. Another issue area that illustrates the second dimension of hardness vividly is that of race. As I discuss in greater detail in chapter 3, race may be a

---

[5] Of course, it could be that the public might simply rely on heuristics or shortcuts when confronted with general questions relating to hard issues such as taxation. For example, most members of the public would prefer lower taxes to higher taxes, as a general rule. Thus, when asked, "Do you think that taxes should be raised or lowered?" most members of the public could use a simple heuristic to respond, "Taxes should be lower." However, as discussions of public policy turn to the more complex issues regarding tradeoffs between competing priorities, such heuristics are not as useful. For example, the same people who like lower taxes may also like high levels of public services, such as social security spending, public highways, and other government services. When confronted with heuristics that lead to competing ends on specific political tradeoffs—such as the social welfare policies discussed in chapter 5—those heuristics might not lead to simple answers (for a discussion of tradeoffs among competing preferences, see Hansen 1998).

cognitively easy issue, but the social stigma attached to expressing certain antiracial sentiments may make it a socially hard policy area for some respondents who hold racially conservative views.

The task for the rest of this book will be to demonstrate that the framework presented here and in the last chapter can reveal the presence of politically consequential opinion distortions and, by so doing, can contribute to our understanding of the place of the mass public in the American political system. In the next three chapters, I turn to an in-depth examination of three diverse issue areas—race, social welfare policy, and war—at particular points in time. I look first at public opinion relating to policies designed to ensure racial integration in the 1990s and the early 1970s. I then examine opinion concerning the proper scope of the social services safety net provided by the federal government in both the 1990s and the 1970s. Finally, I investigate opinion concerning the U.S. involvement in the Vietnam War across the period from 1964 to 1972.

The choice of these cases speaks directly to the two-dimensional typology of issue difficulty advanced above. The cases occupy different places in that typology, depending on the issue area under consideration and the particular social and political context surrounding that issue at a given time. Figure 2.2 represents graphically the classification of cases.

The increase in the bias in measurement of opinion on racial policy over the last quarter of the twentieth century also demonstrates the effects of social difficulty on bias. Racial policy—and, more specifically, school integration—is Carmines and Stimson's prototypic cognitively easy issue. Although racial issues may be cognitively easy, in the modern era, clear norms governing discussions of race have developed. Thus, over the past thirty years, questions of policies designed to ensure racial equality have become socially difficult areas of public policy for some respondents who hold, on balance, anti-integration sentiment (Mendelberg 2001). Thus, even on cognitively easy issues, such as school integration, the social costs associated with the survey setting may undermine the measurement of public sentiment. The effect of the larger political environment in fostering bias can also be seen in the case of Vietnam. As elite rhetoric shifted over the course of the 1960s, and politicians began to give those citizens with anti-intervention sentiment a way to link their interests to the ongoing issue controversy, the issue became less cognitively difficult for those respondents. As a result, the pro-intervention bias in opinion that existed in the early-to-mid-1960s disappeared by the beginning of the 1970s.[6] On the other

---

[6] The classification of the Vietnam case does not perfectly match that of Carmines and Stimson. While we both classify Vietnam as a hard issue through 1968, Carmines and Stim-

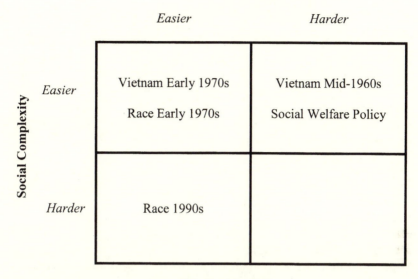

FIGURE 2.2. Case Analysis.

hand, social welfare policy has remained a cognitively difficult issue for liberals over the last thirty years. The pro-conservative bias in that opinion has remained steady as well. In sum, the choice of cases here demonstrates how the individual survey-answering process interacts with the larger social and political environment to create bias in public opinion. Taken together, these empirical projects demonstrate that we need to attend to both the cognitive and the expressive difficulty of an issue when assessing how well we can gauge public sentiment of all citizens on a particular issue.

Methods and Measures

Moving from the theoretical enterprise laid out in the first half of the book to the empirical projects of the subsequent chapters requires some discussion of the techniques I will use to examine bias in public opinion in these issue areas. In the rest of this chapter, I discuss the

son argue that Vietnam was a hard issue in 1972. The differences arise because Carmines and Stimson are primarily interested in assessing the effect of future action in Vietnam on vote choice, while I focus on retrospective evaluations of the war effort at that time.

methodological and theoretical issues involved in measuring the presence and nature of bias in opinion.

To determine the nature and extent of bias in public opinion, we need to measure the opinions of those individuals who answer survey questions, and those individuals who abstain from the questions. Measuring opinions among the first group is straightforward: we can simply look at the answers they give to the interviewer. On the other hand, measuring the sentiment of the second group is rather difficult: we must impute interests and opinions to the set of individuals who claim to have no opinion on the particular question asked of them. In effect, we must ask, "What would these individuals have said, had they given voice to their underlying sentiment?"

The Imputation of Attitudes: Paths to Bias

This task is difficult, but not impossible. While we do not have measures of the attitudes of the question abstainers, we do know a great deal about their personal characteristics and beliefs.[7] This information helps us impute or predict their responses to these unanswered questions. In effect, we can use what we know about the opinions of the question-answerers and what we know about the differences between the question-answerers and the nonanswerers to characterize the opinions of those individuals who declined to answer the survey questions. Consequently, we may gauge what the opinions of the *don't know* respondents might have been had they given voice to their underlying sentiments.

The differences between the question-answerers and the question-abstainers may take one (or both) of two forms. First, our estimates of the weights used to translate and combine beliefs and interests into opinions might be incorrect if we look only at the sample of people who give answers to particular questions. Thus, when determining these weights, we may need to use procedures that account for the respondents who say they *don't know* their opinion. Statisticians commonly refer to this concern as selection bias.[8] Second, answerers and abstainers might differ on the very characteristics that shape the types of political judgments people make. We therefore must also take a close look at these ingredients of opinion and see how the measured factors

[7] More precisely, we have detailed information about the demographic and political characteristics of many of the respondents, such as partisanship, ideological identification, political values, race, gender, and religious affiliation.

[8] To be precise, these weights are determined by conditioning on the measures included in the models. Selection bias is therefore a property of the data conditioning on the model, not the data alone.

that determine the direction of response are related to the measured factors that determine whether the respondents will offer an opinion on a given question. As argued above, insofar as these two sets of factors are closely related, the potential for the creation of misrepresentative public opinion is great. In the discussion that follows, I refer to this concern as "opinion ingredient bias."

To give the intuition behind selection bias, I turn to an example from a medical setting. Say, for example, I am interested in studying the effect of a particular drug on all cancer patients, but I test the drug only on those patients who have not responded to any previous treatments. My results will likely be tainted by selection bias, because chances are that patients who have not responded to available treatments will, on balance, be harder to treat than those patients who have not undergone any treatment.

The problem of selection bias has increasingly interested scholars of politics over the last fifteen years (see Achen 1986 and Brehm 1993 for comprehensive treatments of the problem of selection bias in political science). The discussion here is somewhat technical, but important. Achen (1986) notes that the effects of selection bias can be avoided in analysis if and only if the *unobserved* factors influencing selection are uncorrelated with the *unobserved* factors influencing outcomes.[9] Such a state of affairs will arise in surveys only if the process by which people decide if they have an opinion and the process by which they decide their opinion are independent, conditioning on the measured characteristics of the respondents.[10] If, for example, we cannot directly measure the social pressures of the interview, and if that pressure caused

[9] Specifically, as Dubin and Rivers (1989/90) note, in the event of selection bias, errors occurring in the outcome equation sample do not have zero mean because the sampling procedure has picked out those observations that are, in terms of the theory, "unusual." Achen (1986) makes the same point in the case where the outcome equation dependent variable is continuous (and is, therefore, estimated using Ordinary Least Squares). Specifically, he notes that if the error terms in the selection and outcome equations—u_{1i} and u_{2i} respectively—are correlated in the censored sample, the disturbance term of the outcome equation u_{2i} has neither mean zero nor zero correlation with the outcome independent variables, even though it has both properties in the full sample. Thus, when the sample selection process is related to the error of the outcome equations, separate estimation of the selection and outcome equation will lead to faulty inferences concerning the effect of the variables of interest in the outcome equation.

[10] Selection bias can also be avoided if *every* variable influencing selection is controlled in the outcome equation. In other words, in theory, the differences between respondents and nonrespondents could be captured in the measured variables in a model. Achen argues that it is often difficult in practice fully to control for the selection mechanism in the outcome equation and achieve this condition. In my work on social welfare policy and Vietnam described in chapters 4 and 5, however, I find that I am able to capture this mechanism with my models.

respondents with particular types of opinions to keep silent rather than express their opinions, we would expect there to be significant selection bias. Such bias could have serious consequences. If the people who do not answer a particular opinion poll question are systematically different from those who *do* answer the question, ignoring the nonrespondents will paint an incomplete picture of public sentiment on that question.[11] The strategy, then, is simple. Selection bias models are important because they allow us to account for the unmeasured (and, indeed, unmeasureable) factors that drive the selection process—here, for example, the social pressures of the survey interview. If there is no selection bias in a given model, we can say that there is nothing special about answering the question that distinguishes the question-answerers from the full population.

While selection bias may create misrepresentative opinion, we must also attend to "opinion ingredient bias." Specifically, we must account for differences between nonrespondents and respondents on those characteristics we *can* measure—what I call here "opinion ingredients." If the same opinion ingredients both increase an individual's propensity to take a particular position and increase the tendency to answer that question in an opinion survey, opinion polls will present a biased measure of public sentiment. In effect, a base of sentiment of a particular kind will be excluded from public opinion.

Both selection bias in the estimation of the weights used to translate interests and beliefs into opinions and systematic differences in opinion ingredients can contribute to the development of bias in public opinion. That is, selection bias and opinion ingredient bias may lead to "exclusion bias." In the case of selection bias, a failure to account for differences between question-answerers and nonanswerers can affect how we understand the weighting of the interests of respondents.

---

[11] As I discuss in the chapters that follow, I am careful to ensure that the differences I find are rooted in systematic factors and not simply a consequence of the particular methods I use to analyze the data. It is important to distinguish between selection bias that results from unmeasurable factors common to both disturbances in the selection and outcome equations and apparent selection bias due to improper model specification. In the chapters that follow, I report model results for a single specification. However I am always careful to check the robustness of those results. I employ different model specifications and, where appropriate, use different forms of sensible exclusion restrictions. For the racial policy questions examined in chapter 3, the finding of selection bias holds across a variety of model specifications. Specifically, the results hold if the same variables are added to the selection and outcome models and if different (sensible) exclusion restrictions are employed (see Berinsky 2000 for further details). However, in the case of the Vietnam questions in chapter 5, what might appear to be selection bias in a limited model specification turns out to be an artifact of the modeling strategy (see the appendix to chapter 5 for discussion).

In the case of opinion ingredient bias, a failure to account for differences in the balance of opinion ingredients may truncate opinion of a particular stripe. In the first case, we misjudge the determinants of the shape of public opinion; in the second case, we misjudge the particular mix of those determinants in the population.

Because this point is central to the analyses that follow, I will restate it in another way. Question-answerers may differ from abstainers in ways that we can directly measure, and in ways that we cannot measure. In the first case, we can determine how the *don't know*s would answer by imputing attitudes based on the knowledge we have about how different opinion ingredients are combined into survey answers. In the second case, we can use what we know about accounting for the nonrespondents to properly assess how the mixes of opinion ingredients are combined to form a survey answer.

It is also important to recognize that this is not an either/or proposition; both of these problems may plague opinion data. Question-answerers can differ from abstainers in ways we can measure, ways we cannot measure, or both. So the analytic strategy in this book accounts for both possibilities. First, I test if the weights given to different ingredients on the shape of opinion are accurately measured through the use of selection-bias models. Second, I use the values of the different opinion ingredients to accurately project the opinions of question-abstainers.[12]

To begin the process of estimating and accounting for exclusion bias, it is first necessary to examine the link between the decision to provide an answer to a given survey question, on the one hand, and the position taken on the question, on the other. I take a close look at both the ingredients of individual opinion and the unmeasured factors—using statistical techniques that account for selection bias—to see how the factors that determine the direction of response are related to the factors that determine whether the respondents will offer an opinion on a given question. Insofar as these two sets of factors are closely related, the potential for the creation of misrepresentative public opinion is great.[13] For example, as I discuss later, I find that measured politically

---

[12] The nontechnically inclined reader may want to think of the aggregate differences between corrected and uncorrected preference distributions as being caused by selection bias. But the term selection bias is a technical one. The correct way to think about the problem addressed in this book is that the aggregate differences are caused by exclusion bias—some combination of selection bias and opinion ingredient bias.

[13] A quick note concerning the selection model choice is in order here. I posit that there are some general factors—such as political engagement—that affect the decision to answer all survey questions. But there are other issue-specific factors that also affect the decision to answer survey questions, such as value conflict in social welfare policy and anticommunist sentiment on questions regarding Vietnam. Thus, the selection models I use are different in each chapter but share many common elements.

relevant resources—such as education and income—that facilitate the formation of coherent and consistent opinions on social welfare policies also predispose citizens to oppose the maintenance and expansion of welfare-state programs. Thus, public opinion on social welfare policy controversies gives disproportionate weight to respondents opposed to expanding the government's role in the economy.

We can then use what we know about the opinions of the question-answerers to characterize the opinions of those individuals who declined to answer the question. In effect, we can determine what the nonanswerers would have said if they were willing and able to give voice to their underlying interests and values. This done, we can compare the unexpressed political voice of these citizens to that of those individuals who answer survey questions.

The Problem of Imputing Attitudes

At this point, the skeptical reader might argue that by imputing attitudes to non-respondents I am overstepping the bounds of proper analysis. Admittedly, generating attitudes for nonrespondents—no matter how technically sophisticated the method used—is a somewhat tricky business. In effect, I ask, "What would these individuals have said if they answered questions that they chose not to answer?"

It might be reasonable to argue that these imputed interests are not valid measures of popular sentiment. Even if we take Converse's (1970) nonattitude hypothesis as too extreme, we do know that people vary in how stable or firm their positions are, with some responses appearing to vary almost randomly over time. This continuum of stability almost certainly varies across issue areas, according to the dimension of cognitive complexity discussed above. It is, therefore, easy to imagine that there are some fairly complex issues on which many people would reasonably and appropriately give a *don't know* response. And even if one accepts my argument about the fluidity of the line between responses and nonresponses, we must acknowledge that, on balance, the respondents who fail to answer particular survey questions fail to do so because they are too far to the "unstable" side of opinion firmness to do so. The question, therefore, is whether the procedure by which we impute attitudes to nonrespondents produces meaningful results.

I argue that the answer to this question is yes. As I discussed in the last chapter, the decision to give a *don't know* response does not indicate that a given respondent lacks politically relevant interests. Some individuals might find it difficult to answer closed-ended survey questions, even if they have politically relevant wants, needs, and desires.

Other respondents may not wish to reveal attitudes that paint them in a poor light. Simply because respondents are unable easily to translate their thoughts and feelings into a summary judgment does not mean that those concerns are irrelevant. After all, as Gallup and Rae (1940, 288) note, "A man might not be able to decipher a Congressional appropriation bill, but he can tell whether or not he approves of the objects for which it is to be passed; a man might not be able to understand the technological causes of his unemployment, but he knows what it means to be out of work, and his experience will contribute to the solution of the general problem." In essence, through my analysis, I ask what would happen if we did not draw the firm line between question-answerers and question-abstainers—what would happen if we assumed that everyone, no matter how muddled their political voice, should be heard as part of the democratic process? How would our view of the political world change? How would our measure of the popular will change?

Ultimately, we might choose to ignore those people who decline to answer survey questions, but without answering questions such as these, we cannot know what types of sentiment we miss in opinion polls by excluding nonrespondents. If opinion polls were the only way we looked at what the public wants from government, we might indeed wish to ignore the *don't know* segment of the population. But when polls are only a piece of the picture—as they are in modern political society—we should make polls as inclusive as possible. After all, there are already many ways in which those with weak and/or ill-formed attitudes are excluded from the public voice. If we were interested only in those who hold relatively strong views, we might, for example, look at the sentiments of people who write to their representative, or those citizens who vote on ballot initiatives. But since we are often interested in the views of all, fully representative opinion polls are vital.[14]

Understandably, not all scholars will accept this position on faith. Thus, in the chapters that follow I undertake additional steps to address potential criticisms of my analytic strategy. In each of the issue areas, I seek external confirmation of the positions I impute to respondents, where possible. In the case of racial policy issues, for example, I demonstrate that the same methods that predict that opinion polls

---

[14] Furthermore, I am not interested in the imputed attitudes of the nonrespondents on a case-by-case basis. I seek instead to tap directly the average balance of considerations of the pool of nonrespondents. So I am not claiming that the imputed positions are "attitude statements" per se. Instead, I am interested in looking at the average opinion of those respondents we miss in our surveys polls, and how that voice is different from the voice of those from whom we hear.

understate opposition to policies designed to ensure racial equality also predict the results of the 1989 New York City mayoral election more accurately than the uncorrected data from the pre-election polls. In the case of social welfare policy, for each measure of social welfare policy liberalism, I look at the answers nonrespondents give to other survey questions on similar topics. In many cases, respondents who abstain from one of the social welfare policy items answer other questions on a related topic. We therefore have a measure of opinion concerning social welfare policy sentiment for some respondents who declined to answer particular scale items. I find that, in line with the liberal attitudes I impute to respondents, those citizens who fail to answer particular social welfare policy items are relatively liberal on those items they do answer. My hope is that this evidence, taken together with my imputation analysis, will persuade even the reader who is skeptical of my empirical enterprise.

THREE

THE DYNAMICS OF RACIAL POLICY OPINION,

1972–1994

THE LESSONS of the previous chapters are straightforward. We should not necessarily embrace opinion polls as a means of discerning the public will. Under certain circumstances, opinion polls may subvert the communication of the public's preferences. These circumstances, as argued in the last chapter, are heavily dependent on the political and social context surrounding specific areas of public policy.

In this chapter, I explore how the individual tendency to edit attitudes at the stage of opinion formation may lead to inaccurate measures of opinion on racial issues. I first use National Election Studies (NES) data from 1990 to 1994 to show that public opinion polls overstate support for government intervention to ensure school integration. Some individuals who harbor anti-integration sentiments are likely to conceal their socially unacceptable opinions behind a *don't know* response. Second, I demonstrate that a similar process leads to an overstatement of support in opinion polls for government intervention to ensure fair treatment for blacks in jobs. To confirm the validity of these findings, I show that the same methods that predict that opinion polls understate opposition to government involvement in school integration and fair employment also predict the results of biracial elections—where the charged racial atmosphere makes accurate polling difficult, if not impossible—more accurately than the marginals of the pre-election polls taken in the weeks leading to the election. Together, these results suggest that survey questions concerning racial attitudes may exclude a significant base of racially conservative sentiment.

Further analysis, however, demonstrates that these findings are driven by the social sensitivity of respondents in the present era. I use data from the early 1970s to show that the strong social desirability effects in the 1990s do not characterize opinion in earlier eras. As I predict, increasing the expressive difficulty of an issue area—in this case racial politics—increases the exclusion bias in opinion concerning that topic. The analyses reported here indicate that while we need to pay attention to and account for the social context surrounding sensitive issues when gauging public opinion, we must also pay attention

to changes in that context over time. All told, these findings have pro-
found implications for the utility of polls on racial policy issues, an
area of great importance on the modern American political scene (Carmines and Stimson 1989).

Racial Issues and Expressive Difficulty

Response effects related to social concerns may contaminate the measures of opinion on some issues. In order for the individual-level social
effects arising at the stage of opinion expression to bias measures of
public opinion, the social context of the survey setting must systematically affect the expressed opinions of a particular group of individuals.
To the extent that individual characteristics systematically affect the
willingness of these respondents to express the political judgments
they construct at the attitude formation stage, surveys may paint a distorted picture of underlying public sentiment. It is important, then, to
identify specific issue areas where we might find such systematic social
effects—that is, issues that are socially difficult.

One area of politics that seems, in the modern era, to contain a good
number of cognitively easy but socially difficult issues is that of policies relating to racial equality. Over the past forty years, a massive
change has occurred in the racial attitudes of the American public. Seg-
regationist and exclusionary principles that were accepted by a large
majority of Americans in the 1940s and 1950s find bare traces of support today (see Schuman et al. 1997). Though overall support for racial
equality has increased greatly since the middle of the century, many
Americans remain profoundly ambivalent about polices that seek to
use government efforts to improve the position of blacks. Thus, although many Americans may support general principles of equality,
large segments of the mass public are ambivalent about programs designed to implement those principles (Jackman 1978; Schuman et al.
1997). Under such circumstances, respondents may be inclined to
hedge and moderate their racially conservative views to avoid appearing to subscribe to racist principles.

Previous work suggests that the level of expressed ambivalence and
hostility to racially liberal policies may be, in part, affected by the social nature of the interview, as described above. For example, Schuman
et al. (1997) find that attitudes in a racial survey administered by mail
appear more racially conservative than attitudes obtained in a more

traditional face-to-face survey setting.[1] As the authors note, this result indicates that at least some (white) respondents feel pressure in an interview setting to give more racially liberal responses than they in fact hold (see also Dovidio and Fazio 1992; Dunton and Fazio 1997; Gilens, Sniderman, and Kuklinski 1998; Hurley 1997; Kinder and Sanders 1996; Krysan 1998; Kuklinski and Cobb 1998). While respondents may have little trouble forming coherent racial policy opinions, they may not feel comfortable freely stating their judgments. To use the typology discussed in the last chapter, issues of race may be cognitively easy but socially hard. Thus, social pressures may lead to survey question abstention at the opinion expression stage. Questions that address racial policies may therefore provide a fertile arena in which to explore the effects of the social pressures of the survey interview setting.

School Integration and Busing: Principles and Policies

A prominent controversy in which the conflict between principles and policies is especially conspicuous is the debate over the proper role of government in ensuring integrated schools. While the American public overwhelmingly supports the principle of school integration, individuals are often ambivalent and sometimes downright hostile toward the use of government authority to ensure that integration occurs.

Sentiment concerning the principle of school integration among white Americans has changed greatly since the 1950s. Elite rhetoric reminiscent of George Wallace's call for "Segregation today! Segregation tomorrow! Segregation forever!" has long since disappeared from the American political scene. The mass public has also embraced a more liberal stance. In 1956 the public was evenly split on the question of whether white and black students should go to the same schools. By 1965, however, 70 percent of Americans supported the integration of schools. In the early 1970s, this rate broke the 80 percent barrier, and by the early 1980s there was almost universal consensus on the merit of school integration (Hochschild and Scott 1998, Schuman et al. 1997). In the present day, then, it is almost impossible to publicly express opposition to the principle of school integration without appearing to be an overt racist.

The public's racially liberal sentiment does not, however, easily extend to the *policies* designed to implement this widely held *principle*. A

[1] By "racial conservatism" I mean opposition to principles of racial equality and policies designed to ensure such equality. Conversely, "racial liberalism" means support for such policies. I use these terms throughout this chapter.

good deal of the hostility toward the implementation of desegregation is focused on one particular type of government action: school busing. In the years immediately following *Brown v. Board of Education*, school integration was viewed primarily as a southern issue. As Hochschild (1984) notes, *Brown* targeted only the legislatively mandated dual school systems most prevalent in the South. Thus, once the school funding provisions of the 1964 Civil Rights Act gave the *Brown* rulings some teeth and school desegregation efforts began in earnest, desegregation action was confined primarily to southern states (Rodgers 1974).

The restriction of government school desegregation action to the South was short-lived. A series of court decisions in the late 1960s and early 1970s moved school integration in general—and busing in particular—onto the agenda of school districts across the country. In *Swann v. Charlotte-Mecklenburg* (1971), the Supreme Court ruled that school boards were obligated to achieve immediate desegregation and, if necessary, to implement busing to achieve "the greatest possible degree of actual desegregation." The *Swann* ruling, important in and of itself, laid the groundwork for extending desegregation efforts outside the South. In *Keyes v. School District No.1 of Denver, CO* (1973), the Court ruled that any school district could be subject to court-ordered desegregation, even if the district did not have a history of legislated dual school systems, as long as it was found that the school board had intentionally segregated its students. While movement toward widespread implementation of busing plans in the North was tempered by the Court's split ruling the next year in *Milliken v. Bradley* (1974), which limited busing across school district boundaries, that decision did not remove busing from the public agenda. The Court's decisions in the early 1970s transformed integration from a "southern issue" into one that was highly contested in the North as well. This development changed the political climate surrounding the integration movement because, as Hochschild (1984, 29) notes, "northern liberals became wary when desegregation moved out of the distant south and onto their own suburban doorsteps."

Busing remained extremely unpopular throughout the 1970s, as many school districts (for example, those in Boston, Los Angeles, and Pontiac, Michigan) experienced hostile antibusing demonstrations and protests that sometimes even exploded into violence. It is no surprise, then, that throughout the 1970s and into the mid-1980s, support for busing rarely rose over 20 percent (Hochschild and Scott 1998).[2]

---

[2] Over time, blacks have also become more ambivalent about busing (see Schuman et al. 1997).

This brief review of the American experience with school integration underscores two important points. First, support for the principle of school integration—in both elite rhetoric and public opinion—has risen steadily over the last forty years, reaching near universal proportions in the present day. Clearly, there is a norm against expressing public opposition to the *principle* of integration in the modern era. Second, at the same time that support for the principle of integration has risen to near universal levels, the specific policy used most often to integrate schools—namely, busing—has found little support among any segment of the population.

Given this conflict between a principle that nearly every American supports—a principle that it is impossible to oppose without appearing archaic—and a policy that few support, it seems that questions that ask about government efforts to integrate schools would be an ideal place to investigate the consequences of the individual process of attitude expression. One venue particularly well suited to an investigation of public opinion concerning school integration is the NES, which is designed to collect a sample of all voting-age members of the American population and, as a result, comes as close as any survey to painting a picture of the public will. Fortuitously for the present purposes, the NES has included measures of opinion on the government's proper role in ensuring integrated schools. In particular, the NES asks if respondents support government intervention to ensure that black and white children go to the same school. This question therefore directly pits the principle of integration against the policies of government action.[3]

Evidence from the 2000 NES Pilot Study lends support to the conclusion that respondents are sensitive to the presentational implication of their answers to survey questions on this matter. In the study, respondents were told: "Some people say that the government in Washington should see to it that white and black children go to the same schools. Others claim that this is not the government's business." One-half of these respondents were asked what answer they would give if they wished to make the best possible impression on the interviewer; the other half were asked what they would say to make the worst possible impression. While there was no clear consensus on what the "best" answer should be, three-quarters of the sample said that claiming that

---

[3] The question reads: "Some people say that the government in Washington should see to it that white and black children go to the same schools. Others claim that this is not the government's business. Have you been concerned (1990: interested) enough in this question to favor one side or the other? [If yes] Do you think the government in Washington should see to it that white and black children go to the same schools, or stay out of this area, as it is not their business?"

TABLE 3.1
1990-1994 School Integration Question Opinion Distribution (Whites Only)

A: With *Don't Knows*

Year	Support	Oppose	Don't Know
1990	27%	33%	40%
1992	28%	36%	37%
1994	24%	38%	38%

B: *Don't Knows* Excluded

Year	Support	Oppose
1990	45%	55%
1992	44%	56%
1994	38%	62%

Source: National Election Studies Cumulative File
Note: Entries do not always add to 100 percent because of rounding.

integration "was not the government's business" was the best way to make a bad impression. As a point of comparison, this figure is approximately the same as the percentage of people who believed that saying they "did not vote" would be the best way to make a bad public impression. Clearly, then, there now exists a high sensitivity to the social norms governing discussion of racial policies (or at least knowledge of those norms). Given previous research in this area, it seems quite likely that some respondents in the present day would hedge, moderate, and perhaps even conceal their racially conservative views on policies to avoid appearing to subscribe to racially conservative principles.

School Integration: Public Opinion in the Modern Era

In the 1990–1994 period, less than half of white respondents who expressed an opinion supported government intervention (see table 3.1). These figures may, however, conceal a deeper story. While approximately one-third of the full sample of survey respondents expressed opposition to government action, another third declined to answer the integration question in each of those years.[4] This high number of *don't*

---

[4] The *don't know* category here includes two types of respondents. The first group— and the overwhelming majority of respondents in this category—is those respondents

know responses may be, in part, a function of the fact that NES uses a full filter for the integration question (see chapter 1). Respondents are first asked if they have an opinion on the integration question and then are asked what that opinion is. This structure gives respondents an opportunity to opt out of the question-answering process at an early stage. To use the language of chapter 1, if respondents are uncomfortable expressing an anti-integration opinion, they may avoid a socially difficult response by saying that they don't know how they feel about the integration question rather than express their opposition to government action to integrate schools.

Before I continue, it is important to note that my argument is not that the white respondents examined here necessarily choose to hide their sentiments concerning school integration behind the *don't know* response because they do not want the world to know they are "racists." Instead, some people might fear that their opposition to school integration might be construed as racist, even though their opposition might result from legitimate policy concerns.[5] The integration question appears well into the survey interview, and respondents by then know that they will not be given an opportunity to explain their opinion. Given these conversational constraints on the process of opinion expression, it may be easier for respondents to choose the *don't know* response rather than tackle the socially difficult question if they suspect they

---

who declined to answer the question when presented with the question filter. A smaller portion of respondents—3.8 percent in 1994, for instance—indicated that they had an opinion on the school integration question but then declined to choose a position when asked their opinion. These respondents must be dealt with in a systematic way in the analyses that follow. Ultimately, respondents who make it through the *don't know* filter but then fail to answer the choice question are conceding that they don't know where they stand on the integration question. It would, however, be a mistake simply to assume that these *no choice* respondents are identical to the respondents who do not make it past the question filter. In the analyses that follow, therefore, I estimated the models two ways. In the first case, I included any respondent who declined to support or oppose government involvement in school integration as a *don't know*. I also ran the model excluding the uncertain respondents altogether. These two approaches yielded parameter estimates that were nearly identical. Because the estimation results are similar across the two models, we can reasonably conclude, for the present purposes, that the *uncertain* respondents do not differ systematically from the respondents who choose the *don't know* option. However, the fact that a small portion of respondents attempt to give a more nuanced response underscores the belief that individuals may choose the *no opinion* response because of the constraints imposed through the regulated structure of the survey interview (see chapter 1).

[5] Thus, given a situation when an attitude could be construed as revealing something unpleasant—and quite possibly untrue—about one's character, it is perfectly reasonable to expect that opponents of school integration might pass rather than placing themselves in a socially difficult situation.

might fall in the camp of the opposition. In sum, the structure of the integration question, combined with the highly constrained social inter-action of the survey interview, should lead respondents to say they have no opinion on the integration question, rather than give a response that could be construed—and quite possibly misconstrued—as racist.

If these intuitions about the school integration question are correct, then a number of respondents who oppose government involvement in school integration might choose to abstain from the integration question rather than reveal an opinion that could potentially be con-strued as socially unacceptable. If this is the case, the sample of indi-viduals who offer an opinion on the integration question will differ in systematic ways from the sample of nonrespondents. Put another way, if some respondents who oppose integration hold their tongue at the stage of attitude expression rather than voice their opposition, those individuals who do answer the integration question will be unusual in the sense that they are more likely to hold favorable attitudes to-ward school integration than the rest of the population. Thus, if my hypothesis is correct, the school integration question-answering pro-cess will be plagued by exclusion bias.

In the case of the school integration question, I believe that this bias will be driven by selection bias because the NES does not have good measures of sensitivity to social norms of respondents.[6] Selection bias, as noted in chapter 2, occurs when the full sample of units in which we are interested (be it opinion poll respondents, patients with a cer-tain disease, criminal trial outcomes, or international conflicts) differs significantly from the particular sample we use for our analysis. The effects of selection bias can be avoided in analysis if and only if the unobserved factors influencing selection are unrelated to the unob-served factors influencing outcomes. Such a state of affairs will arise only if the process by which people decide if they have an opinion and the processes by which they decide their opinion are related merely through those factors we can observe, such as the gender, education, and social background of the respondents.[7] Analyses that account for selection bias allow us to see if (and how) the nature of the question-answering process differs between those citizens who provide re-sponses to survey questions and those who do not. Such information

[6] The appropriateness of such measures has been debated in psychology but has found limited success in political science (see Berinsky 2003 for a discussion of social desirability measures).

[7] In other words, in the case of the school integration data, selection bias can be avoided only if the decision to offer an opinion on the school integration question is independent of one's opinion on that question, controlling for the observed characteris-tics of the respondents.

will enable me to test directly my hypothesis concerning the effects of the survey interview setting on expressed opinion. In particular, selection models will measure the extent and nature of the link between the decision to offer an opinion on school integration and the decision to take a position on that issue.

If the estimates reveal that selection bias does not exist in the school integration question-answering process, then we must move to an examination of the opinion ingredients we can measure to see if my hypothesis concerning the link between social desirability concerns and the *don't know* response is incorrect. On the other hand, to the extent that my statistical analysis reveals the presence of selection bias, we may reasonably infer that the social context of the survey interview leads some individuals to suppress their preferences at the stage of attitude expression and offer a *don't know* response instead.[8] More importantly, the results of these analyses can also be used to determine the nature of the preferences concealed by the *don't know* responses arising in opinion expression.

Model Construction

In the analyses that follow, I model the individual question-answering process to discern the effects of the social milieu of the survey interview on school integration opinion. I look first at the process by which individuals decide whether they have an opinion they are willing to express to the survey interviewer (the opinionation model) and then at the process by which they decide what their opinion is (the opinion position model).

I constructed this model using data from 1992 with two concerns in mind. First, I included variables that would provide a good representation of the respondent's decision to give an opinion and decide upon a policy position. I also included a series of demographic variables in both the model of opinion holding and the model of opinion position.[9] I took this step to ensure that any selection bias estimated was not simply an artifact of omitting explanatory variables common to both pro-

[8] Of course, the finding of selection bias does not mean that my hypothesis is necessarily correct. Selection bias could occur in the data for a variety of reasons. A finding of selection bias is, however, consistent with my hypothesis concerning the effect of the social forces at work in the survey interview.

[9] For a discussion of the potential costs associated with the addition of these variables and appropriate robustness tests, see appendix to chapter 3.

cesses.[10] While including these variables may decrease the parsimony of the results, by adopting an overly inclusive modeling strategy I can be reasonably sure that any selection bias I estimate is not an artifact of model misspecification. Instead, any bias is endemic to the social interactions of the question-answering process—a factor that is critical to the conception of the survey response advanced in chapter 1, but one that existing data do not permit us to measure (as noted above).[11]

I modeled the decision to express an opinion as a function of three types of variables. I first used variables that proxy for general political engagement because, as discussed in chapter 1, individuals who are more engaged with the political system are better able to draw links between their personal concerns and political controversies and, as a result, are more likely to form coherent political judgments and answer survey questions.[12] Second, I included measures indicating how diffi-

---

[10] Specifically, I included measures of a respondent's age, age squared, race, sex, education, income, number of school-age children, area of residence, religion, occupation, and home ownership status. The addition of these variables may, admittedly, not provide a complete model of the process by which people decide to answer the integration question. But, following Bartels (1996, 208), with the addition of the demographic variables, this equation "might be thought of as a reduced form model corresponding to some more elaborate, more realistic, but unspecified structural model in which proximate political attitudes mediate between demographic and social characteristics on the one hand" and the decision to offer an opinion on the other.

[11] The reason I adopt this inclusive modeling strategy is that I do not believe that I have measures of the factors that influence both the selection and outcome processes—namely, the social factors at work in the survey interview setting. In my analyses, I do not want to confuse these selection effects—which, given the set of variables in the NES data, are unmeasurable—with simple bias that arises from model misspecification. As Breen (1996, 35) notes, "the correlation [between the errors in the selection and outcome equations, measured by ρ] should be thought of as intrinsic to the model. In other words, we assume $\rho \neq 0$ in the theoretical model that we posit for the population and not simply for the sample in which we may have omitted the measurement of a variable common" to the selection and outcome equations. The errors, therefore, covary *despite* proper model specification. The cause of the correlation should, then, be unmeasurable. "In essence," Breen concludes, "both equations are affected (in part) by the same random perturbations (or random perturbations that tend to covary)."

[12] To measure general political engagement, I included the respondent's level of political information (see Zaller 1992), a dummy variable measuring whether the respondent will place himself or herself on a liberal-conservative scale, and a measure of how often the respondent discusses politics. To measure how difficult it was to contact the respondent, I included measures of whether the respondent was sent a "refusal conversion" letter, whether the respondent received a "persuasion" letter, and the number of calls required to secure the interview. Some critics have suggested that excluding political information from the outcome equation is unreasonable because politically informed individuals would be more sensitive to racial policy questions. I argue that this exclusion is valid because while information should increase the probability of giving an answer, it should have no effect on opinion direction independent of socialization experiences

cult it was to contact the respondents, on the assumption that those who are difficult to reach would also be less likely to answer specific survey questions (Brehm 1993). Finally, as discussed above, I included the variables that measure the demographic characteristics of the respondents. I modeled the decision to take a particular stand on the integration question as a function of general political affiliations, material interests, and political principles (see Kinder 1998).[13] In addition, as above, I included the demographic measures to control for model misspecification. Finally, in these analyses—as in the analyses for the rest of the chapter—I used only the sample of white respondents, under the assumption that white and black respondents would be subject to different types of social pressures in the survey interview. Using the full sample of respondents, as expected, weakens somewhat the power of the results. But, as demonstrated in my previous work (Berinsky 1999, 2002a), the main pattern of the results is robust to such respecification.

Model Estimation and Interpretation

At the micro level, an important question is whether those individuals who volunteer an opinion on the school integration question differ systematically from those who do not. It is this question, after all, that will help determine whether my hypothesis concerning the effects of the social milieu of the survey interview is correct. The short answer to

---

such as class and education. There is, in fact, no relationship between information and opinion direction once income and education are controlled for. The exclusion restriction adopted here, then, is reasonable.

[13] To measure material interests, I included a measure of the number of children the respondent had in school. To measure political affiliations, I included measures of the respondent's partisan identification and ideological self-placement (or nonplacement). To measure political principles, I included measures of the respondent's level of trust in government, support for equality, racial resentment, and moral conservatism (I included measures of the respondent's level of religious engagement to disentangle "strong traditional religious conviction" from the "moral conservatism" concept in which I am interested). The use of the racial resentment measure may seem somewhat problematic in the present context. The six items that comprise the racial resentment scale, after all, directly probe the respondent's opinions concerning racial matters. It could be argued that individuals concerned about presentational appearances would decline to answer these questions. However, such concerns do not seem to pose a problem here, for two reasons. First, the racial resentment scale is designed to unobtrusively measure racial attitudes. Its measurement, therefore, should not be contaminated by the same presentational concerns as the integration question. Second, and more conclusively from an empirical standpoint, models that omit the racial resentment measures (along with other measures of political values) yield results essentially identical to the full model results (see Berinsky 2000).

this key question is an unequivocal "yes." Statistical analysis demonstrates that the question-answering process is contaminated by selection bias. The hypothesis that selection bias does not exist in the data can be rejected at a high level of confidence. The full results are presented for the interested reader in appendix tables A3.1, A3.2, and A3.3.[14] Thus, the process by which individuals decide to offer an opinion is not independent of the process by which they decide that opinion. Instead, as I hypothesize, the unmeasured factors that lead respondents to reveal their answer to the survey interviewer also lead them to take a more supportive stance on the integration issue. Conversely, individuals who harbor anti-integration sentiments are likely to hide their opinions behind a mask of indifference.

Identifying the presence of selection bias, though valuable, is only half the story. A more important objective is ascertaining the effects of that bias. Substantively, accounting for selection bias alters the estimated effects of many of the predictors of an individual's predicted opinion direction.[15] For example, correcting our predictors of opinion direction in 1992 for selection bias decreases the power of the gender variable, indicating that female respondents are more hostile toward government involvement in school integration than the uncorrected estimates suggest.[16] The uncorrected estimates suggest that a respondent

[14] Admittedly, the selection equation—the decision to offer a response on the integration question—does not do a great job of predicting who answers the item. Ideally, it would be better to have selection equations that perform as well as that in the 1989 New York City mayor's election analysis. That said, the results presented here are valid for several reasons. First, the selection model contains a great number of variables that should plausibly affect the decision to answer the question—there are no predictors available in the NES that are obviously missing from that model. Second, and more importantly, the findings of selection bias are consistent across years and across questions, indicating that the finding of selection bias is not simply a fluke of the data. Finally, the selection equation model used in the 1990s analysis is no worse than that used for the 1972 analysis presented below. The fact that the selection bias found in the 1990s analysis is absent in the 1972 analysis (see below) indicates that there is nothing about the relatively weak fit of the selection equation that necessarily leads to a finding of selection bias.

[15] Correcting the outcome equation for the selection bias present in the opinion expression process alters the model estimates in several ways. A comparison of the independent probit results and the bivariate probit results indicates that using the bivariate probit correction alters the substantive performance of many outcome equation variables. While none of the substantively significant coefficient estimates change sign, the substantive power of many of the coefficients is altered by the selection bias correction.

[16] A careful observation of the results in appendix table A3.2 reveals that a number of other relationships change in significant ways once the correction for selection bias is implemented. For example, the predictive ability of the "value" variables—racial resentment, trust in government, and moral conservatism—is attenuated, in some cases by up to 20 percent. This result suggests that correcting for selection bias reduces the differences among groups in their attitudes concerning school integration. This makes the in-

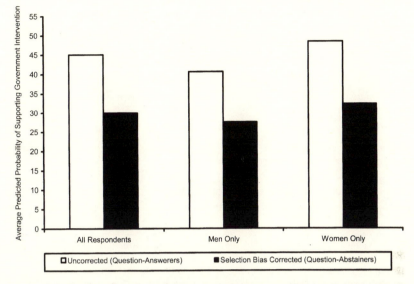

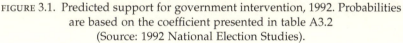

FIGURE 3.1. Predicted support for government intervention, 1992. Probabilities
are based on the coefficient presented in table A3.2
(Source: 1992 National Election Studies).

who is average in every way (where "average" means possessing the
average characteristics of the full sample) and female is just over 7 percent more likely to support integration than an otherwise similar male.
However, the corrected estimates indicate that the average female is 5
percent more likely to support integration than the average male.

The movement of the predicted effects of the various opinion ingredients once selection bias is accounted for is significant, but what is
more impressive is the movement of the predicted baseline opinion.
Once selection effects are accounted for, respondents become more
likely to oppose school integration.[17] Figure 3.1 presents a comparison

dividuals in the sample appear to behave more alike than in the independent probit
estimation—they all like school integration less. Similar trends appear to hold for other
blocks of variables, such as the census region variables.

[17] While the intercept in the school integration choice outcome equation is approximately zero in the separate probit model, it is highly negative in the bivariate probit
selection model. This result should not be taken as a failure of the bivariate probit selection technique. Simulations undertaken by Brehm (1993, chap. 3) indicate that selection
based on the value of the dependent variable and selection based on independent variables directly related to the value of the dependent variable both affect the constant in
ways consistent with the results presented here. In the present context, then, we might
see the movement in the constant term if the decision to withhold an opinion was deter-

of the expected levels of support for the average respondent using the uncorrected estimates (question-answerer) and the selection bias corrected estimates (question-abstainer) for 1992. As expected, correcting for selection bias reduces the net probability of supporting government efforts to integrate schools. In addition, the differences work in predictable ways among subgroups of the respondents. Correcting for selection bias minimizes the difference between men and women, for example (though both groups are less likely to support integration).[18]

Having demonstrated the presence and effects of selection bias in the school integration question-answering process using the 1992 NES data, I sought to replicate my results using data from 1990 and 1994.[19] Consistent with the results found in 1992, there was strong evidence of selection bias in the question-answering process. Again, these full model results are presented in appendix table A3.2. The process by

---

mined by one's opposition to school integration and/or factors that led to such opposition. The attenuated constant result here is most likely the result of the omission of those measures that could capture individual variation in the selection effects found here. Specifically, I hypothesize that the constant is attenuated because we do not measure the respondent's sensitivity to the social environment of the survey. As noted in chapter 1, some individuals are more likely than others to react to social pressures. The effects estimated here, however, compound interindividual variation in sensitivity to social concerns into a single aggregate effect. In other words, the absence of measures of social sensitivity drives the selection effects into the constant term. Thus, the attenuation of the constant term should not be taken to mean that *everyone* approaches the school integration question-answering process the same way. Rather it should be construed as an indication that those measures that capture the differences in how people answer survey questions—such as levels of self-monitoring—are not in the outcome equation. Unfortunately, the NES does not contain such measures. Thus, given the limitations of data, it is impossible to unpack the heterogeneity in respondent reaction to the social milieu of the survey interview. That said, the model estimates provide strong support for the hypothesis that selection bias exists in the question-answering process. Furthermore, and more importantly for present purposes, we can confidently trace out the effects of this selection bias on the shape of aggregate public opinion.

[18] These results are robust across a variety of equation specifications. The basic pattern found in the results presented above—a significant ρ and a reduced constant term once the correction for selection bias is introduced—holds across more restricted specifications of the selection and outcome equations. Specifically, in each of five restricted specifications, ρ is greater than 0.75 and is statistically significant at the 0.05 level. Thus, it appears that the selection effects estimated here are endemic to the question-answering process and not simply an artifact of the group of variables used in estimation. The consistency of these results is especially heartening because selection models tend to be extremely sensitive to changes in model specification.

[19] The 1990 sample is much smaller than the 1992 and 1994 samples because only half of the 1990 sample was asked the school integration question. Because respondents were randomly assigned to the form with the school integration questions, it is valid to draw inferences from that sample to the full population. The results presented here also replicate in 1986. They are available from the author upon request.

which people come to express their attitudes on the school integration question, then, is surely contaminated by a bias that conceals significant anti-integrationist sentiments behind the veneer of a *don't know* response. Put simply, as expected, some opponents of government efforts to integrate schools appear to censor their judgments at the opinion expression stage.

Consequences for Public Opinion

To draw out the implication of my individual-level analysis for our understanding of public opinion on school integration, I ran a series of simulations in which I predicted support for government involvement in school integration among those respondents who failed to offer an opinion.[20] In this way, the predicted behavior of the entire sample of citizens can be used to gauge the effect of selection bias arising from the social concerns at play in the survey interview.[21]

This strategy differs from the one I adopted in my earlier published analyses (Berinsky 1999, 2002a). In those pieces, I compared the pre-

---

[20] More specifically, I used my coefficient estimates from the equations reported above to generate each respondent's predicted probability of supporting school integration. I then took the average of this probability across the sample to measure mean support for school integration. To be precise, I ran my simulations in several steps. First, I used the estimates of the βs from the bivariate probit to generate a predicted probability of supporting school integration for each individual in the sample of question-answerers, conditional on selection. Next I used the βs from the bivariate probit results to compute the mean probability of giving a supportive response, for all non-answerers.

[21] Here, as in the chapters that follow, I compare the imputed attitudes for the nonrespondents with the predicted opinion positions (generated by the model estimates) of the respondents. That is, I use probit results (and later my regression results) to impute the mean responses of *both* the question-answerers and question-abstainers. I believe that this method is preferable to comparing the imputed opinions of nonrespondents with the given opinions of respondents (see, for example, Althaus 1998). The regression and probit models used in this book are not perfect. Like all statistical models in political science, they are not designed to explain *all* the variation in human behavior. Using predicted estimates allows me to control for imperfections in my models of opinion direction and hold constant the predictive power of those models across the estimates of public opinion. This strategy leads to somewhat different results than would be obtained by comparing actual answers with predicted answers. For example, the estimates of predicted support for school integration among question-answerers in table 3.2 are somewhat different from expressed levels of support detailed in table 3.1b (though still within one percentage point). I think that this strategy is the appropriate approach; unlike Althaus (1998), I do not believe that it is wise to compare average predicted probabilities of giving a particular response with the percentage of people in the population who actually gave that response because I wish to control for the fact that my model of opin-

TABLE 3.2
Predicted Support for Government Intervention in School
Integration, 1990–1994

Year	Respondents	Nonrespondents	Difference
1990	45	33	12
1992	44	30	15
1994	39	31	7

Note: Entries are the average predicted probability of supporting school integration. The differences in the last column do not always represent the differences between the first two entries because of rounding.

dicted levels of support under two conditions: one where it was assumed that selection bias did not exist in the data, and the second where the estimates were corrected for selection bias for *all* respondents. Here, I account for the fact that some respondents did in fact choose to answer the survey question. Specifically, I incorporate the indirect effect of the decision to offer a response to the school integration question on the direction of that response. In effect, this method makes allowances for the possibility that respondents who give racially liberal answers actually support racially liberal policies, as they say they do. This method generates somewhat different aggregate results from those in my previously published work, but, as I will demonstrate below, even with this more stringent standard, the estimates of racial liberalism in the population are significantly different once selection is accounted for.[22]

Table 3.2 demonstrates that across all years, there is significant exclusion bias. The predicted support for school integration is much lower for nonrespondents than for those citizens who answered the school integration question. On average, this difference is 11 percent. Thus, as expected, the underlying sentiment of the respondents differs greatly from the sentiment of the nonrespondents.

The next step in my analysis is to trace out the aggregate effect of these differences. The imbalance in collective opinion induced by excluding nonrespondents is the amount that measure of opinion would

ion formation is imperfect. By using predicted values generated by a model, I hold constant the predictive power of that model across the estimates of public opinion.

[22] To be precise, for those independent variables that appear in both the selection and outcome equations, there are two effects on the predicted outcome. First, there is a direct effect on the outcome, which we estimate through the βs in the outcome equation. But there is also an indirect effect of those independent variables on the predicted outcome via their effect through the selection equation. In previous work, I estimated only the direct effect and ignored the indirect effect.

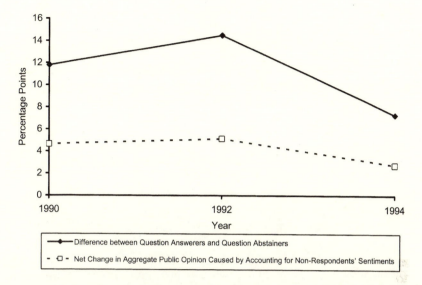

FIGURE 3.2. Bias in measured support for government intervention. Probabilities are based on the coefficient estimates presented in tables A3.1–A3.3 (Source: 1990, 1992, 1994 National Election Studies).

change if we accounted for the sentiment of nonrespondents. The degree of this net change in aggregate public opinion depends on the proportion of question-abstainers in the sample and the difference between the mean of the answerers and the mean of the abstainers.[23] With measures of these quantities, then, we can estimate the degree of bias in school integration opinion. All of this information is readily available.

The estimates of the differences between question-abstainers and question-answerers and the net aggregate change in collective opinion that results by accounting for the change are presented in figure 3.2. As the graph makes clear, accounting for the sentiments of nonre-

[23] This mean may be expressed, following Kalton (1983), as:

$$\bar{Y} = W_r\bar{Y}_r + W_m\bar{Y}_m$$

where $\bar{Y}$ is the population mean, $\bar{Y}_r$ is the population mean for the respondents, $\bar{Y}_m$ is the population mean for the nonrespondents (the subscript r denotes respondents, and the subscript m—for "missing"—denotes nonrespondents), and W_r and W_m are the proportion of the population in these two groups ($W_r + W_m = 1$). Since the survey fails to collect data for the nonrespondents, it estimates $\bar{Y}_r$, not the population mean $\bar{Y}$. The difference between $\bar{Y}_r$ and the population parameter $\bar{Y}$ is the bias that results from using the respondent mean in place of the overall mean and is given by:

$$BIAS = W_m (\bar{Y}_r - \bar{Y}_m).$$

spondents alters our picture of public opinion. Both the differences between respondents and nonrespondents and the net aggregate change
are large. On average, collective opinion moves over four points in the
racially conservative direction once the projected opinions of nonrespondents are taken into account. To be precise, on average, the majority opposed to government involvement moves from 57.6 percent to
61.8 percent.[24]

An Independent Confirmation: Fair Employment

To this point, I have presented what I hope is compelling evidence of
the consequences of opinion withholding on public opinion concerning school integration. However, it remains to be shown that the findings presented above can be extended beyond that issue domain to
other racially sensitive controversies. Fortunately, there exists a question on the NES survey well suited to such replication—the fair employment question.

In the 1992 NES survey, respondents were asked whether they
thought that the federal government should see to it that blacks get
fair treatment in jobs.[25] Like the school integration question, this
question was asked with a full filter. More importantly, like the integration question, the fair employment item pits a widely supported
principle—equal opportunity in employment—against a less popular
policy, namely, a particular use of government authority to achieve
such equality.

By 1972, 97 percent of whites agreed with the statement that "Ne-
groes should have as good a chance as white people to get any kind
of job," rather than the statement "White people should have the first
chance at any kind of job," indicating wide opposition to the principle
of white preference in hiring.[26] However, as is the case with school inte-

---

[24] In 1990, opinion moves from 55.5 percent opposed to government intervention to
60.1 percent opposed. In 1992, opinion moves from 55.8 percent to 60.9 percent
opposed. In 1994, opinion moves from 61.5 percent opposed to 64.2 percent opposed.

[25] The question reads: "Some people feel that if black people are not getting fair treatment in jobs, the government in Washington ought to see to it that they do. Others feel
that this is not the federal government's business. Have you had enough interest in this
question to favor one side over the other? [If yes] How do you feel? Should the government in Washington see to it that black people get fair treatment in jobs or is this not
the federal government's business?"

[26] This is a very strict application of the principle of equal hiring because it asks if
whites should be given preference in hiring over blacks, not whether blacks and whites
should have equal opportunities to secure jobs.

gration and busing, the near unanimous subscription to a political principle does not necessarily translate to widespread support for the use of government action to ensure that principle. In 1993, almost three times as many whites thought that blacks should receive no special treatment from the U.S. government as thought that the government should help blacks (see Schuman et al. 1997).[27] As the political debate over equality in hiring moved to a discussion of affirmative action in the mid-1970s, this tension between a popular principle and an unpopular policy increased.[28] Thus, the dynamics of the fair employment question-answering process should follow the basic pattern of the integration question-answering process, in part because both questions address racially sensitive controversies, but also because the two issues have evolved in similar ways over the last twenty-five years. By examining the fair employment data using the same models of selection employed above, then, I can determine whether my findings can be extended past the area of school integration into other racially sensitive political controversies.

As was true with school integration, expressed support for federal government intervention was rather slim among whites. Of those who answered the question, 50.8 percent, a bare majority, supported such action. Again, the rates of question abstention are relatively high; 33.8 percent of the respondents chose not to give any answer to the fair employment question. In short, it appears that the fair employment question would exhibit many of the properties of the school integration question. I therefore proceeded to repeat my school integration analyses using the fair employment data.

To make sure I mimicked as closely as possible my analyses across the two racial policy items, I employed the same model specifications I used to predict opinion on school integration to predict responses to

[27] It is interesting to note that in modern times, blacks also have increased in their opposition to affirmative government action. By 1992, 42 percent of black respondents opposed special preferences in hiring and promotion for minorities (Schuman et al. 1997). Thus, it could be that in the 1990s blacks have their own reasons to be skeptical of federal intervention to ensure job equality but might be loath to express such dissenting sentiments when those policies come in conflict with a deeply held principle.

[28] The salience of concerns relating to affirmative action programs in the NES fair employment question-answering process was, in all likelihood, especially high in 1992 because respondents were asked their opinion on affirmative action right before they were asked the fair employment question. Specifically, they were asked: "Some people say that because of past discrimination, blacks should be given preference in hiring and promotion. Others say that such preference in hiring and promotion of blacks is wrong because it gives blacks advantages they haven't earned. What about your opinion—are you for or against preferential hiring and promotion of blacks?"

the fair employment question.[29] The results of this analysis are straight-forward and clear; the pattern of selection bias in the fair employment question closely follows that of the school integration question.[30] Once again, there is strong evidence that the process by which individuals decide to offer an opinion is not independent of the process by which they decide that opinion. Furthermore, as was the case for government involvement in school integration, predicted support for fair employ-ment is much lower for nonrespondents than for question-answerers. Predicted support among respondents is 51.3 percent, while it is 36.6 percent among nonrespondents. Finally, accounting for these differ-ences alters our picture of public opinion in a meaningful way. Collec-tive opinion moves 4.7 points in the conservative direction once the preferences of the nonrespondents are figured into the picture. Thus, predicted support for fair employment drops from 51.3 percent to 46.6 percent once nonrespondents are taken into account. Accounting for unspoken preferences paints a different picture not only of the strength of support or opposition to fair employment, but also of the direction of aggregate opinion on that question. While the important finding here is the differences between the sentiments of respondents and those of nonrespondents, in some cases these differences can lead to significant effects in collective opinion.

From Attitudes to Behavior: The 1989 New York City Mayoral Race

At this point, one topic of concern may remain for the skeptical reader. While the findings concerning the effects of the social transaction in the survey interview replicate well across different questions and years, these results are admittedly somewhat incomplete because I have not presented an observable check on my results. That is, I cannot compare the opposition to government involvement concerning school integration and fair employment with the observable behavior of the mass public. In this section, I demonstrate that the same model I used above predicts inaccuracies of reports of individual behavior in so-cially sensitive situations.

---

[29] I did, however, remove the school-age children variable because it was not directly relevant to the fair employment question.

[30] The full model results are presented in appendix table A3.4. There, ρ is positive and highly significant. Moreover, the constant in the outcome equation is attenuated greatly once selection bias is accounted for.

Candidate Choice and the Don't Know Response
in Biracial Elections

Just as opponents of government efforts to integrate schools and ensure fair employment might hide their opposition behind a *no opinion* response, pre-election polls in electoral contests that involve candidates of different races offer a situation where individuals might be loathe to express their true candidate preferences for fear of appearing racist. Work by Reeves (1997) suggests that individuals who are uneasy or apprehensive about voting for black candidates may "vacate the field" in pre-election polls and declare themselves undecided rather than come out and say that they oppose a black candidate. While Reeves does not demonstrate a direct link between the *undecided* option and support for white candidates, he presents the results of a survey experiment that suggest such a link. He finds that the percentage of voters who claim to be undecided doubles in a hypothetical biracial contest compared with an identical race where both candidates are white. The fact that antiblack sentiment exerted a statistically significant effect on whites' willingness to express their voting preferences in a biracial election suggests that an undecided response may be a covert vote preference for the white candidate (see also Cavanagh 1983; Pettigrew and Alston 1988).

Such a process would explain seemingly inexplicable pre-election polling results in the 1989 New York City mayoral election. In that contest, black candidate David Dinkins held a fourteen to eighteen point advantage over his white opponent, Rudolph Giuliani, in polls taken only days before the election but ended up winning the race by less than two percentage points (McConnell 1990; Rosenthal 1989). The reason for the fallibility of the pre-election polls in the New York race has been much debated (Clymer 1989; Rosenthal 1989). However, the concealment of pro-Giuliani sentiment behind the *don't know* response among a substantial portion of the public may have led to the failure of the surveys.

The 1989 election presented a difficult choice for many voters. Though New York City is an overwhelmingly Democratic city, Giuliani's moderately conservative policy positions and his reputation as an effective prosecutor gave him substantial crossover appeal. At the same time, given a series of racially charged incidents in the summer of 1989—most notably the racially motivated murder of a black youth by whites in Bensonhurst, Queens—it was impossible to remove the factor of race from the electoral environment. Thus, though there may have been many valid reasons to support Giuliani in the election, given the tenor of the times, it may have been difficult to perceive a Giuliani vote as anything but an antiblack vote (see McConnell 1990). This was especially true of the older Jewish voters whose preferred candidate, incumbent Mayor Ed Koch, was defeated in the Democratic primary. In short, many respondents—those who supported Giuliani but were not members of his typical constituency, and sensitive to social context—may have had an incentive to say they were undecided rather than reveal their pro-Giuliani sentiments.

The 1989 New York City mayoral race, then, parallels many of the conditions found in the context of the school integration question. In both cases, a large number of respondents abstained from offering their opinion or candidate choice. In both cases, the broader social climate made expressing a racially conservative opinion—a vote for Giuliani or opposition to government involvement in school integration—a difficult act. With the New York mayoral race, however, we have the advantage of being able to check how well the selection bias correction that I used to examine the school integration data works in a case where we can observe an actual outcome—in this case, the actual election results. Specifically, we can see how well the predicted results from the selection bias correction conform to the true election outcome. Of course, we should not expect these results to predict the election perfectly. As previous analysts have noted (see Arian et al. 1990; Flemming and Parker 1998; Kohut 1999; Pettigrew and Alston 1988; Richards 1989), the concealment of antiblack sentiment behind an *undecided* response is only one of several reasons why pre-election polls fail in biracial contests.[31] But if my hypothesis is correct, correct-

[31] There are several reasons why pre-election polls may fail to predict the winner of biracial contests. Some authors attribute polling errors to unforeseen patterns of voter turnout (Arian et. al. 1990; Richards 1989). As these authors note, pre-election polls are generally drawn from the population of all registered voters. Thus, the sample of respondents in any given pre-election poll may not accurately reflect the demographic makeup of those individuals who actually vote on election day. In particular, certain groups might be underrepresented in the pre-election polls relative to the size of their ultimate voting block. If those groups eventually turn out to vote for the white candidate, the pre-election polls will paint a distorted picture of the final outcome. In the 1989 New York City mayoral election, for example, some exit polls found that turnout was especially high among Jewish and white respondents—who were likely to cast votes for Giuliani—in part explaining the discrepancy between the polls and the final tally (Richards 1989). Other analysts have argued that polls in biracial contests fall short of the mark because surveys fail to capture the preferences of a significant portion of voters predisposed to the white candidate. Several authors (Flemming and Parker 1998; Richards 1989; Pettigrew and Alston 1988) have argued that people who refuse to participate in surveys are likely to be older and more conservative than those who take part in the polls. Consequently, individuals who are less likely to take part in surveys are inherently predisposed to oppose the black candidate. As a result, systematic bias in the pattern

ing for the concealment of anti-Dinkins sentiment at the opinion expression stage should bring the estimate of the poll closer to the actual election results.

Data and Methods

To gauge the presence and effect of selection bias in the 1989 mayoral pre-election polls, I used data from a poll conducted by ABC News and the *New York Daily News* from October 31 to November 6. This poll found that 45.9 percent of registered voters said they supported Dinkins, 35.4 percent supported Giuliani, 4.8 percent supported another candidate, and 14.0 percent were undecided. Thus, the pre-election poll indicated that Dinkins had 56.4 percent of the two-party vote—a seemingly commanding lead of almost thirteen percentage points. Among whites, 42.4 percent of those who expressed a preference said they would vote for Dinkins, while 16.0 percent said they were undecided. These results conform to the results of other pre-election polls (see Reeves 1997) but not to the true results of the election held just one day after the poll ended. It appears likely, then, that the same type of selection bias found in the integration and fair employment data might contaminate these polling data.

To test this hypothesis, I employed the same strategy as in the school integration and fair employment cases to analyze the expressed preferences of nonblack registered voters. Here, my model posits that candidate choice (the outcome equation) is a function of the respondent's party of registration, ideology, education, age, religion, income, gender, and Hispanic ethnicity. The willingness to offer a choice (the selection equation) is a function of these variables, as well as certainty of voting.[32]

Statistical analyses indicate that we can say with a high degree of confidence that the 1989 New York pre-election polling data are indeed contaminated by the same selection bias as the school integration data

---

of survey nonresponse may lead pre-election polls to understate support for the white candidate, thereby painting an inaccurate portrait of the electoral environment in biracial elections. Evidence from the 1989 New York City experience seems to bear out this hypothesis. Andrew Kohut, then of the Gallup organization, found that weighting pre-election survey data to adjust for unit nonresponse significantly decreased the projected levels of support for Dinkins in that contest (Kohut 1999).

[32] The respondent's self-reported certainty of voting in the mayoral race (controlling for previous voting behavior) was a strong predictor of whether he or she would offer a candidate choice but did not affect the direction of that choice. It could be argued that, under some circumstances, a respondent's certainty of voting could predict the direction of vote choice. In a race where one candidate did a better job than the other of mobilizing supporters in the weeks leading to the election, we might expect such a pattern. In the New York City election, however, there is no evidence to suggest this was the case.

(see appendix table A3.5 for details). This result indicates that those people who were likely to express a voting preference were—by simply answering the preference question—more likely to say they supported Dinkins. Conversely, the *don't know* option showed significant support for Giuliani. Unlike the school integration question, the effects of the selection bias in the pre-election polling data are not captured in the baseline estimate of the support. Rather, the selection bias affects the estimates of the predictors of opinion.[33] Thus, we can ascertain precisely which types of individuals concealed their pro-Giuliani sentiments. For example, correcting for selection bias increases the predictive power of age by over 50 percent. To illustrate the magnitude of this effect, while the uncorrected estimates suggest that a respondent who was average in every way and 75 was just over 5.8 percent less likely to support Dinkins than the same individual who was 25. However, the corrected estimates indicate that the average 75-year-old was about 10.6 percent less likely to support Dinkins than the average 25-year-old. Similarly, correcting for selection bias indicates that Jewish voters were more likely to support Giuliani than the data indicate.[34] These results indicate that respondents who were older and Jewish—those groups who, in the wake of Koch's defeat in the primary, would gravitate to Giuliani but might be reluctant to express their anti-Dinkins sentiment—were more likely to support Giuliani than the uncorrected probit estimates suggest. Moreover, the analysis indicates that those individuals who refused to reveal information about themselves—those who would not identify their religion or income levels—were less likely to support Dinkins than it would initially appear.

What is especially interesting about these patterns of uncertainty in candidate choice is that they are inconsistent with the respondents' self-reported likelihood of voting in the election. While older respondents and Jewish respondents are less likely to reveal their candidate choice than other respondents, they are more likely to claim they would ultimately vote in the mayoral election. Table 3.3 shows that almost 22 percent of Jewish respondents claimed to be undecided as to how they would cast their vote, but 90 percent of those respondents also said they would definitely vote in the election. By contrast, about 11 percent of non-Jewish respondents said they did not know who they would vote for in the election, but 84 percent said they would vote in the election.

---

[33] In other words, in the New York City case, we are able to discern the specific factors that are correlated with the selection effects.

[34] This result makes sense because these individuals were also less likely to reveal for whom they planned to vote in the election. Accounting for the effects of their reticence on the coefficient estimates yields a pro-Giuliani stance that appears larger than it is at first glance.

TABLE 3.3
Undecided and Intended Voting Rates for Key Demographic Groups,
New York City Mayoral Race, 1989

	Do Not Offer Candidate Preference	Will Definitely Vote	N
Jewish	21.8%	90.2%	482
Not Jewish	10.5%	84.0%	2027
Age 50+	19.8%	89.4%	915
Age<50	8.5%	82.7%	1594
Jewish and 50+	29.5%	92.5%	241

Similarly, twice as many respondents over 50 years of age gave a *don't know* response to the candidate preference question compared to younger respondents. At the same time, a greater number of older respondents said they would definitely cast their vote on election day. These results suggests that, at least for some individuals, a *don't know* response really meant "I think I know, but I don't want to tell you."

Electoral Implications

While the results from the 1989 data may differ in specifics from the school integration and fair employment results, they are similar in spirit. In both cases, the *no opinion* response seems to be a cover—for at least a significant proportion of the sample—for opposition to racially liberal policies and particular candidates in elections that are racially sensitive.

The similarity between the school integration and fair employment results and the 1989 pre-election poll results continues with a simulation predicting respondents' candidate choice. As before, the average predicted probability of supporting Dinkins is estimated separately for nonrespondents and respondents. The predicted level of support for white respondents is 42.0 percent. This result conforms to the poll marginals but is inconsistent with the election results—even if we assume that every black respondent who did not give a candidate preference ultimately voted for Giuliani (an extremely unlikely scenario), the projected level of support for Dinkins is still over 54 percent. However, projected support for Dinkins among white nonrespondents is only 33.7 percent, indicating the strong underlying base of support for Giuliani. If we account for the predicted preferences of these nonrespondents, the projected support for Dinkins drops by 1.4 percent. This prediction still overstates Dinkins' true level of support, but, as noted above, there are several reasons why support for the black candidate might be overestimated in biracial elections. What is important is that accounting for the fact that some respondents hide their socially unacceptable choices behind a *don't know* response reduces the projected margin of victory of Dinkins. Thus, the major point to take from this analysis is that accounting for exclusion bias yields a predicted estimate of Dinkins support closer to the truth—that the race that Dinkins seemed to have in the bag was, in fact, closer than was apparent from the pre-election polls.[35]

Because the estimates corrected for selection bias do a better job of predicting the actual election results than the uncorrected estimates, it is clear that the selection bias correction provides a more reliable estimate of the true vote intentions than the preferences expressed in the survey.[36] Given that the circumstances surrounding the biracial elections are similar to those of the school integration and fair employment setups, we can then have greater confidence that the corrected estimates for the school integration and fair employment data in the modern era are closer to "the truth" as well.

The Dynamics of Racial Policy Opinion

The analyses up to this point have demonstrated that the presence of bias in the process of opinion expression may lead to significant bias

---

[35] I have also replicated the basic tenor of this result with data from the 1982 California gubernatorial election (see Berinsky 2000).

[36] Some have argued that the results presented here are evidence of genuine ambivalence on the part of the respondents rather than willful preference misrepresentation. However, I believe that my results are not consistent with such an explanation, for two reasons. First, if the respondents who said they did not know how they were going to vote were truly ambivalent, we would not see the patterns of selection bias in the data that my analyses have uncovered. The *don't know* response does not arise because respondents are conflicted over which candidate to support. Instead it arises because respondents are conflicted between their support for the white candidate and their fear that such support could be construed as racist. Second, evidence from exit polling in the 1989 Virginia gubernatorial election supports the hypothesis that some voters misrepresent their preferences to pollsters. Traugott and Price (1992) found that exit polls that employed traditional face-to-face interviewing techniques overstated support for the black candidate, Doug Wilder, while polls that employed a self-administered questionnaire accurately predicted the election outcome. This result suggests that respondents will, as I suggest here, willfully misrepresent their preferences in situations where they must directly reveal their candidate choice to the interviewer. In this situation, there is no possibility that such behavior arises from ambivalence: the respondents have, after all, just cast their votes. This result suggests that polls in biracial contests are contaminated by willful preference misrepresentation, not simple ambivalence.

in opinion poll data. The fact that some individuals held their tongue in the 1990s rather than express conservative positions on policies designed to ensure racial equality means that opinion polls may not accurately measure public sentiment on racial issues. These analyses, while persuasive, are not demonstrations of universal truths. The inherent expressive difficulty of an issue, as discussed in chapter 2, is a product of the larger social context in which that issue is situated. It is, after all, the interaction of the individual psychological processes of the question-answering process with the larger political world that makes a particular issue difficult or easy. As a society evolves and changes over time, the ways in which individuals approach the survey interview should change as well.

The climate surrounding racial policy questions in the 1990s was very different from that of the late 1960s and early 1970s. In the 1990s and today, as noted above, social pressures exist that make it difficult to talk frankly about race. However, such strong traditions have not always existed in the United States. Over the last thirty years, Americans have become increasingly sensitive to issues of race. Consider, for example, the comparative performance of McConahay's Modern Racism Scale in the 1970s and 1990s (see also Kinder and Sanders 1996). McConahay was concerned that direct measures of "old-fashion prejudice"—for example, agreement with the statement, "Generally, do you feel blacks are not as smart as whites?"—would elicit socially desirable, rather than truthful, answers. The Modern Racism Scale was therefore developed to measure basic attitude toward blacks in such a way that minimized the respondent's sensitivity to social pressures. In other words, the Modern Racism Scale was designed to be nonreactive on questions explicitly concerning matters of race (McConahay 1986). Experimental studies by McConahay and his colleagues in the 1970s indicated that the Modern Racism items possessed this quality (see McConahay 1986 for a review of these studies). But what was true in the 1970s does not necessarily hold in the modern era. Experiments conducted by Fazio et al. (1995) using college students indicate that the Modern Racism Scale is now a highly reactive measure.[37] Thus, while there may have been indications of social desirability pressure in the early 1970s on some matters explicitly concerning the abilities of blacks, today that pressure extends even to more implicitly racial questions.[38]

---

[37] In addition, a recent study by Swim et al. (1995) finds that the Modern Racism Scale is no longer empirically distinct from the "old-fashion prejudice" scale. This result suggests that the Modern Racism Scale may currently be as reactive as the more blatant racial items.

[38] We can see this increased sensitivity not only in experimental data, but also in records of conversations with ordinary citizens. Bob Blauner (1989), for example, com-

Put simply, over the last thirty years, racial policy has become a more socially difficult issue. Today's world is different from the early 1970s in ways that should affect how people react to survey questions on issues concerning racial policy. It is plausible, if not likely, that these differences could have affected how respondents approached the NES integration question. To assess the effects of changes in the larger social context on the process of opinion expression, I replicated my school integration analysis with data from the 1972 NES to see just how the findings of bias in integration opinion hold up over time.[39]

The overall shape of public opinion on the school integration question in 1972 was very different from that in the early 1990s.[40] Only 19 percent of respondents failed to give an opinion on the question in 1972, compared with about one-third through the 1990s. Of those who did express a preference, 45 percent supported government intervention, compared with 49 percent in 1992. Among whites, in particular, these differences are just as stark—19 percent declined to give an answer, and of those who expressed an opinion, only 39 percent expressed support for integration. Though the differences in the marginals across the two eras may be interesting, the more critical question for the present purpose is how well those marginals represent underlying public sentiment on the integration issue. For this task, I returned to the model I used above. If my hypothesis concerning the effect of the social climate of the 1970s is correct, data from the early 1970s will lead to a different result: the unmeasured factors that influence whether a respondent will offer a response to the school integration question (the selection equation) will be independent of the unmeasured factors that lead that respondent to support or oppose government efforts to integrate schools (the outcome equation).

While I would ideally like to replicate faithfully my analyses using the 1972 data, the dataset from 1972 lacks certain measures—

---

piled a series of interviews concerning race relations with a group of respondents in San Francisco in 1968. He then followed up with these respondents in 1979 and 1986. Even a casual glance at the transcripts reveals that the change in the rhetoric of some of the respondents is striking.

[39] The results presented here are not specific to the 1972 dataset. Analyses using data from 1968 yield results substantively similar to those presented here (results are available from author upon request).

[40] The school integration question reads: "Some people say that the government in Washington should see to it that white and black children are allowed to go to the same schools. Others claim that this is not the government's business. Have you been concerned enough about this question to favor one side over the other?" [If yes] Do you think the government in Washington should see to it that white and black children go to the same schools, or stay out of this area, as it is not their business?"

such as the values and predisposition scales—that strongly predicted opinion direction in contemporary times. However, the fact that these measures are missing does not jeopardize the analyses. As noted above, the critical finding from the analyses of integration opinion in the 1990s does not depend on the particular specification of the question-answering process.

With these concerns in mind, I estimated a model of the question-answering process in 1972 that followed the spirit, if not the letter, of my earlier analysis. I modeled whites' decision to offer an opinion on the integration question as a function of respondents' level of political information, their level of psychological and personal involvement with the presidential campaign,[41] a dummy variable measuring whether they placed themselves on a liberal-conservative scale, and the same demographic variables used in the 1992 analysis.[42] I modeled the respondents' choice on the integration question as a function of party identification, ideological self-identification, trust-in-government, efficacy, and demographic control variables. I include the efficacy and trust in government scales in these analyses in an effort to compensate for the predictive power of the missing value scales. The basic thrust of the results remain the same if I exclude them from analysis.

As expected, the results do not replicate the findings from the 1990s. In fact, the results from the 1970s are strikingly different. (The full results are presented in appendix table A3.6 for the interested reader). The selection bias that was so clearly present in the question-answering process in the 1990s is entirely absent. We can reject the hypothesis of selection bias with a high degree of confidence and move to examining the effects on opinion of the measured characteristics of citizens.

Even accounting for measured differences between respondents and nonrespondents, the difference in the preferences of respondents and nonrespondents is insignificant. The probability of giving a supportive response among respondents is 39.5 percent, while among nonrespondents it is 41.0 percent. This gap of 1.5 points pales in comparison with that found in the 1990s data and is in the opposite direction as well.

---

[41] This measure is a scale of interest in the campaign and the performance of five campaign acts: (1) voting in the presidential election; (2) trying to convince other people they should vote for one of the parties or candidates; (3) attending political meetings; (4) doing work for one of the parties or candidates; and (5) wearing a button supporting one of the parties or candidates. This scale has a reasonable alpha of 0.60.

[42] I included measures of age, age squared, sex, education, income, number of school-age children, area of residence, and religion. I also included measures of the SMSA size of the respondent's neighborhood because I believed that respondents who lived in suburbs and cities might be less supportive of integration efforts than other respondents.

In short, unlike in the 1990s, the projected sentiment of nonrespondents was almost identical to that of the respondents.[43]

Additional analyses indicate that these results are not a fluke of the school integration question. A similar analysis using the fair employment question demonstrates that the pattern of selection bias in that question closely mimics that of the school integration question in 1972. Again, we can reject the hypothesis of selection bias with a high degree of confidence. These analyses (presented in appendix table A3.7) indicate that in the fair employment analyses, as in the school integration analyses, the bias found in the 1992 data is absent from the 1972 results. Not surprisingly, then, the predicted behavior of the collective sample is nearly identical across the case where potential selection bias is ignored and where it is taken into account and estimated. The probability of supporting government involvement is 47.3 percent among respondents and 45.6 percent among nonrespondents—an insignificant difference of under two percentage points.[44] Thus, accounting for the sentiment of the nonrespondents does not at all change our view of public sentiment on this issue.[45]

In sum, the results from the 1972 data speak as loudly as those from the 1990s but tell a very different story. In the early 1970s, unlike the

[43] Correcting aggregate opinion for this bias moves opinion an insignificant amount—less than two-tenths of one percentage point.

[44] Again, correcting collective opinion for this bias leads to a change of only two-tenths of one percentage point.

[45] At a more technical level, these results also provide suggestive evidence that the selection bias found in the school integration case in 1992 is endemic to the question-answering process and not simply the result of a change in question wording from 1972 to 1992 described by Schuman et al. (1997). The school integration question has been asked by the NES in one form or another for much of the last thirty years. NES kept constant its school integration question wording from 1964 to 1978. When the item reappeared on the 1986 NES after an eight-year absence, it did so in a somewhat different form. Until 1978, the filter to the school integration question read: "Some people say that the government in Washington should see to it that white and black children are allowed to go to the same schools. Others claim that this is not the government's business. Have you been concerned enough about this question to favor one side over the other?" When the question was resumed in 1986, the phrase "are allowed to" was dropped from the filter. Schuman et al. (1997) argue that the removal of the phrase highlights the salience of active government action and may effectively change the school integration item into something closer to an affirmative action question. The fair employment question, on the other hand, was asked in an active form in 1972 and 1992. Thus, the fair employment question can be exploited to gain some empirical purchase on the relative validity of the Schuman "question wording" hypothesis and my preferred "political context" hypothesis. Because the pattern of selection bias in the fair employment question changes across the two eras, we can say with a fair amount of confidence that the lack of selection bias in the school integration question in 1972 is, at least in part, the result of changes in the

present day, respondents did not withhold their views. *Don't know* really meant "I don't know." Thus, it appears that the change in the larger social and political environment surrounding issues of race from the 1970s to the 1990s changed the individual process of attitude expression. As issues surrounding policies designed to ensure racial equality increased in social complexity over the last quarter of the twentieth century, the bias in opinion increased as well.[46]

Conclusion

Across a variety of policies and datasets, I have demonstrated that opinion polls may paint an inaccurate picture of public sentiment on racial issues in the present day. The unspoken opposition to government integration efforts revealed in my analyses indicates that the *don't know* response conceals strong anti-integration sentiment. In addition, this latent opposition appears to contaminate measures of support for government fair employment policies. The finding of these effects in two distinct realms of racial policy underscores the difficulty involved with measuring public sentiment on racial policies more generally. Furthermore, the results from the 1989 New York City analysis provide a compelling account of the failure of pre-election polls in biracial elections. In New York, certain groups of individuals—older respondents, Jews, and those respondents who were reluctant to reveal personal information—chose to keep silent rather than voice their opposition to Dinkins.

Finally, as expected, differences in the norms governing the discussion of racial issue between the early 1970s and the 1990s led to significant differences in the way in which individuals approached the question-answering process. The concealment of anti-integration sentiment behind the *don't know* response that is present in the current era appears to be absent in the earlier era. Thus the results presented in this chapter underscore the importance of attending to the effects of

---

larger political context surrounding these contentious racial policy issues, not a result of the changed question wording.

[46] This is not to say that all issues of race were socially easy in the early 1970s. Some questions—those dealing with principles of racial equality and the tenets of old-fashion racism—may have been socially difficult for certain groups of people at that time. But, at the same time, it is easy to forget how different the norms governing the discussion of race were in the early 1970s. For example, 31 percent of white Americans in 1972 subscribed to the view that blacks were disabled by virtue of their biological inheritance (Kinder and Sanders 1996), and 50 percent of whites in 1970 favored laws against intermarriage (Schuman et al. 1997).

the social environment of the survey interview—the "social complexity" of a particular issue, to use of the language of chapter 2—when investigating public opinion. Sometimes, as demonstrated in this chapter, polls can fail us in systematic ways.

This failure could have serious consequences for political representation in the United States. For example, the school integration results may explain, in part, the unfinished legacy of the school integration efforts begun in the 1950s (Hochschild 1984). While Americans may express overwhelming support for the principles of integration, there appears to be a strong undercurrent of opposition to government intervention that is not visible in the marginals of opinion polls, but that might become visible when it comes to participating on issues that deal with the education of one's children (see, for example, Green and Cowden 1992). Polls that misrepresent public sentiment could subvert the processes of policy formation and implementation if elites use polls to serve as a barometer of the public's wishes on sensitive policy controversies, as some scholars suggest they might. Polls on racial policy issues not only carry incorrect information concerning the public's preferences on those controversies, they also carry information that can mislead representatives who seek to establish effective communication with their constituents. Just because it might be rational for an individual to withhold his or her opinion at the opinion expression stage in the survey setting does not mean that it will always be rational to withhold that opinion.

As racial issues move to the forefront of the policy agenda and politicians begin to implement changes in public policy, keeping silent when one's interests are directly threatened may appear to incur tangible costs. Thus, individuals may act in ways that we could not predict with opinion polls.

We can see this most clearly in the context of the biracial elections examined in this chapter. When the costs of opinion expression change—as they do when we move from the (semi-) public forum of the survey to the complete anonymity of a polling booth—political action diverges substantially from the prediction of opinion polls. Thus, the divergence between public statements and private sentiment is not merely the residue of a process where individuals play different "roles" in their public and private lives (Bogart 1967). Rather, this divergence may serve as an indication of things to come. In the day-to-day goings-on of political society, where the costs and benefits of action and inaction may differ from those of the survey interview, the public may take political action, such as protest and acts of civil disobedience, which could surprise politicians. The questions examined in this chapter are important because they exemplify the types of hard choices between popular principles and unpopular policies that must be made by government.

As a result, politicians may be unprepared for a strong public backlash that unpopular policies might spark. As the costs of inaction for individuals rise, and the opponents of unpopular policies in sensitive issue areas are mobilized, politicians might eventually obtain an accurate picture of the public's will by watching their constituents' actions. Such a picture will come too late for representatives to respond to the public will. For if representatives are unaware that they are out of step with public sentiment, they will not provide the leadership and explanation of their actions that enable representative systems to function. Representatives will not know they are out of step with popular sentiment until they have committed to an unpopular course of action. In short, opinion distortions arising from social factors have the potential to fracture the ongoing communication between representatives and their constituency and, in the process, may subvert effective political representation.

FOUR

SOCIAL WELFARE POLICY AND

PUBLIC OPINION, 1972–1996

IN THE LAST CHAPTER, I considered how the social processes at work in the survey interview could bias measures of opinion on support for policies designed to ensure racial equality. In this chapter, I move to a discussion of the consequences of problems at the stage of opinion formation. I examine a cognitively difficult issue area—social welfare policy—and demonstrate that both inequalities in politically relevant resources and the larger political culture surrounding that issue disadvantage those groups who are natural supporters of the welfare state. These supporters—the economically disadvantaged and those who support principles of equality—are less easily able to form coherent and consistent opinions on such policies than those well endowed with politically relevant resources. Those predisposed to champion the maintenance and expansion of welfare state programs are, as a result, less likely to articulate opinions on surveys. This result underscores the importance of attending to the implications of opinion distortions arising at the stage of attitude formation. On some cognitively hard issues, public opinion may mirror the inequalities of voice found in other realms of the political arena.

The findings of this chapter suggest that the inequalities in voice uncovered in studies of political participation are not simply the result of the direct and tangible costs associated with traditional forms of opinion expression, such as contacting representatives and donating money to campaigns. At a more basic level, inequalities arise when citizens try simply to come to grips with particular political controversies—when they attempt to link their personal concerns to the world of politics. Some individuals are better able to map their personal concerns onto political controversies. These citizens will be advantaged with regard to their political voice, regardless of how low the costs of opinion expression fall. When examining the quality and composition of political voice, then, we should not only ask if relevant interests are expressed but also examine possible sources of bias arising from the manner in which those interests are formed.

Social Welfare Policy and Bias

In chapter 2, I discussed how cognitively hard issues can foster distortions in the process of opinion formation. As issues increase along the dimension of cognitive complexity, those individuals who have difficulty linking their interests and values to the goings-on of the political world will be more likely to offer a *don't know* response. To the extent that the factors that make it difficult to answer survey questions overlap significantly with factors that produce opinion of a particular type, the full spectrum of the public's preferences may not be heard. One area where the presence of such effects seems especially likely is the realm of social welfare policy.

Since the Great Depression, the American welfare state has grown tremendously. While the legitimacy of government involvement in the economy has not been seriously challenged for more than half a century, setting the proper scope of the public support net provided by government has proven to be extremely controversial. Compared to other industrialized democracies, support for social welfare programs in the United States is weak (Shapiro and Young 1989).

McClosky and Zaller (1984, 2) suggest that one reason for the controversial nature of the welfare state in the United States is the political creed that has developed over the last two centuries—what they term the "American ethos." Americans, they argue, hold deeply two sets of inherently contradictory values. On the one hand, Americans are taught to revere democracy, a belief that "all people possess equal worth and have the right to share in their own governance." On the other hand, the tenets of capitalism—"a substantial measure of laissez-faire, and market determination of production, distribution, and economic reward"—are also highly valued in the United States.[1] These tenets clash especially strongly in the arena of social welfare policy.

The impetus for the expansion of the welfare state, McClosky and Zaller argue, comes from the more egalitarian democratic aspect of the ethos, the belief that society should assist those in distress. As they write, "Although democratic theory does not explicitly require that the

---

[1] Certainly, the reduction of the American political tradition to a twofold typology is an extreme simplification. As Rogers Smith (1993, 550) notes, there is no single political "tradition." Instead, "American politics is best seen as expressing the interaction of multiple political traditions, including liberalism, republicanism, and ascriptive forms of Americanism." However, what is important for the present purposes is that social welfare policies tap values—egalitarianism and individualism—that are revered in American political society but lead to contradictory policy prescriptions.

community guarantee the prosperity of every individual, it is a natural extension of the democratic concern for human well-being and equality to contend that all individuals should be assured the material necessities for a decent and fulfilling life" (279). However, the flip side of that creed—the capitalist notions of individualism, self-help, and limited government involvement—provides a counterweight to the development of the welfare state. State-run assistance programs, under such a view, infringe on the market's allocation of resources to members of a society and, as a result, can only hinder the efficient functioning of the economy. Thus, according to McClosky and Zaller, the welfare state remains deeply controversial in the United States because the programs that encompass the welfare state run across, rather than along, the grain of the American ethos.[2]

Empirical work has born out McClosky and Zaller's predictions about the role played by the conflicting values of democracy and capitalism in determining social welfare policy opinion. Feldman and Zaller (1992) find that, in answering social welfare policy questions, individuals draw on the principles of capitalism, individualism, and opposition to big government and the principles of democracy (fairness and egalitarianism) when asked what kinds of things come to mind. Similarly, Hochschild (1981) finds that when discussing distributive justice, people draw upon both norms of equality—arguing that all people may legitimately make the same claims on social resources—and norms of differentiation—believing that some individuals have a greater right to social resources than others. Furthermore, Hochschild finds that individuals differ not merely from each other; they are deeply ambivalent in their views on which of these norms is most important.

The effect of the value conflict on the types of opinions people form on social welfare policy is not, however, constant across the population. Both liberals and conservatives must deal with the inherent tensions in the American political culture.[3] But, as Feldman and Zaller note, ambivalence and inconsistency in the areas of social welfare policy are not found with equal frequency in all segments of the population. Social welfare conservatives, they find, exhibit less value conflict than liberals. Liberals, they argue, must reconcile their humanitarian democratic impulses with the capitalist impulses toward individualism and limited government. Thus, liberals must balance two equally important, but

[2] Other authors have made similar observations but use different labels for the underlying values highlighted by McClosky and Zaller. Ladd and Lipset (1980), for example, discuss social policies in terms of conflict between the values of egalitarianism and achievement.

[3] The terms "liberal" and "conservative" are used here to describe particular positions on social welfare policies, not as labels for more encompassing political ideologies.

contrary, values when evaluating social welfare policy programs. As Tetlock's (1986) "value pluralism" model of ideological reasoning demonstrates, such conflict in deeply held values will lead individuals to be less certain of their political judgments. Conservatives, on the other hand, are able to oppose social welfare policies while at the same time endorsing equality of *opportunity* rather than the economic equality of results (Verba and Orren 1985). In this way, social welfare policy conservatives are able to appeal to a single value and need not necessarily suffer from the same value conflict as their liberal opponents (for a more detailed explication of this argument, see Feldman and Zaller 1992; Hochschild 1981; Tetlock 1986). In short, issues of social welfare policy are difficult for those tending toward the liberal side of the spectrum.

It is not simply the larger political culture that disadvantages the natural supporters of social welfare policies. Those individuals who are victims of resource inequalities—those who do not share fully in society's benefits—are natural supporters of the welfare state.[4] However, these resources—such as the education and free time that enable individuals to become informed about politics—are especially important in enabling individuals to resolve value conflict and uncertainty in forming coherent political opinions.

Thus, those individuals who, by dint of their values or personal characteristics, would support social welfare are disadvantaged. Some are more prone to the value conflict that leads to ambivalence and difficulty in resolving their issue positions. Others lack the resources that allow them to resolve their uncertainty and form political opinions well connected to their personal wants, needs, and desires. And still others suffer from both of these problems.

Because of these circumstances, social welfare policy seems to fit the criteria for an issue area where significant bias in the underlying voice of the people could exist. Social welfare policy liberals are, for a variety of reasons, more prone than conservatives to opinion distortions arising from confusion, ambivalence, and uncertainty when forming opinions about the welfare state. As a result, liberals will be less likely to answer the social welfare policy questions. Public opinion should, therefore, suffer from the truncation of liberal social welfare policy opinion.

Data and Introduction to Analyses

To examine the presence and nature of the compositional bias in opinion concerning social welfare policy issues, I draw again on data from

[4] Though, of course, they are not the only supporters of such a state.

the National Election Studies from the mid-1990s. As in the last chapter, the NES data are well suited to my purposes because the NES is designed to represent the entire voting-age American public. Any conclusions regarding the presence of missing political voices may be extended to the "mass public" as a whole.

I begin my analysis with the 1992 and 1996 studies. The 1996 study is especially appropriate for my purposes because it contains a number of questions concerning social welfare policies. The analysis below will, therefore, draw primarily upon the 1996 data. In particular, I will examine possible bias in three questions that gauge opinion concerning the proper level of social redistribution of economic resources—the Guaranteed Jobs, Services, and Redistribution scales.[5] The Guaranteed Jobs scale asks respondents to place themselves on a seven-point scale measuring whether the government should "see to it that every person has a job and a good standard of living." These scales, common in the NES, give respondents two extreme options, labeled "1" and "7." Respondents are then asked to choose one of these extreme positions, or an intermediate position. The Services scale uses a similar question format and asks if the government should "provide many more services even if it means an increase in spending." Finally, the Redistribution scale asks whether the government should "reduce income differences between the rich and the poor."[6] Together these scales tap three sepa-

[5] Empirically, the three NES items seem to tap an underlying social welfare policy opinion dimension. The interitem correlations of the items are fairly substantial in 1996 (0.394 between the Services and Guaranteed Jobs scales; 0.362 between the Services and Redistribution scales; 0.475 between the Redistribution and Guaranteed jobs scales). Moreover, a scale constructed from these items is reasonably reliable (alpha = 0.67). Finally, the items have common background correlates, thereby providing additional evidence that the questions tap the same underlying dimension (see below). These results are consistent with Feldman and Zaller's (1992) analysis of these questions in the 1987 NES. Also, in recent work Jacoby (2000) finds that the Services scale taps general social welfare policy preferences.

[6] The Guaranteed Jobs scale reads: "Some people feel the government in Washington should see to it that every person has a job and a good standard of living. Suppose these people are at one end of a scale, at point 1. Others think the government should just let each person get ahead on their own. Suppose these people are at the other end, at point 7. And, of course, some other people have opinions somewhere in between, at points 2, 3, 4, 5, or 6. Where would you place yourself on this scale, or haven't you thought much about it?" The full wording of the Services scale reads: "Some people think the government should provide fewer services even in areas such as health and education in order to reduce spending. Suppose these people are at one end of a scale, at point 1. Other people feel it is important for the government to provide many more services even if it means an increase in spending. Suppose these people are at the other end, at point 7. And, of course, some other people have opinions somewhere in between, at points 2, 3, 4, 5, or 6. Where would you place yourself on this scale, or haven't you thought much about it? (List 7-point scale)." The Redistribution scale reads: "Some people think that the government

rate but interrelated facets of the welfare state. For the purposes of the analyses below, I have rescaled these seven-point scales to make 1 the most conservative response and 7 the most liberal response. Thus respondents who choose a value on the scale greater than 4 believe welfare state programs should be expanded, while those who choose values less than 4 believe such programs should be reduced.

The American public, on the whole, took a position just somewhat to the conservative side of the center on social welfare policy questions in the mid-1990s. In 1996, the average respondent placement on the Guaranteed Jobs scale was 3.54; on the Redistribution scale, 3.72; and on the Services scale, 3.89. The average respondent in 1992 was somewhat more liberal: 3.69 on the Guaranteed Jobs scale and 4.11 on the Services scale (the Redistribution question was not asked in 1992).

At the same time, a significant portion of the population abstained from the NES social welfare policy items.[7] Nine percent of respondents claimed that they could not place themselves on the Guaranteed Jobs scale, 14 percent did not take a position on the Services scale, and 23 percent—almost one-quarter of the sample—said they did not know where they stood on the issue of income redistribution. These figures are even higher in 1992 (19 percent for the Services question and 13 percent for the Guaranteed Jobs item).

If my hypothesis concerning the presence of exclusion bias in social welfare policy opinion is correct, the picture of moderation evident in the NES surveys may present a somewhat misleading view of the underlying preferences of the American public. If supporters of broader government involvement in economic affairs gravitate to the *no answer* response at disproportionate rates—as previous work suggests they might—it could be that the process of collecting opinion on social welfare policy through opinion surveys obscures a base of underlying liberal sentiment among nonrespondents on those issues.

---

in Washington ought to reduce income differences between the rich and the poor. Suppose these people are at one end of a scale, at point 1. Other people think that the government should not concern itself with reducing income differences between the rich and the poor. Suppose these people are at the other end, at point 7. And, of course, some other people have opinions somewhere in between, at points 2, 3, 4, 5, or 6. Where would you place yourself on this scale, or haven't you thought much about it? (List 7-point scale)."

[7] Here, I include respondents who "haven't thought much" about a particular social welfare policy question in the *don't know* category. These respondents are accepting the interviewer's invitation to pass on a particular question and, in effect, are saying they don't know where they stand on that question. I do not, however, include the "not ascertained" responses in the *don't know* category because it is not clear how these responses were generated. Sometimes, for example, the interviewer simply forgets to ask a particular question. The term *don't know* as used in this chapter can therefore be thought of as "question-abstainer."

As discussed in chapter 2, to explore the roots of such bias, it is necessary to examine the link between item response and opinion position. We need to take a close look at the ingredients of individual opinion and see how the factors that determine the direction of response are related to the factors that determine whether the respondents will form an opinion. Insofar as these two sets of factors are closely related, the potential for exclusion bias is great.

To this end, I looked at the determinants of opinionation (whether the respondent was able to form an opinion on the social welfare policy item) and opinion direction (where he placed himself on the seven-point scale for each of the NES surveys). Previous work suggests that the roots of exclusion bias may lie both in the values that individuals hold and in the types of personal resources they bring to the survey setting that enable them to link their personal concerns to the world of politics.

I therefore examined the decision to offer an opinion and the direction of that opinion as a function of the values held by the respondents and their level of politically relevant resources.[8] First, I included measures of support for equality and limited government, which correspond roughly to McClosky and Zaller's democracy and capitalist values, respectively. I also included a measure of the amount of conflict between these values on the idea that liberals would experience greater value conflict than conservatives.[9] To capture resources, I included measures of a respondent's level of education, income, and employment status.[10]

One issue remains, however. Simply modeling the decision to answer a question and the particular placement on a question independently is not always a wise strategy. We must also attend to issues of selection bias. In the last chapter, I demonstrated that accounting for item nonresponse on questions measuring support for policies designed to ensure racial equality alters our understanding of the structure of opinion on those policies. It is important to ensure that the social welfare policy data are not contaminated by selection bias that

---

[8] The decision to answer the question is modeled as a probit, while the decision to take a particular stand on the social welfare policy question is modeled with Ordinary Least Squares. The results are not different if social welfare policy position is modeled using ordered probit.

[9] The equality and limited government value scales are coded from 0 to 1. Conflict is given as 1 minus the absolute value of the difference in placement on these two scales. The conflict measure takes a value of 0 if the respondent places himself or herself at opposite ends of the two value scales and increases as the similarity between placements on the scales increases. Alvarez and Brehm (2002) use this same measure in their study of public opinion, though they call their measure "competition" rather than "conflict."

[10] These results are robust to respecification including other demographic controls, such as age, race, and gender.

could arise from unmeasured factors relating to nonresponse. Selection bias, after all, will arise in any situation where the sample of observed cases differs in systematic ways from the sample of unobserved cases, in ways that we cannot directly measure. In the case of the social welfare policy items, I believe that I can adequately capture the differences between the question-answerers and the question-abstainers. I therefore expect to find no selection bias here—only opinion ingredient bias. Indeed, this is the case; given the measures of values and politically relevant resources included in the model, the opinion-direction and opinion-giving processes are independent and can be considered separately.[11] We can therefore proceed to examining the direct links between the *measured* variables in the two processes.

Social Welfare Policy: The Roots of Bias

I first investigated the effects of these various opinion ingredients using data from the 1996 NES. Table 4.1 presents the results of these analyses. The entries in this table represent the average effect of the different opinion ingredients—or variables—across the three social welfare policy questions. The first column lists the variables used to predict both the direction of opinion and the decision to give an opinion.[12] The second column indicates the effect of the different variables on the probability of offering an answer to the social welfare policy questions. These values are calculated to represent the effect of moving from the minimum value of a given opinion ingredient to the maximum value of that ingredient.[13] For example, the effect on the probabil-

[11] I used a Heckman selection bias model (see Greene 1997) and estimated (1) the determinants of item response, (2) the determinants of expressed issue position, and (3) the link between *unmeasured* factors affecting the two processes. The full model results are presented in appendix table A4.1. This result may, at first glance, seem somewhat puzzling. The analyses in table 4.1, after all, show that nonresponse and the direction of response share common predictors. But selection bias occurs only when the *unobserved* factors predicting selection are correlated with the *unobserved* factors predicting opinion direction. In the analyses presented here, I observe many of the factors that predict both opinion direction and selection. So the lack of selection bias should be expected.

[12] The full model results are presented in appendix table A4.1 (see also Berinsky 2002b).

[13] The estimates are derived by calculating, for each of the three social welfare policy items, the difference in the predicted probability of item response between the minimum and maximum value of a particular variable (while holding all other variables at their mean value). These estimates are derived separately for each question from the coefficient estimates in appendix table A4.1, then averaged to generate the entries in table 4.1. The pooling of the coefficients to present the average effect is appropriate because in most cases the coefficients are similarly signed and of similar magnitude. In only one instance

TABLE 4.1
1996 Results

Variable	Average Change in Likelihood of Answering Question (in Percentage Points)	Average Change in Issue Position (on 7-Point Scale)
Education	+9	−0.26
Income: <$12,000	−1	+0.49
Income: $12,000–$21,999	−3	+0.37
Income: $22,000–$49,999	−2	+0.14
Income: $105,000+	+3	+0.05
Income: Not Ascertained	−4	+0.19
Unemployed	−6	+0.39
Liberal	+4	−0.01
Conservative	+3	−0.15
No Ideology	−12	+0.17
Limited Government	+6	−0.94
Equality	0	+1.95
Valve Conflict	−6	+0.17

Note: Entries are the average partial effect of the independent variables on the probability of answering the social welfare questions (column 2) and the position on the 7-
point social welfare policy scales (column 3). The income variables are a series of dummy
variables that compare the effect of being in a particular income class with that of having
an income in the $50,000–$104,999 range. The coefficient estimates used to derive these
effects are presented in table A4.1.

ity of answering the social welfare policy questions of raising a respondent's education from the grade school level to a college degree is an
increase of about nine percentage points. The third column presents
the average effect of the different opinion ingredients on the respondent's issue position.[14] Again, this value is calculated to represent the
effect of moving from the minimum to the maximum value of that in-

(the "liberal" dummy variable in the outcome equation) do I average coefficients that are
of opposite signs and statistically significant. This procedure generates conservative estimates of the predicted effect of the variables. This is because the average response rate to
the social welfare policy questions is fairly high. Therefore, the effects are calculated in
the upper tail of the cumulative normal, far from the point of maximal effect.

[14] This entry is the average regression coefficient from appendix table A4.1.

gredient. For instance, increasing a respondent's education from the grade school level to the college level moves the respondent's opinion a quarter-point in the conservative direction (on the seven-point scale).

The analyses in table 4.1 indicate that, as expected, the ability to form an opinion and the direction of that opinion are closely linked through the determinants of both processes. First, the larger political culture plays a strong role in determining which types of opinions are heard in the realm of social welfare policy, and which fall by the wayside. Those individuals who subscribe to values that lead them to the conservative end of the seven-point scales—those respondents who believe strongly in limited government—are more likely to answer the social welfare policy questions than those individuals who support a larger role for government.[15] For example, individuals most firmly committed to the tenets of capitalism are, on average, 6 percent more likely to answer the social welfare policy questions. And when they do answer those items, they take a position that is almost one point more conservative than the position of those who reject such values. However, while those individuals who support the democratic values of equality are more likely to take a liberal position on the social welfare policy scales, unlike those respondents who subscribe to the tenets of capitalism, they are no more likely than those with low equality scores to offer an opinion on the social welfare policy question. Finally, as the work of Feldman and Zaller and Hochschild suggests, those individuals who experience value conflict are less likely to answer the social welfare policy questions but tend to the liberal end of the seven-point scales.[16] The results presented in table 4.1 are not specific to 1996; the basic pattern of these findings can also be found in the 1992 data (see appendix table A4.2).

As predicted, the existence of resource differentials between the natural supporters and opponents of social welfare policies exacerbates the effects of the larger political culture. By and large, those individuals who possess personal characteristics that would incline them toward the liberal positions on the seven-point scales—the unemployed and those with low incomes—are less likely to offer opinions on the social welfare policy questions.[17] Again, these results replicate in 1992.

[15] Though the coefficient on the limited government measure is not always statistically significant, it is in all cases substantively large and in the expected direction.

[16] Though the effects do not always reach conventional levels of statistical significance, they are always in the expected direction.

[17] Though the coefficients on those variables do not always reach statistical significance, the coefficients have the anticipated sign in both the choice and item response equations for all the models. This trend holds for all three questions but is strongest for the Redistribution item.

It appears, then, that many of the same factors determine the decision to give an opinion on the social welfare policy questions and the direction of that opinion. As expected, certain types of opinion ingredients both drive individuals toward the conservative end of the policy spectrum *and* enable them to answer the social welfare policy questions. Those individuals who avoid the fault line in the larger political culture between capitalism and democracy—those who subscribe only to the capitalist principle of limited government—are more likely to voice opinions, and opinions with a conservative bent. Furthermore, those individuals advantaged in the resources that allow one to relate one's personal concerns to the larger political stage and form coherent summary judgments on survey questions are also more likely to express opposition to the welfare state. Thus, there is reason to believe that the (fairly substantial) population of respondents who abstain from the issue placement questions because of high levels of uncertainty and ambivalence differ from the population of respondents in their political preferences concerning social welfare policy.[18]

Bias in Social Welfare Policy Opinion: Estimation and Interpretation

It is possible to compute the degree of bias in social welfare policy opinion. Because the bias works through the factors that we can measure, we can use what we know about the opinions of the question-

[18] It is sensible to expect, as I do here, that extreme ambivalence and uncertainty would lead respondents to abstain from answering survey questions. There are, however, many reasons why individuals might choose to abstain. Thus, it is desirable to confirm through empirical analysis that the hypothesized link between uncertainty and ambivalence at the stage of opinion formation, on the one hand, and item nonresponse, on the other, does indeed exist. A variety of techniques have been used to measure uncertainty and ambivalence in individual opinion (for a review, see Alvarez 1998). However, one set of techniques that has gained prominence in recent years is statistical procedures that model the variance of individual opinions (see, for example, Alvarez and Brehm 1995). These techniques presume that individuals vary not simply in their mean responses to survey questions, but also in the variances of their responses to those questions. Presumably, those groups of individuals who are more uncertain and ambivalent about their opinion exhibit higher error residual variances than those individuals who are certain about their political judgments. Thus, we can observe uncertainty and ambivalence by comparing response variances across individuals. Statistical analyses (available from the author upon request) demonstrate that uncertainty and ambivalence not only lead individuals to abstain from questions, but also may increase their propensity to give more variant answers. Specifically, many of the same opinion ingredients that increase the likelihood that an individual will abstain from issue placement questions also increase individual variance for the three questions.

TABLE 4.2
Predicted Issue Placement Positions

1992			
	7-Point Placers	*Nonplacers*	*Difference*
Services	4.07	4.37	0.30
Guaranteed Jobs	3.66	3.92	0.26
1996			
	7-Point Placers	*Nonplacers*	*Difference*
Services	3.84	4.26	0.42
Guaranteed Jobs	3.50	3.90	0.40
Redistribution	3.65	4.12	0.47

Note: The use of T-tests to gauge the difference between the two groups is inappropriate because this table compares projected issue placements to actual issue placements. But predicted positions generated using the Clarify program (King, Tomz, and Wittenberg 2000) indicate that these differences are significant at the .01 level.

answerers to characterize the opinions of those individuals who declined to answer the question. In effect, we can determine what the nonanswerers would have said if they were able to overcome their uncertainty and ambivalence and give voice to their politically relevant wants, needs, and desires.[19] We can then compare this sentiment with the collective judgment of those individuals who place themselves on the issue scales to gauge the extent—not simply the presence—of compositional bias in social welfare policy opinion.[20]

Table 4.2 indicates that, as expected, the differences in the average opinions of scale placers and those individuals who do not answer

[19] Specifically, I use the coefficients presented in table 4.1 to predict the issue positions of the nonrespondents. This approach is valid because, as noted above, there was no selection bias in the data. The betas for the sample under analysis (the sample that excludes people who do not choose a position on the seven-point scale) are therefore the full sample betas. Thus, the relationship between the independent and dependent variables is not different for the people who answer the social welfare policy question compared with those who are unable to form coherent opinions on those issues. I also replicated these analyses using both models of opinion direction that included more variables and those that included fewer variables. In all cases, the predicted differences between the *scale placer* group and the *don't know* group remained stable.

[20] Though the predictors of item response do not always reach statistical significance in the analyses, the placers and nonplacers differ significantly in the composition of their opinion ingredients. Put another way, at a bivariate level, all predictors of opinion holding in table 4.1 are significant.

items are significant across all the social welfare policy questions. Issue placers are almost one-half a point more conservative on the seven-point scales than our best estimate of the mean position of those who abstain from the issue placement questions in 1996. Though the differences in 1992 are of a somewhat smaller magnitude, the same basic pattern is obtained. Thus, the differences between the respondents and the nonrespondents on the various opinion ingredients—the resources and values that determine social welfare policy positions—have real consequences for the types of social welfare policy opinions we would expect them to hold.

Validating the Results

Given that I assessed the differences between scale placers and non-placers using opinion placements constructed, in part, by imputing interests to individuals who opted out of answering survey questions, a healthy degree of skepticism is understandable. However, such skepticism is unfounded: the finding of a proconservative tilt among the population of issue placers extends from the imputed interests to expressed opinions.

While some respondents declined to answer all three of the social welfare policy items in 1996, other respondents who abstained from one item answered one or two of the other items. We therefore have a measure of social welfare policy sentiments for some respondents who declined to answer particular social welfare policy items. For example, of the 350 respondents who did not answer the Redistribution question, 81 percent answered the Guaranteed Jobs item, and 68 percent placed themselves on the Services and Spending scale. The actual answers these "partial respondents" gave can be compared with the answers of the item placers to see if the differences found in table 4.2 are mirrored in measured opinions.

In table 4.3, I present the social welfare issue placement positions for respondents and nonrespondents in 1996. Replicating the differences found in table 4.2, those individuals who were not able to form an opinion on one of the issue placement scales were more liberal than placers on those items they did answer. For example, Services scale nonplacers were almost one-half point more liberal than placers on the Guaranteed Jobs scale and over three-quarters of a point more liberal on the Redistribution scale. Again, similar differences are found in the 1992 data. Thus, once again, it is clear that the bias in opinion is not

TABLE 4.3
Social Welfare Policy Item Placements, 1996

Services			
	7-Point Placers	*Nonplacers*	*Difference*
Guaranteed Jobs	3.49	3.94	0.45**
Redistribution	3.64	4.49	0.84**
Guaranteed Jobs			
	7-Point Placers	*Nonplacers*	*Difference*
Services	3.87	4.20	0.32**
Redistribution	3.66	4.58	0.91**
Redistribution			
	7-Point Placers	*Nonplacers*	*Difference*
Services	3.74	4.39	0.65**
Guaranteed Jobs	3.44	3.75	0.31**

* = $p < .10$; ** = $p < .05$ (one-tailed test).

an artifact of the political climate in 1996; rather, it pervaded measures of opinion through the 1990s.[21]

This difference between placers and nonplacers extends not only across different social welfare policy items asked in the same survey, but also to the same items asked at different points in time. The 1992 and 1996 NES data examined above are separate datasets, but they are also part of a three-wave panel survey conducted in 1992, 1994, and 1996. That is, some respondents to the 1996 survey were also interviewed in 1992 and 1994. We therefore have measures in 1992 and 1994 of the social welfare policy opinions for some individuals who in 1996 said that they did not know where they stood on the Services and Guaranteed Jobs scales. For instance, we have measures of self-placement on the Services scale in 1992 and/or 1994 for 74 percent of those respondents who declined to answer the item in 1996. It is possible, then, to use these data to validate further the differences in the social welfare policy opinions of respondents and nonrespondents found above.[22]

[21] The full results for 1992 are presented in appendix table A4.2.

[22] To measure the social welfare policy sentiment of nonplacers, I constructed a scale that measured the average scale position for each respondent in the sample on one item

TABLE 4.4

Summary of Average Over-Time Issue Placement, 1992–1996

	7-Point Placers (1996)	Nonplacers (1996)	Difference
Services	3.76	4.08	0.32**
Guaranteed Jobs	3.45	3.82	0.36*

* = $p < .10$; ** = $p < .05$ (one-tailed test).

As table 4.4 demonstrates, the pattern of liberal social welfare policy sentiment among the *don't know* respondents uncovered in tables 4.2 and 4.3 continues. While the differences between the placers and non-placers over time are not as great as the differences presented above, individuals who did not answer the social welfare policy items in 1996 gave answers that were one-third point more liberal than those respondents who took a position in 1996 (again, similar results are found in an analysis of the 1992 data).[23]

In sum, the analysis of both simulated and measured opinions of the NES survey respondents leads to the same conclusion. Those individuals who—due to uncertainty and ambivalence surrounding the social welfare issues examined here—are unable to answer the Guaranteed Jobs, Services, and Redistribution scales are more favorable to policies that support the welfare state than those who are able to form opinions on the NES issue placement questions. Thus, when the mass public speaks through opinion polls, a portion of liberal sentiment on social welfare policy questions is not heard.

Aggregate Consequences

The analyses presented above show that respondents and nonrespondents differ in their social welfare policy sentiment, but the effect of correcting for individual-level opinion distortions on the shape of collective social welfare policy opinion remains to be determined. The estimates of the net aggregate change caused by accounting for the senti-

---

across the entire series. If respondents answered an item in any year of the panel, then, I have a measure of their score on that particular scale.

[23] Additional analyses confirm that the differences between placers and nonplacers are driven by differences in social welfare policy sentiment, rather than general liberalism. Nonplacers are significantly more liberal than placers on the NES item that taps beliefs about spending on the "poor." However, the two groups are identical in their beliefs regarding spending on "blacks" and "crime," as well as their position on whether the federal government should enact laws to protect homosexuals.

TABLE 4.5
Estimated Sample Mean Bias

	1992	1996
Services	−0.06	−0.06
Guaranteed Jobs	−0.03	−0.04
Redistribution	—	−0.11

ments of the nonrespondents are presented in table 4.5. These estimates are calculated in units of the seven-point NES issue scales. As expected, the estimates indicate that the sample mean overestimates the American public's conservatism on social welfare policy issues. The direction of this bias is consistent across issues and across years. However, the degree of this bias is rather small, ranging from the equivalent of one-half to two points on a hundred-point scale. Nonrespondents therefore differ significantly from respondents in their social welfare policy preferences, but in the aggregate this difference does not seem to change significantly our measures of collective opinion.

These results may initially seem reassuring for those concerned with the ability of opinion polls accurately to gauge public opinion. But they are less reassuring if we pull our frame of analysis back to a lower level of aggregation. Take, for example, opinion at the level of census region. The misrepresentation of aggregate opinion on the Redistribution question in the South in 1996 is 0.17, a figure that is almost three times the comparable bias in the Northeast.[24] More importantly, the bias of opinion polls echoes the patterns of inequality found in traditional forms of political participation. As table 4.6 demonstrates, the differences between placers and nonplacers on the social welfare policy items mirror

[24] Moving to a more explicitly political context, consider opinion at the level of the state. If senators from some states receive signals more reflective of the underlying social welfare policy sentiment of their constituents than others, the clarity of the voice of the mass public will vary greatly across states, even if such differences largely wash out at the aggregate level. The NES data reveal that a wide range of exclusion bias may exist at this level. For example, there is almost no exclusion bias in the redistribution question in New Jersey—0.05 to be precise. In Arkansas, on the other hand, opinion on redistribution understates liberal sentiment by almost one-half a point on the seven-point NES scale—the equivalent of almost six points on a hundred-point scale. These aggregate differences exist because the distributions of the key predictors of nonresponse and response direction differ in these geographic areas. Given the relatively small sample sizes at the state level and the fact that the NES sampling procedures do not ensure random samples below the regional level, it would be a mistake to take this evidence as anything more than suggestive. However, these cross-sectional differences indicate that the existence of exclusion bias in aggregate public opinion is not necessarily innocuous.

TABLE 4.6
Issue Placement Differences by Political Participation Level, 1996

	Voting		
	Voters	*Nonvoters*	*Difference*
Services	3.76	4.18	0.42**
Guaranteed Jobs	3.39	3.88	0.49**
Redistribution	3.60	4.15	0.55**
	Campaign Participation		
	Participators	*Nonparticipators*	*Difference*
Services	3.64	3.98	0.34**
Guaranteed Jobs	3.28	3.62	0.33**
Redistribution	3.57	3.80	0.23**

Note: A participator is a person who said he or she engaged in at least one of the four following activities: (1) trying to convince other people they should vote for one of the parties or candidates; (2) attending political meetings; (3) doing work for one of the parties or candidates; and (4) wearing a button supporting one of the parties or candidates.
  $* = p < .10$; $** = p < .05$ (one-tailed test).

the differences between participators and nonparticipators in both direction and size. Nonvoters are about one-half point more liberal on all the social welfare policy questions than are voters. Those who fail to participate in campaigns are one-third of a point more liberal than campaign activists.[25] In short, in polls, as in other avenues of public expression, it is the voice of the disadvantaged that is muted.[26]

Continuity in Opinion: Social Welfare Policy Opinion in the 1970s

Having established the presence and nature of the bias in social welfare policy opinion in the present day, as in the last chapter, I now ex-

[25] Participators are persons who said they engaged in at least one of the four following activities: (1) trying to convince other people they should vote for one of the parties or candidates; (2) attending political meetings; (3) doing work for one of the parties or candidates; and (4) wearing a button supporting one of the parties or candidates.

[26] The empirical record concerning the representativeness of the attitudes of political participants may be somewhat mixed (Bennett and Resnick 1990; Ginsberg 1986; Verba et al. 1993; Wolfinger and Rosenstone 1980), but here the data support the notion of an accumulation of inequality in political voice.

amine the dynamics of this bias over time. The factors that make social welfare policy a cognitively difficult issue for liberals did not change over the last quarter of the twentieth century. Thus, in contrast to the dynamic changes in the school integration results over the last twenty years, our expectation should be that the bias in measures of opinion concerning social welfare policy should remain constant from the 1970s to the 1990s.

The fault line in the American political tradition between the tenets of capitalism and those of democracy, described by McClosky and Zaller (1984), is an enduring one. Given this stability, it would be surprising, to say the least, if the ideological tensions underlying social welfare opinion changed significantly over the last twenty years. Indeed, the similarity between Hochschild's (1981) conclusions—reached using data collected in the mid-1970s—and Zaller and Feldman's (1992) conclusions—reached using data from the late 1980s—suggests that stability in the patterns of uncertainty and ambivalence in opinion formation is the rule in the realm of social welfare policy opinion.

The continuity in political culture over this period, moreover, should be mirrored by a similar constancy in the resource inequality between opinion holders and nonholders. The relationship between resources such as education and political information, on the one hand, and opinion holding, on the other, is not an artifact of the present day; as noted above, a large body of research dating back to the 1970s has underscored the importance of such a link. Moreover, there is no reason to suspect that those who most benefit from social welfare policies—the resource poor—would have opposed those policies in an earlier era. In sum, there is much to suggest that the pattern of the social welfare question-answering process—and the resulting exclusion bias arising at the stage of opinion formation—should follow the same pattern in the 1970s as it does in the present day.

As with the school integration issue, replicating the 1990s social welfare policy analysis in the 1970s is not straightforward. The 1972 and 1976 datasets are missing several measures that proved to be strong predictors of contemporary social welfare policy opinion. Most critically, the measures of the values of equality and limited government that lie at the heart of the theoretical enterprise above are lacking. Moreover the Services versus Spending item was not added to the NES question battery until 1982.

Even with these limitations, it is possible to examine the impact of resource inequalities and liberal/conservative ideologies on the respondents' ability to form social welfare policy opinions. In this way, I can determine whether, as I suspect, the pattern of exclusion bias found in social welfare policy opinion in the 1990s also existed twenty years earlier. I therefore sought to replicate, as best I could, the analyses presented above using the Guaranteed Jobs item from 1972 and 1976.

As in the 1990s, the American public, in the whole, took a moderate to slightly conservative view on social welfare policy questions in the 1970s. The average respondent placement on the Guaranteed Jobs scale was 3.70 in 1972 and 3.57 in 1976, figures that are comparable to those of the present day (remember again, that 4 is the midpoint on the scale). Similarly, a significant portion of the population abstained from the NES social welfare policy items in those years. In 1972, 14 percent of respondents claimed that they could not place themselves on the Guaranteed Jobs scale; in 1976, this figure rose to 20 percent. While the proportion of *don't know*s is higher in the 1970s than in the present day, it is not significantly higher. In sum, the data from the 1970s is remarkably similar to that from the 1990s.

To see if these similarities lead to a comparable conservative bias in the earlier era, I examined the determinants of the social welfare policy question-answering process. I considered the ability to form an opinion as a function of the same politically relevant resources (education, income, and employment status) and political values (partisanship and liberal/conservative identification). I predicted the decision to answer the question as a function of the same politically relevant resources used to predict the direction of opinion.[27]

In line with my expectations, the basic pattern of these results largely mirrors that found in the present day. The results of these individual-level analyses for 1972 and 1976 are presented in appendix table A4.3.[28] Thus, the basic result from the 1990s appears to hold at the individual level in the 1970s, even with the limited nature of the replication.[29] Those who lack the resources necessary to draw clear links between their personal lives and the political world are more supportive of social welfare policies but are less likely to form opinions on the Guaranteed Jobs question. Thus, the roots of exclusion bias appear to exist in individual-level behavior in the 1970s.

---

[27] To capture general political engagement, I used information about politics and interest in the campaign. As before, I used the Heckman estimation technique to account for possible selection bias, though I did not expect the presence of such bias.

[28] For example, those individuals with lower incomes are more likely to support social welfare policies than those in higher income brackets. While income levels do not appear to predict opinion holding in 1972 (though they do in 1976), this apparent nonrelationship arises because other factors in the model—most notably political information—are correlated with opinion holding *and* levels of income.

[29] As was the case in the 1990s, the Guaranteed Jobs question does not appear tainted by selection bias; ρ is indistinguishable from zero in both a statistical and a substantive sense.

The more important question, however, concerns how these roots play out in the construction of public opinion. Here again, there appear to be significant similarities between the 1970s and the present. Respondents who are able to form opinions on social welfare policy questions differ in important ways from individuals who are unable to form such judgments. While the differences between the placers and nonplacers on the simulated Guaranteed Jobs placement is smaller than in the 1990s, this difference is in the expected direction. Those respondents who are unable to form attitudes on social welfare policy issues are significantly more liberal—by about a quarter point on the seven-point scale—than those who answer the Guaranteed Jobs item. Respondents to the item took a position of 3.71 in 1972 and 3.59 in 1976. By comparison, nonrespondents are predicted to take a position of 3.88 in 1972 and 3.92 in 1976.

Because only the Guaranteed Jobs item was asked in the 1970s, I cannot validate the predicted opinions with actual opinions using cross-sectional data, as I did in the 1990s. However, because the 1972 and 1976 datasets are the endpoints of a three-wave panel study, it is possible to verify the differences I find using the answers given by the panel respondents. As in the analysis from the 1990s, I constructed a scale of opinion on the Guaranteed Jobs question across the panel.[30] I then compared the scores of opinion placers and nonplacers. The results of this analysis again support the findings of greater liberalism among nonplacers. In 1972 and 1976, those individuals who did not answer the Guaranteed Jobs question were significantly more liberal than scale placers when they did answer the question in other years. Respondents to the item in 1972 took an average position of 3.57 across the panel, while nonrespondents to the Guaranteed Jobs question in 1972 took a position of 3.73. The comparable placements for 1976 are 3.55 for respondents and 3.77 for nonrespondents.

Finally, the findings carry over to the aggregate level. Given the somewhat smaller difference between the placers and nonplacers, but the slightly higher nonresponse rates in the early 1970s, I would expect roughly similar aggregate effects as I found in the present day. Indeed this is the case. The Guaranteed Jobs item has a conservative bias of −0.02 in 1972 and −0.05 in 1976. Again, though the size of the aggregate bias is small, it is present and in the expected direction.

In sum, as expected, I find the same pattern of exclusion bias in the 1970s as I did in the 1990s. In both eras, a bias that is determined by resource inequality exacerbates the gap between the views of those

[30] To measure the social welfare policy sentiment of nonplacers, as before, I constructed a scale that measured the average scale position for each respondent in the sample on one item across the entire series. If a respondent answered the Guaranteed Jobs

who are able to form opinions on the social welfare policy items and those who are unable to construct such judgments. Exclusion bias on social welfare policy opinion is therefore a persistent feature of the American political system.[31]

Conclusion

The results presented here deepen our understanding of biases in opinion polls in particular, and political participation more generally. As hypothesized, those respondents who are able to form opinions on social welfare policy issues are more conservative than those respondents who are not able to come to such coherent judgments. The natural supporters of the welfare state are, therefore, more likely to abstain from polling questions on the welfare state. Thus, the larger political culture surrounding social welfare policy questions in combination with significant resource differentials that fall along, not across, this political fault line understates support for an expanded social welfare state.

When aggregated at the national level, as demonstrated above, this bias does not appear to threaten significantly the representativeness of public opinion signals. However, the fact remains that those who keep silent on social welfare policy issues would—if they gave opinions—speak in a different manner than those who answer social welfare policy questions. This result is especially important because it mirrors the patterns of inequality found in traditional forms of political participation, such as writing to government officials. The true costs of participation lie not just in the expression of opinion, but also in the *formation* of opinion. Social welfare policy is a cognitively difficult issue for those who support the expansion of the welfare state. Thus, the resources that enable individuals to make meaningful links between their personal interests and values, on the one hand, and controversies in the political world, on the other, are as important as the more tangible costs of participation. Thus, reducing the direct costs of opinion expression will not, in and of itself, necessarily give equal voice to all groups. Opinion polls, contrary to the claims of Gallup and Verba, do not always make up for the inegalitarian shortcomings of other forms of political participation. Under some circumstances, they echo and may even reinforce those shortcomings.

---

question in any year of the panel, then, I have a measure of his or her score on that particular scale.

[31] These results also replicate in the mid-1980s, further confirming that the bias found here is a persistent feature of aggregate public opinion concerning social welfare policy.

FIVE

THE CHANGING CONTEXT OF PUBLIC OPINION

CONCERNING THE VIETNAM WAR, 1964–1972

SCHOLARS have long suspected that the intensity of the public's attention declines when the focus of policy turns to foreign affairs. Navigating America's place on the international scene involves complicated policy decisions. The public is by and large ill informed about events in other countries and, as a result, is poorly positioned to make such difficult choices. Even if the mass public's views concerning American involvement abroad are not formless and malleable (Almond 1960), the balance of empirical evidence indicates that public opinion concerning foreign policy is less structured than opinion concerning domestic policy (see, for example, Hurwitz and Peffley 1987; for recent surveys of public opinion concerning foreign policy, see Foyle 1999; Holsti 1996; Sobel 2001). Thus, for much of the public, foreign policy is a cognitively hard issue area.

In the realm of foreign policy, therefore, there is a great deal of room for political leadership to affect the shape of public opinion. The nature and balance of elite rhetoric may affect the character of public opinion. If elites speak in a unified voice on foreign affairs, those citizens with underlying predispositions in line with the prevailing message will be able to give voice to their interests. For these individuals, foreign policy will become a comparatively easier issue. However, individuals who hold predispositions discordant with that message will tend to fall by the wayside. As a result, the creation of a bias in public opinion in line with dominant discourse is highly likely. In this chapter, I argue that such a situation characterized public opinion in the early years of the war in Vietnam. However, antiwar messages became more common in the public sphere in the years after 1968. The war therefore became a cognitively easier issue for those citizens who opposed intervention abroad, and the pro-intervention bias disappeared.

Elite Rhetoric and The Vietnam War

Walter Lippmann began his classic work, *Public Opinion*, with a parable concerning an island where the residents—collectively of English, German, and French descent—did not learn that their native lands were engaged in the First World War until almost six weeks after it began. This parable captures an essential element of public opinion concerning foreign affairs—the distance between the average citizen and the events that occur on the world stage. No matter their level of concern or interest, citizens can rarely draw upon their personal experiences when evaluating the policy choices of the government. As Lippmann argues, "The world that we have to deal with politically is out of reach, out of sight, out of mind. It has to be explored, reported, and imagined" (1922, 18).

Such processes carry important political implications. Most of what Americans know about affairs abroad comes to them through the debate and dialogue of elites with interests in foreign events. It is especially important, therefore, to attend to the tenor and tone of elite discourse when considering the nature of public opinion concerning foreign policy. The discussion in chapter 1 suggests that the presence of elite discourse on one side of a controversy will aid the expression of opinion supportive of that position. Similarly, the absence of such rhetoric will hinder the expression of opinion conducive to that view. To reiterate the argument made previously, this is not to say that elites can create waves of public sentiment out of thin air. Instead, elite discourse stimulates the expression of opinions because that discourse resonates with the underlying predispositions of particular segments of the mass public.

In the case of Vietnam, elite rhetoric played an especially large role. Conflict in Vietnam began shortly after World War II as a colonial war between France and revolutionary forces in Vietnam. In the summer of 1954, the French government ended its century of rule over Vietnam by agreeing to the Geneva Peace Accords, which partitioned Vietnam at the 17th parallel. This arrangement was supposed to be temporary but, under President Eisenhower, the United States sought the creation of a counterrevolutionary government south of the dividing line—the Republic of Vietnam (or South Vietnam). This government proved unstable, and in the late 1950s and early 1960s a revolutionary movement known as the National Liberation Front emerged to fight the South Vietnamese government, with at least the tacit support of the Democratic Republic of Vietnam (or North Vietnam). In response, President Kennedy increased U.S. military involvement in Vietnam, through arms and advisers. This buildup continued under President Johnson.

Direct U.S. involvement in the conflict began in 1964. In response to apparent attacks by North Vietnam in August of that year, Congress passed the Gulf of Tonkin Resolution. This bill was supported unanimously in the House and met with only two dissenting votes in the Senate. The Gulf of Tonkin Resolution gave the president broad war powers to pursue the conflict in Vietnam, and in March 1965 the first American combat troops were sent to Vietnam. The United States was now fully committed to supporting the weak South Vietnamese government. More importantly for the purposes of the analyses to follow, given the strong support for the Gulf of Tonkin Resolution, the American government was fully united behind an interventionist strategy. Individuals predisposed to take aggressive action to protect American interests could find support for their position in a steady and largely unchallenged stream of rhetoric reminiscent of Lyndon Johnson's contention that the issue of Vietnam "is the future of southeast Asia as a whole. A threat to any nation in that region is a threat to all, and a threat to us. . . . This is not just a jungle war, but a struggle for freedom on every front of human activity."[1]

This strong pro-intervention flow of elite communication continued through the mid-1960s. Zaller's (1992) content analysis of news magazine coverage of the Vietnam War finds that the prowar message was much stronger than the antiwar message in the period from 1964 to 1968, reaching its high point of disparity in 1966.

However, with hearings held by Senator William Fulbright in 1966, opposition to the war began to emerge within the U.S. government. In 1967 there were some attempts in Congress to cut off funding for the war. As Zaller (1992) notes, the defeat of these bills by large margins indicated continuing strong support for the war within the government. By the late 1960s, however, antiwar sentiment had penetrated the elite level. In the years after 1968, the anti-intervention message signaled by Fulbright's actions gathered steam. By the turn of the decade, the proportion of pro- and anti-intervention messages, while not quite balanced, contained strong messages to appeal both to those groups predisposed to support the war and to those predisposed to oppose the U.S. effort.

If the argument made in this book is correct, the dynamic changes in the volume and salience of elite messages concerning the Vietnam War should have led to a differential balance of the expression of predispositions at different points in the war because different groups would be differently advantaged by elite discourse enabling them to link their political predispositions to the political controversies of the Vietnam War. In the early years of U.S. involvement in Southeast Asia, individuals who on balance held predispositions that conformed to prowar rhetoric would be more likely to be heard in opinion polls. On the other hand, respondents who possessed predispositions that did not fit with the dominant prowar message should have been underrepresented in public opinion. To use the language of this book, in the first portion of the war, public opinion should have suffered from a pro-intervention bias. That is, on balance, anti-intervention sentiment

---

[1] President Johnson's Message to Congress, August 5, 1964. *Department of State Bulletin*, August 24, 1964.

would have been excluded from public opinion.[2] Over the course of the war, as the balance of the volume and salience of elite rhetoric changed and both pro-intervention and anti-intervention views were represented in public discourse, the size of this bias should have reduced and eventually disappeared. In short, as the mix of elite rhetoric concerning the war changed over time, the nature of bias in public opinion should have changed as well.

Previous scholars have not directly addressed the nature of the sentiment that may have been lost by excluding question-abstainers from public opinion concerning war. But some suggestive evidence exists. In a study of public opinion concerning the Korean War, Modigliani (1972) finds that the incidence of *don't know* responses was highest among respondents who—on the questions they did answer—tended to oppose international involvement. Moving to more directly relevant evidence, Jackson (1993) performed an in-depth investigation of opinion concerning the Vietnam War. He modeled the respondents' decision to take a position on Vietnam and their propensity to choose a *don't know* response (which he terms uncertainty). Jackson finds that respondents who answered survey questions but were uncertain of their preference on U.S. policy toward Vietnam were more likely to take a dovish position, as opposed to a hawkish position. He concludes that this pattern of guessing created a picture of aggregate public sentiment that was more dovish than true public sentiment. But this view assumes that we should strip out uncertain respondents from our measures of public opinion. In this book, I take the opposite view. If these uncertain doves reflected the sentiments of the abstainers from the Vietnam placement questions—as my hypothesis suggests—then it could be that true sentiment toward American policy in Vietnam might have been *more* anti-interventionist than opinion polls indicated. In sum, the hypothesis of a pro-intervention bias in public opinion in the early years of the Vietnam War is promising and deserves close investigation.

The Roots of Bias in Opinion Concerning the War

To explore the roots of exclusion bias, we must examine commonalities in the determinants of item response and opinion position. Two factors

---

[2] This is not to say that there were necessarily "doves" that remained silent. Rather, people who were uneasy with the war effort could not find a rhetoric recipe to match their sentiments to the Vietnam conflict. So the sentiment that was missing in the early part of the war was not so much an active call for disengagement as a general unease with the war effort.

stand out. The first, and more obvious, is the direct effect of exposure to elite rhetoric. In the early years of the war, when the balance of rhetoric largely favored U.S. involvement, we would expect that exposure to such rhetoric would enable those with pro-intervention predispositions to see how their underlying interests and values related to the conflict in Vietnam. Those individuals predisposed to favor intervention would be likely to answer questions concerning Vietnam. On the other hand, respondents who held underlying predispositions that led them to oppose intervention would find little in elite discourse to enable them to link their personal concerns to the Vietnam controversy. These individuals would have a difficult time finding their political voice on opinion surveys. Thus, in the early part of the war, respondents who were highly exposed to elite accounts of American involvement in Vietnam should have been more likely to support American involvement *and* should have been more likely to answer questions concerning the war.

Second, we should identify the types of individuals who hold those predispositions from which elite rhetoric would resonate. In some cases, it is possible to measure directly who holds these predispositions. One might, for example, measure the tendency of certain individuals to take a firm and aggressive stand toward foreign nations. But we can also look at the characteristics of individuals to determine the kinds of groups that might be particularly receptive to a pro-intervention or an anti-intervention message.[3]

At first glance, such a search does not seem especially promising. One striking finding of early scholarship investigating public opinion concerning the Vietnam War was the minimal structuring of that opinion. As Verba et al. (1967, 323) write, "Unlike candidate preferences in an election, or opinions on domestic policies, attitudes on the war in Vietnam do not pattern along the standard dimensions of social structure. The respondent's social characteristics—class, party, place of residence—have little relationship to preference." Though opinion on Vietnam may have not followed the standard political cleavages of the 1960s, some important cleavages did exist. First, Verba and his colleagues found that men were more likely than women to support policies that escalated U.S. involvement in Vietnam, while women were more likely than men to support policies of de-escalation. These conclusions were largely supported by Mueller's (1973) analysis of Gallup data from the late 1960s. Mueller found that women were gen-

---

[3] The characteristics of individuals are not intended here to serve as causal factors. Rather, they serve as a signal of membership in groups who hold predispositions that, on balance, would lead them to be particularly favorable or unfavorable to the war.

erally less favorable to escalation of war efforts than men and were less likely to oppose de-escalatory policies.[4] Second, researchers found that race was a significant determinant of preferred Vietnam policy. Verba et al. found a racial gap in opinion similar to the gender gap. Blacks opposed escalation more than whites and were more likely to support de-escalation policies. Again, Mueller's analysis supports these conclusions. Finally, some indicators of group membership show a significant, though somewhat weaker, relationship to pro-intervention predispositions. Contrary to popular perceptions, younger Americans tended to take a more hawkish position on the war than did older citizens. Mueller (1973) and Rosenberg, Verba, and Converse (1970) both find that age had a negative relationship with support for taking an aggressive position vis-à-vis North Vietnam.

These groupings do not necessarily break principled doves from principled hawks. At a more basic level, they may separate those supportive of aggressive U.S. policy abroad from those uncomfortable with such positions. Work by Schuman (1972) is suggestive on this point. In a 1970 Detroit area survey, Schuman included an item asking respondents if it "was a mistake to get involved in Vietnam"—a question asked by several survey organizations in that period (see below). Respondents who replied that they thought such involvement was a mistake were then asked why they believed that to be so. Schuman found that women, blacks, and older respondents were more likely to take what he called a "pragmatic isolationist" position than an ideologically driven dovish position. Older respondents, for example, tended to oppose the war because it "causes trouble." Women were likely to have reservations about American involvement because they were uncomfortable with the deaths of American soldiers. Thus, opposition to the war tended to originate from an uneasiness with the general war effort, based on diffuse interests. Regardless of its underlying source, however, real divisions along these dimensions existed in the mass public.

The work of these scholars, therefore, allows us to identify some basic factors that may have served to generate exclusion bias in opinion concerning the war. While not as involved and detailed as in the study of social welfare policy in the last chapter, these factors do give us a rough sense of whether the roots of bias exist, and whether such bias could damage our ability to properly assess public opinion concerning the war in Vietnam. If the roots of bias can be found in mea-

---

[4] However, Mueller finds that they were only slightly more likely to take an opposition view. Thus Mueller concludes that "the sexual difference is mostly manifested in women's relative unwillingness to voice support for wars, not in their expressed opposition to them" (146).

sures of exposure to elite rhetoric and membership in groups that possess prowar predispositions, it will be possible to move forward and examine the implications of this bias for the shape of public opinion on the Vietnam War.

Bias in the Early War Years: The Public Opinion and the War in Vietnam Study

The literature reviewed above suggests that exclusion bias would be relatively large in the early years of the war. Zaller's work indicates that the balance of elite rhetoric should have excluded dovish sentiment from collective opinion concerning Vietnam in the years before 1968. Fortunately, data appropriate to such a purpose are available. In late February and early March 1966, Verba and his colleagues directed the "Public Opinion and the War in Vietnam Study." This survey is well suited to gauge the presence and nature of exclusion bias in opinion because it asked a series of questions concerning the proper direction of future U.S. involvement in Vietnam. These questions measured sentiment concerning actions that would escalate involvement in the Vietnam war—such as "having 200,000 troops in South Vietnam" and "bombing military targets in North Vietnam"—and actions that would de-escalate the U.S. presence in Southeast Asia—such as "holding free elections in South Vietnam even if the Viet Cong might win" and "gradually withdrawing our troops and letting the South Vietnamese work out their own problems."[5] The researchers asked a total of eight

[5] At first glance, it is not apparent why such of division of items is necessary. Most retrospective accounts of the mass response to the Vietnam War, including my account above, have attempted to separate the American public into two clear camps. On one side of the divide lie the hawks—those individuals who believed we should escalate our involvement in Vietnam. On the other side are the doves—those citizens who argued that the United States should actively seek to reduce its military commitment in the pursuit of peace. While these distinctions may serve as convenient rhetorical groupings, previous empirical work suggests these groupings may not be differentiated enough to accurately characterize the opinions of the public at large. In early 1966, Verba et al. (1967) conducted a survey of public attitudes toward future involvement in Vietnam. The investigators found that few respondents took strict hawk or dove positions. Instead, they found that many individuals held a somewhat conflicted attitude toward the war. The investigators discovered that individual sentiment toward the Vietnam War was best characterized by two correlated but independent factors: one related to escalating involvement in the war (escalation), and the other related to withdrawal from Southeast Asia (de-escalation). Respondents varied in their positions on these scales, and in some cases they could hold both pro-escalation and pro-de-escalation beliefs. Such individuals were not dim-witted. A respondent could, for example, believe that America should either win the Vietnam War or get out entirely (see Rosenberg, Verba, and Converse 1970).

questions relating to escalation and eight questions related to de-escalation. Thus, a close examination of the data can give us a clear picture of opinion bias in 1966, a critical early moment in the war.

Individual-Level Analysis

I began by constructing separate models of opinionation (whether the respondents answered the question concerning future action in Vietnam) and opinion direction (whether they supported a dovish position).[6] I also employed models that account for selection bias. In each of the analyses that follow, I tested for the possibility that selection bias existed in the question-answering process. Taken as a whole, there is no evidence that such bias is present in the process.[7] I therefore

---

Modigliani's (1972) study of public opinion on the Korean War suggests that this two-dimensional structuring of attitudes toward war is not limited to Vietnam. Modigliani factor analyzed a series of questions from Gallup Polls in 1955 and 1956 concerning American involvement in Korea. Like Verba and his colleagues, he finds that the items measuring desired future action separate into two distinct clusters of questions—one relating to disengagement, the other relating to escalation. Modigliani labels the first dimension "international interventionism"—which captures how committed individuals are to an interventionist foreign policy—and the second dimension "administration distrust"—how dissatisfied the individual is with the performance of government. Attempts to collapse opinion concerning prospective courses of future action into a single hawk/dove dimension may not necessarily accurately characterize public sentiment toward the war (see also Mueller 1973). My expectation is that, on balance, dovish (meaning pro-de-escalation and anti-escalation) opinion was missing from collective opinion in the early years of the war. But to represent properly the Verba et al. data in their original form, in the analyses that follow, I will separately consider sentiment toward escalation and de-escalation.

[6] The decision to answer the question is modeled as a probit, and the decision to take a particular stand on the question is modeled as a probit.

[7] For some questions, it appeared that selection bias might be present. However, such conclusions occurred when only a few factors—such as race, gender, and age—were used to predict item response and opinion positions. When more fully specified models were used, the apparent selection bias disappeared entirely. In the analyses that follow, I use the more fully specified models to project opinion positions. The more limited analyses presented in appendix table A5.2 are intended to illustrate the common roots of opinion giving and opinion direction. The projected opinion positions are robust to model respecification; no matter which variables are used to predict opinion, the results are virtually identical. In short, the empirical analysis confirms what theory suggests—the Vietnam policy question-answering process is uncontaminated by selection bias.

To check the robustness of the "nonfinding" of selection bias, I ran a number of models of question-answering process for each of the items below. For example, in the analyses for the NES "mistake" question, I ran a series of models that grew increasingly complex as I added additional variables to both the selection and outcome equations. Some of the more limited models showed evidence of selection bias. For example, one of the smaller models for the 1964 NES Mistake question had a $\rho = 0.56$ with a standard error

proceed to looking at the measured factors that could drive bias in measures of public opinion.

As discussed above, exposure to elite rhetoric and prowar predispositions should make it more likely first that respondents will offer an opinion on particular questions and, second, that they should offer an opinion favoring continued intervention in Vietnam. In the Public Opinion and the War in Vietnam Study, there are a number of factors that measure these quantities of interest. First, there are direct measures of receptivity of elite rhetoric. The study contains a number of questions testing the respondents' factual knowledge of the Vietnam War. As Zaller's (1992) work has shown, factual knowledge of politics is a good measure of exposure and reception of elite rhetoric. The measure of information is especially advantageous here because the questions directly gauge exposure to elite rhetoric concerning Vietnam.[8]

In addition to measures of exposure to elite rhetoric on Vietnam, the Public Opinion and the War in Vietnam Study contains both direct and indirect measures of hawkish predispositions. First, the study contains a measure of the respondents' general anticommunism tendencies. The study asks whether the U.S. policy toward Russia, China, and Cuba has been "too tough, just about right, or too soft."[9] The survey also contains indirect measures of predispositions through membership in groups that, on balance, would favor a hawkish position toward U.S. involvement, namely, whites, younger citizens, and men.[10]

---

of 0.39. However, adding variables to both the selection and outcome equations yielded a $\rho = 0.01$ with a standard error of 0.73. Similarly, for the 1966 analysis, a limited model of the question-answering process yielded a $\rho = 0.90$ with a standard error of 0.11—strong evidence of selection bias from both a substantive and a statistical standpoint. However, adding variables omitted from both equations in this limited specification greatly reduced the point estimate and precision of ρ ($\rho = 0.29$; standard error = 0.64). Thus, the apparent selection bias is merely an artifact of model misspecification. In the analyses that follow, therefore, I report only the non–selection bias specifications.

[8] The six items used to create the information scale are: (1) "What is the capital of South Vietnam?" (2) "What is the capital of North Vietnam?" (3) "As far as you know, are we currently bombing any targets in North Vietnam?" (4) "As you understand it, who are the Viet Cong—the government we are supporting in South Vietnam, the South Vietnamese Communists, North Vietnamese, or who?" (5) As you understand it, was the current South Vietnamese government freely elected by the people?" and (6) "As far as you know, has the Congress declared war in Vietnam?" These items scale together well. An exploratory factor analysis indicates that a single factor solution is appropriate, and the scale created from the six measures has a reasonable alpha ($\alpha = 0.60$).

[9] These three items scaled together well ($\alpha = 0.69$), so I created a single additive measure of hawkish predispositions to use in my analyses.

[10] It should again be noted that the role of group membership is not causal. Instead, the group labels indicate the kinds of people that, on average, would hold political predispositions of a particular type.

TABLE 5.1

1966 Public Opinion and the War in Vietnam Data Opinion Ingredient Analysis

	Escalation Questions	
Item	*Average Change in Likelihood of Answering Question (in Percentage Points)*	*Average Change in Likelihood of Giving a Dovish Answer (in Percentage Points)*
Vietnam Information Level	+9	−3
Too Soft on Communist Countries	+2	−25
Black	−0	+10
Female	−2	+14
Age	−8	−4
	De-escalation Questions	
Item	*Average Change in Likelihood of Answering Question (in Percentage Points)*	*Average Change in Likelihood of Giving a Dovish Answer (in Percentage Points)*
Vietnam Information Level	+8	−14
Too Soft on Communist Countries	+2	−20
Black	−1	+18
Female	−2	+3
Age	−7	+12

Note: Entries are the average partial effect of the independent variables on the probability of answering Vietnam escalation questions (column 2) and the probability of giving a dovish response (column 3) estimated from minimum to maximum value.

I therefore modeled both the decision to offer an opinion and the direction of opinion as a function of information about the Vietnam War, anticommunist tendencies, race, gender, and age. These analyses reveal that, as expected, the tendency to offer an opinion on the Vietnam policy questions and the direction of that opinion are closely linked through these measures. The full results of these analyses are presented for the interested reader in appendix table A5.2. Table 5.1 presents the overall results in a more easily interpretable manner. The entries in the top portion of the table represent the average effect of

the different opinion ingredients—or variables—across the eight escalation questions. The entries in the bottom portion of the table present
the average effects for the variables across the eight de-escalation
items. The first column lists the variables used to predict the direction
of opinion and the decision to give an opinion. The second column
indicates the average effect of the different variables on the probability
of offering an answer to the Vietnam questions. These values are calculated to represent the effect of moving from the minimum value of a
given opinion ingredient to the maximum value of that ingredient (see
chapter 4 for details on the procedures used for these simulations). So,
for example, the effect on the probability of answering the escalation
questions of raising a respondent's Vietnam information level from no
information to high information is an increase of about nine percentage
points. The third column presents the average effect of the different
opinion ingredients on the respondent's probability of choosing a dovish position. Again, this value is calculated to represent the effect of
moving from the minimum to the maximum value of that ingredient.
So, once more using Vietnam information as an example, increasing a
respondent's level of information from no information to high information decreases the likelihood of giving a dovish responses by about
three percentage points, on average.

It appears, then, the same factors in part drive the decision to give
an opinion on the Vietnam questions and the direction of that opinion.
Those individuals who are exposed to elite rhetoric on Vietnam are
more likely to express opinions, and opinions with a hawkish bent.
Furthermore, those individuals who are likely to hold hawkish predispositions—whites, men, younger respondents, and respondents with
strong anticommunist views—are more likely to answer survey questions. Thus, there is some evidence that the population of respondents
who abstain from the issue placement questions differ from those respondents who answer the items in their political preferences concerning what should be done on the question of Vietnam. Given this state
of affairs, to represent fairly public sentiment in the early part of the
war, we need to somehow correct for this uneven expression of political predispositions.

Opinion Bias: Estimation and Interpretation

It is possible to compute empirically the degree of bias in Vietnam
opinion and determine just whose political voice is missing from opinion polls. As in the last chapter, because there is no selection bias in

TABLE 5.2

1966 Public Opinion and the War in Vietnam Data Predicted Opinion Positions

| | Mean Predicted Probability Of Anti-Escalation Response | | |
Item	Respondents	Nonrespondents	Difference
Disapprove of 200,000 American troops in South Vietnam?	34%	39%	5%
Disapprove of bombing military targets in North Vietnam?	17%	26%	9%
Disapprove of half a million troops in South Vietnam?	50%	55%	5%
End involvement in Vietnam if it means fighting the Chinese Army?	38%	45%	8%
End involvement in Vietnam if it means a ground war in China?	65%	68%	3%
End involvement in Vietnam if it means atomic war with China?	69%	74%	5%
End involvement in Vietnam if it means atomic war with Russia?	76%	76%	0%
End involvement in Vietnam if it means total mobilization of U.S. Army?	56%	61%	5%

the data, we can use what we know about the opinions of the question-answerers to characterize the opinions of those individuals who declined to answer the question.

As expected, the differences in average opinion between scale placers and those individuals who do not answer items are significant across almost all of the escalation and de-escalation items (see table 5.2). In fourteen of the sixteen cases, the mean predicted probability of giving a dovish response is higher for nonplacers than placers. This difference is almost five percentage points, on average, and is especially significant because nonrespondents show consistently more dovish positions on both the escalation and de-escalation items. In short, table 5.2 demonstrates that the differences between the respondents and the nonrespondents on the various opinion ingredients—the resources and values that determine positions on the war—have real consequences for the types of Vietnam policy opinions we would expect them to hold.

TABLE 5.2 *(cont'd)*
1966 Public Opinion and the War in Vietnam Data Predicted Opinion Positions

Item	Mean Predicted Probability Of Anti-Escalation Response		
	Respondents	Nonrespondents	Difference
To end fighting, form South Vietnam govt. in which Viet Cong takes part?	59%	62%	3%
To end fighting, hold elections in South Vietnam even if Viet Cong may win?	62%	56%	–6%
To end fighting, a truce with each side holding the territory it now has?	76%	82%	6%
To end fighting, troop withdrawal and let South Vietnam work it out?	40%	52%	11%
End fighting, if it means Viet Cong eventually controlling South Vietnam?	31%	37%	7%
End fighting, if it means loss of independence for Laos and Thailand?	15%	19%	4%
Approve American negotiations with Viet Cong, if they were willing?	91%	95%	3%
Approve if Pres. Johnson withdrew troops letting communists rule?	15%	22%	6%

Note: The use of T-tests to gauge the difference between the two groups is inappropriate because this table compares projected issue placements with actual issue placements.

Moving to the collective level, it is possible to estimate the effect of including the sentiments of the nonrespondents. Using the methods described in the last two chapters, I estimate the degree of bias to be comparable to that found in social welfare policy, ranging from approximately one-half to two points across the escalation and de-escalation questions.

Validating the Imputation

As in the case of social welfare policy opinion, I sought to confirm the findings of the imputation analysis by examining the expressed opinions of the nonrespondents to particular questions. Many respondents who abstained from one of the Vietnam placement items answered at least one of the other seven items in the escalation or de-escalation scales. We therefore have some measure of opinion concerning future

TABLE 5.3
1966 Public Opinion and the War in Vietnam Data, Anti-escalation
and Pro–De-Escalation Scores

	Mean Anti-Escalation Score on Items Answered (0–100)		
Item	*Respondents*	*Nonrespondents*	*Difference*
Disapprove of 200,000 American troops in South Vietnam?	53	61	8**
Disapprove of bombing military targets in North Vietnam?	55	74	19**
Disapprove of half a million troops in South Vietnam?	50	60	9**
End involvement in Vietnam if it means fighting the Chinese Army?	52	62	10**
End involvement in Vietnam if it means a ground war in China?	49	51	2
End involvement in Vietnam if it means atomic war with China?	49	41	–8
End involvement in Vietnam if it means atomic war with Russia?	48	38	–11
End Involvement in Vietnam if it means total mobilization of US Army?	50	54	4

* = *p* <.10; ** = *p* <.05.

action in Vietnam for almost all of the individuals who answered *don't know* to particular questions. For example, of the 139 respondents who did not answer the question of whether half a million troops should be sent to South Vietnam, 95 percent answered at least one of the other items. The actual answers these "partial respondents" gave can be compared with the answers of the item placers to see if the differences found in table 5.2 are mirrored in measured opinions. To this end, I created escalation and de-escalation scales for each item on the survey (see table 5.3). These scales represent the average support for the escalation and de-escalation positions on the scale items answered. For example, for the first entry in the table, "Disapprove of 200,000 American Troops in South Vietnam?" the scale is the average anti-escalation score across the other seven antiescalation tables. The scales range from 0 to 100, with higher values indicating more dovish positions.

TABLE 5.3 (*cont'd*)
1966 Public Opinion and the War in Vietnam Data, Anti-escalation
and Pro–De-Escalation Scores

	Mean Anti-Escalation Score on Items Answered (0–100)		
Item	*Respondents*	*Nonrespondents*	*Difference*
To end fighting, form South Vietnam govt. in which Viet Cong takes part?	47	55	8**
To end fighting, hold elections in South Vietnam even if Viet Cong may win?	47	53	6**
To end fighting, a truce with each side holding the territory it now has?	46	48	3
To end fighting, troop withdrawal and let South Vietnam work it out?	50	53	3
End fighting, if it means Viet Cong eventually controlling South Vietnam?	53	63	12**
End fighting, if it means loss of independence for Laos and Thailand?	53	69	16**
Approve American negotiations with Viet Cong, if they were willing?	43	46	3
Approve if Pres. Johnson withdrew troops letting communists rule?	54	74	20**

* = $p < .10$; ** = $p < .05$.

Replicating the differences found in table 5.2, those individuals who were not able to form an opinion on one of the issue questions were significantly more dovish than placers on those items they did answer. Across the eight items in the antiescalation scale, nonrespondents are on average four points more dovish than question-answerers. Three-quarters of the items show differences in the expected direction, and one-half of the items have statistically significant differences. Turning to the pro-de-escalation scale, all eight items show differences in the expected direction, 63 percent of these differences are statistically significant, and the nonrespondents are, on average, nine points more dovish than respondents. All told, these results confirm the findings of my earlier analyses. In the early years of the war, a base of anti-intervention opinion was excluded from public opinion.

Tracing Trends over Time: 1964–1972

The Public Opinion and the War in Vietnam data give evidence of bias in the expected direction in the early years of U.S. involvement in Vietnam. But the existence of such bias in the early part of the war is only half the story. Previous work suggests that as the balance of hawkish messages in elite rhetoric changed over the course of the war, the nature of bias should have changed as well. To see if this prediction is supported by the data, it is necessary to move to a dynamic examination of public opinion concerning the Vietnam War.

Two series of datasets exist that are useful for these purposes. The first is the bi-annual NES data. The second is a series of opinion polls conducted by the Gallup organization. Both of these data series contain repeated measures of an item that asks whether it was a "mistake" for the United States to become involved in Vietnam. The NES asks, "Do you think we did the right thing in getting into the fighting in Vietnam, or should we have stayed out?" The Gallup survey asks, "In view of the developments since we entered the fighting in Vietnam, do you think the U.S. made a mistake sending troops to fight in Vietnam?"[11] While these questions are worded in different ways, they should capture similar sentiment concerning the war. Indeed, analysis by Mueller (1973) demonstrates that the question marginals move in similar ways over time.

The Mistake question is by no means perfect. It cannot, for example, allow us to gauge respondents' beliefs concerning the proper course of future U.S. action. On the other hand, the Mistake question does have certain advantages: it can serve as a measure of broad support or opposition to the war effort. As Mueller (1973, 43) argues, "the question always asks for the respondent's general opinion on the wisdom of the war venture itself, and thus it seems to be a sound measure of a sort of general support for the war." The question is phrased to highlight the overall assessment of the war effort and may tap an overall retrospective evaluation of the war effort (Fiorina 1981). More importantly, the Mistake question was asked often by various survey organizations over the course of the war and is therefore well suited to capture the dynamics of general unease with the war effort in the 1960s and 1970s. While these data are not as rich as the Verba study, they do enable us to trace opinion using a broad summary question over the course of the war.

---

[11] This question is the central dependent variable in Mueller's classic analysis of opinion on Korea and Vietnam.

The analyses begin here with the NES data. The first step is to see whether the roots of exclusion bias can be found in the ingredients of opinion, as was the case with the Verba data. The expectation is that in the early years of the war, the same factors that led individuals to say that becoming involved in Vietnam was not a mistake would also lead them to offer an opinion on the question. Over time, however, the relationship between opinion direction and opinion giving should weaken. Empirical analysis indicates that this is indeed the case (see appendix table A5.3 for the full results). Over the course of the war, certain variables, such as gender, are consistent predictors of opinion giving and opinion direction. Other factors, such as race, wane in their influence.[12] The more interesting story, however, lies in our predictions regarding the size and direction of the bias in opinion concerning the Vietnam War. Based on Zaller's work, we would expect that in the early years of the war, public opinion concerning Vietnam would exclude a base of dovish opinion. Over time, however, the disparity between expressed and unexpressed opinion should diminish.

To gauge the size of the difference in the opinions of these two groups, I computed predicted opinion positions for both respondents and nonrespondents, as I did for the Public Opinion and the War in Vietnam study. These results are presented graphically in figure 5.1. As expected, the question-abstainers are more dovish than the question-answerers in the early part of the war. This gap, in fact, rises from 1964 to 1966, mirroring the difference in elite rhetoric found by Zaller. After 1966, however, the gap shrinks consistently, and by 1972 the difference disappears almost entirely.

The reason for this decline is not a mystery. To return to Schuman's (1972) analysis of the Mistake question, the underlying base of missing sentiment in the early years of the war was quite possibly composed of Schuman's pragmatic isolationists—those individuals who expressed a general unease with the war effort, based on diffuse interests. It would make sense that the behavior of individuals with such sentiment would change over time. For such respondents, Vietnam became a cognitively less difficult issue. Individuals may have been uncomfortable with the war in the early to mid-1960s, but without elite rhetoric to guide their unease to a specific policy position, they chose the *don't know* response. By the time of Schuman's investigation in the 1970s, elite rhetoric had shifted to provide a platform for their sentiments. At that time, they were able to express their underlying unease with the war.

---

[12] There is some evidence that the change in the predictive power of race is due to a change in how African American elites framed their discussions of the Vietnam conflict. I discuss this matter in detail below.

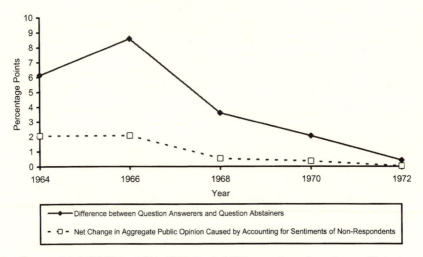

FIGURE 5.1 NES Data, 1964–1972. Probabilities are based on the coefficient estimates presented in Table A5.3 (Source: 1964–1972 National Elections Studies).

Respondents and nonrespondents clearly differ in their sentiment toward the Vietnam War. Following the same empirical procedures as previous chapters, an estimate of this bias is presented graphically in figure 5.1. As expected, the aggregate bias is present in the early part of the war but shrinks over time to less than one percentage point after 1968.[13]

The pattern of results found in the NES data is mirrored in the Gallup data. Figure 5.2 replicates the analyses presented in figure 5.1.[14] Though the pattern is not quite as clean as it was for the NES data, the level of exclusion bias and the bias in opinion is relatively large in the 1965–1967 period but grows smaller over the course of the years. These results are important because they provide additional evidence that the trend found in the NES surveys is genuine, and not simply an artifact of the data.

[13] The NES used a full filter to the Mistake item in 1964 and 1966. Respondents were first asked, "Have you been paying any attention to what is going on in Vietnam?" Only those who responded "yes" were asked the Mistake question. I included respondents who were filtered out at the first stage in the *don't know* pool (20 percent of the sample in 1964; 7 percent in 1966). Excluding these respondents from analysis reduces somewhat the estimated bias in Vietnam opinion but does not change the basic results of the empirical analysis.

[14] The probit coefficients used to impute these results are available from the author upon request.

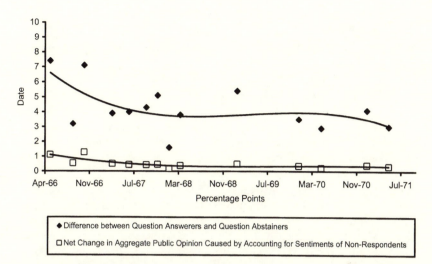

FIGURE 5.2 Gallup Data, 1966–1971. Probabilities are based on probit analysis available from author upon request. The trend line is fitted with a third degree polynominal (Source: Gallup data 1965–1971, studies 728, 734, 737, 744, 748, 752, 755, 758, 760, 774, 797, 807, 821, 830).

A Case Study of Elite Rhetoric: African American Opinion

To this point, I have presented suggestive evidence indicating that a change in the volume and salience of elite rhetoric over the course of the Vietnam War caused the dynamic changes in the levels of bias in opinion concerning that war. I close this chapter with more direct evidence of this hypothesis. I argue that a change in the volume of antiwar messages among African American elites directly led to a reduction in bias among blacks in the years after 1967.

In the early to mid-1960s, civil rights leaders tread carefully around the issue of the Vietnam War. Leaders refrained from open opposition to the war, for fear of diluting their equal rights message and compromising their legitimacy as patriotic Americans. In 1967, however, this began to change. In March of that year, at an Easter peace march in Chicago, Martin Luther King, Jr., spoke out for the first time against U.S. involvement in Southeast Asia, calling the Vietnam War "a blasphemy against all that America stands for." King's stand was certainly controversial, and not all civil rights activists followed suit. The NAACP, for example, voted unanimously the next week against uniting the civil rights and antiwar movements. However, many leaders—including the Southern Christian Leadership Council—followed

King's lead (Zaroulis and Sullivan 1984). In the African American community after 1967, therefore, there was a marked change in the nature of rhetoric concerning the war (see also Gartner and Segura 2000; Holsti 1996).

The question most relevant here is whether this shift in rhetoric was mirrored in an increase in the voice of African American opposition to the war. Based on the argument presented above, we would expect that the change in the volume of antiwar rhetoric among black elites would decrease the rate of *don't know* responses among blacks but should have had no effect on the direction of their opinions—blacks should always oppose the war.

This prediction is strongly born out in the NES data. Figure 5.3 demonstrates that African Americans held higher levels of opposition to the war than whites. The size of this difference is, in fact, almost completely stable over time.[15] What did change over the eight-year period was the willingness of blacks to offer responses to the Vietnam question. Over the course of the war, in fact, the gap between blacks and whites on question-answering rates closes completely. As predicted, the largest drop in this gap occurs between 1966 and 1968, coinciding with the shift in rhetoric among African American elites.

Figure 5.4 replicates the analysis presented in figure 5.1, but for blacks only. As expected, the trend in figure 5.4 largely follows that of figure 5.1; the question-abstainers are more dovish than the question-answerers in the early part of the war. The size of the bias is, however, larger for the blacks-only sample. Thus, while the analyses presented in figures 5.3 and 5.4 are by no means conclusive, they are highly suggestive. As predicted, a sudden change in the balance of rhetoric among African American elites led to a similar change in exclusion bias among blacks in the United States.

Conclusion

The results offered in this chapter deepen our understanding of biases in opinion polls in particular, and political participation more generally. The balance in the volume and salience of elite rhetoric on given issues may greatly impact the shape of opinion in politically consequential ways. In the case presented here, analyses that use very different data sources converge to the same conclusion. A significantly dov-

---

[15] The trend in the graph is not simply a trick of the eye. The null hypothesis of no difference in opinion direction among blacks by year of the survey cannot be rejected at any conventional level of significance.

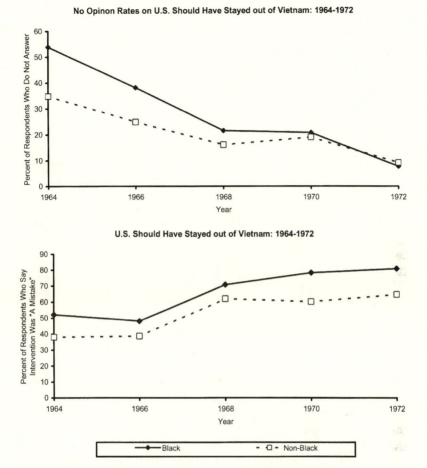

FIGURE 5.3 African American Analysis (Source: 1964–1972
National Elections Studies).

ish segment of the population was excluded from opinion concerning
Vietnam in the early part of the war. The reason for this bias is suggested by the analyses presented in this chapter. Respondents who
were uncomfortable with U.S. involvement abroad had few elite arguments to pin their concerns to in the early to mid-1960s. For these respondents, Vietnam was a cognitively difficult issue.

However, the nature of the issue changed over the second half of the
1960s. Over time, antiwar messages became more common in the public sphere. As the flow of elite rhetoric reached a balance reflective of
the underlying predispositions of the American public, a more com-

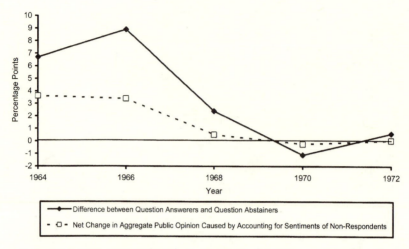

FIGURE 5.4 NES, 1964–1972 (Blacks Only). Probabilities are based on the coefficient estimates presented in table A5.3 (Source: 1964–1972 National Election Studies).

plete picture of the public's views was expressed. The increase of elite antiwar messages not only cued that segment of the mass public who consistently answer survey questions (Zaller 1992) but also allowed an important segment of the public to give voice to their politically relevant wants, needs, and desires. Certainly, not all government officials viewed this change as a positive development. The more conspiratorial-minded might suggest that the restriction of elite dialog did not cause harm but rather allowed the government to manipulate public opinion to serve its policy interests (see, for example, Page and Shapiro 1992, chap. 9). In any event, the shift in rhetoric after 1967 aided the expression of anti-Vietnam sentiment.

Certainly the exclusion bias found in this chapter was not the only effect of the imbalance in elite rhetoric in the pre-1967 period. As Zaller has convincingly demonstrated, change in the flow of elite rhetoric after 1967 contributed to the conversion of citizens from the pro-intervention to the anti-intervention camp. In fact, this process of conversion had a greater effect on the shape of opinion than the exclusion bias I find. But my findings indicate that the shift in the nature of discussion among politicians greatly reduced the differences in the sentiment toward war between the question-answerers and the question-abstainers. As the Vietnam conflict became a less difficult issue for those Americans who held dovish predispositions, their voice was more clearly heard in opinion polls.

CONCLUSION

PUBLIC OPINION AND POLITICAL VOICE

PUBLIC OPINION polling undoubtedly has changed the face of politics in America. Opinion polls provide a direct channel of communication between the mass public and political elites. Policymakers may attend to the information carried through opinion polls, or they may ignore it, but the fact remains that opinion polls will continue to play a central role in the American political system.

This increased flow of information concerning the preferences and perspectives of the mass public comes with a cost. Though opinion polling may be more inclusionary than traditional forms of mass participation, the lesson of this book is that polls are far from perfect. Certainly, measures of public opinion may, under certain circumstances, accurately reflect the wants, needs, and desires of the mass public. But in some cases, opinion polls may silence the political voice of segments of the mass public.

Individual Political Cognition and the
Creation of Public Opinion

In this book, I have argued that the key to understanding the formation and development of bias in pubic opinion is to pay close attention to both the way in which individuals answer survey questions and the impact of the larger political and social world on that process. My investigation began in chapter 1 with an examination of individual political cognition in the survey interview—how it is that individuals approach the tasks put before them by the interviewer. I considered both how respondents construct their preferences concerning current political controversies—that is, how respondents form their opinions on the issues of the day—and the social and psychological processes that determine how respondents express those preferences to the survey interviewer. In many cases, it is reasonable to expect that respondents will faithfully reveal their judgments in surveys. However, under certain circumstances—in those cases where respondents might fear the costs of freely speaking their minds—they may edit and sanitize their opinions before revealing them to the interviewer.

Adopting this conception of the survey response provides a framework to understand why individuals would choose to remain silent when asked their opinions in the survey interview. The key is to consider the costs involved with providing a response. In some cases, individuals may choose the *don't know* response because they are unwilling or unable to pay the cognitive costs necessary to form a coherent view on a particular political controversy. In other cases, individuals might say they have no opinion because they fear the costs—be it physical punishment or simply the scorn of others—involved with freely speaking their mind. In both cases, by choosing the *don't know* response, respondents thwart the collection of their politically relevant wants, needs, and desires.

I next considered the implication of individual cognition for public opinion. I began with the conjecture that, under some circumstances, the sentiments individuals express in the survey interview may poorly reflect their underlying political predilections. However, the probability that the interview will foster such distortions varies greatly across individual respondents. Some individuals carefully attend to developments in the political world and will easily link their personal concerns to ongoing controversies, arriving at positions that reflect their underlying predispositions. Other individuals will shy away from the political world and—even though they possess politically relevant concerns—will find it difficult to draw clear links between their private affairs and the political world. As a result, they will abstain from questions on those issues. Similarly, some individuals will freely reveal their opinions to the survey interviewer, no matter what the topic of conversation. Others will hold their tongue on certain subjects rather than express a sentiment that runs contrary to popular norms of acceptable behavior. Thus, the incidence of opinion distortions will vary greatly according to the personal characteristics of the respondent.

If there is a systematic pattern to the decision to abstain from a particular survey question, the underlying interests of certain groups of respondents may be excluded from opinion polls. And if the same factors that determine an individual's willingness to express an opinion also drive the direction of that opinion, the existence of individual distortions in survey answers may serve to exclude a particular type of sentiment on that issue. Thus, the very process of measuring and collecting individual attitudes through opinion polls may undermine the egalitarian promise of those polls.

Of course, opinion polls will not always be plagued by biases. The central question, then, is when we should expect opinion polls to paint an accurate picture of the underlying wants and desires of the American public as a whole, and when we should expect them to fail. To answer this question, we need to place our understanding of individual political cognition in the context of the events of the political world.

In chapter 2, I followed this path by developing a twofold typology of issue difficulty. As Carmines and Stimson (1980) aptly noted, issues range greatly in their cognitive difficulty. Some issues—those that require the careful consideration of technical alternatives—are hard in the cognitive sense. Many respondents may struggle to form coherent and well-grounded opinions, even though they possess predispositions that relate to those controversies. On the other hand, other issues, those long in the public eye, are cognitively easy. Even individuals with only a passing interest in politics should be able to form opinions on those issues with little effort.

Issues may be difficult in not just a cognitive sense, but also in a social or expressive sense. Some issues touch upon particular norms and therefore may be difficult for the respondent to navigate in the context of the survey setting. Thus, respondents may find it difficult to express the opinions they have formed. Other issues are not affected by norms and are therefore socially easy issues.

This multidimensional conception of issue difficulty allows us to classify political controversies and determine those instances where we would expect opinion bias to occur (see fig. 6.1).[1] On easy issues, polls might accurately measure the sentiments of all citizens. But as the difficulty of a particular issue increases—in both a cognitive and expressive sense—the gap between the relevant interests and values of individuals and the opinions they express in opinion polls may grow. Put simply, issues that are relatively hard will foster opinion distortions among significant portions of the population. Public opinion on those issues may, therefore, be contaminated by significant exclusion biases.

To determine when public opinion excludes certain groups of the mass public, we need to pay close attention to the larger social and political context within which the survey interview takes place. We must ask whether issues are difficult only for those citizens with opinions of a particular stripe. Under such circumstances, the potential for bias is great. The realm of social welfare policy, for example, is a difficult issue area for those citizens who seek the expansion of the welfare state. As I demonstrated in chapter 4, this property leads to the creation of a conservative bias in public opinion.

At the same time, we need to pay close attention to dynamic changes in particular issue areas. We cannot assume that the particular context

---

[1] This typology should not be thought of as a strict two-by-two table. Instead, as noted in chapter 2, the cognitive and expressive difficulty scales should be thought of as continuous dimensions.

Cognitive Complexity

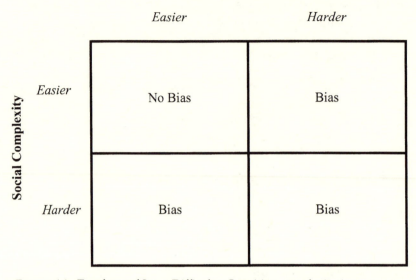

FIGURE 6.1. Typology of Issue Difficulty. Cognitive complexity increases as the technical complexity of an issue increases. Social complexity increases as norms governing "acceptable speech" develop around a given issue. As issues become harder for certain portions of the population, the potencial for bias in collective opinion measures develops.

surrounding a specific issue has a constant effect. That is, issue difficulty may vary not simply across different issues, but also across time within the same issue area, as was the case in the evolution of social context surrounding race over the last thirty years. In this way, we can account systematically for the effect of the larger political and social context on the processes of political cognition at the individual level and determine when public opinion may suffer from exclusion bias.

Summary of Findings

The three chapters that comprise the second half of this book show the value of adopting the theoretical framework advanced in the first three chapters. By first starting with an individual-level model of the survey response and then accounting for the effects of the political and social context of American society, we can not only identify those cases where respondents and nonrespondents to particular questions should differ,

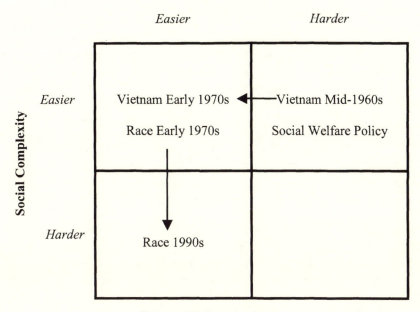

FIGURE 6.2. Case Analysis.

but also measure and account for the effect of these differences in creating bias in public opinion polls.

Figure 6.2 presents the classification of cases examined in this book into the twofold typology of issue difficulty. The prediction made in chapter 2 was that issues that are easy in both a cognitive and a social sense should be untouched by bias. As expected, this was true for Vietnam opinion in the late 1960s and early 1970s, and for racial policy issues in the early 1970s. As issue difficulty increases for individuals who hold opinions of a particular stripe, bias grows as well. This development of bias occurs for issues that are difficult in a social sense—as demonstrated by the case of race in the 1990s—and for those that are cognitively difficult—as shown by the cases of social welfare policy opinion and opinion toward Vietnam in the early 1960s.

In chapters 4 and 5, I found that distortions in opinions on cognitively difficult issues might threaten the representativeness of opinion polls. In the realm of economic policy, certain types of individuals—the resource-poor and those who subscribe to an expansive view of the government's role in the management of public policy—are more likely to adopt liberal positions on social welfare policy questions. These same individuals are also less proficient at linking their personal concerns to their social welfare policy judgments and, consequently, are more likely to abstain from such questions. In this way, the measurement and aggregation of the social welfare policy opinions of individuals introduce a bias into public opinion, which inadvertently silences those individuals predisposed to support the policies of the welfare state.

While respondents who say they don't know where they stand on social welfare policy questions may be uncertain or ambivalent, they are not without politically relevant concerns. The analyses presented in chapter 4 demonstrate that those who keep silent on particular social welfare policy questions would, if they gave voice to their concerns, speak in a different manner from those who are able to form opinions on those questions. These findings are underscored by the fact that the same respondents, when they do give answers to social welfare policy questions—be it on a different social welfare policy item, or on the same question at a different point in time—do express more liberal concerns than those individuals who form opinions on the social welfare policy items. The resulting exclusion bias in aggregate opinion, though not of great magnitude, is real and politically significant. Moreover, this aggregate bias is an enduring feature of opinion on social welfare policy; the same pattern of bias found in the 1990s was also present in the 1970s.

In chapter 5, I provided further evidence that it is important to attend to bias when examining opinion on cognitively difficult issues. In the early years of the Vietnam War, elite rhetoric enabled those supportive of U.S. intervention to easily find links between their underlying interests and the policy interest on the table. Such guidance, however, was unavailable to those who held anti-intervention sentiment. As a result, a pro-intervention exclusion bias could be found in opinion concerning the war. Over time, elite rhetoric achieved a greater balance, and both sides of the debate were able to find arguments for their point of view on the political stage. For those citizens with an anti-intervention balance of predispositions, Vietnam became a cognitively easier issue, and the bias of the early war years dissipated. Thus, chapter 5 provides a dynamic demonstration of the effect of changing issue difficulty on the levels of bias in public opinion.

The findings concerning the existence of exclusion bias on issues that are moderately difficult in a cognitive sense have implications for mass political involvement more generally. Research on political participation (Rosenstone and Hansen 1993; Verba and Nie 1972; Verba, Schlozman, and Brady 1995) has effectively demonstrated that measures of the public will obtained through traditional forms of participation—such as writing letters to officials and participating in community action groups—are biased because those groups rich in politically relevant resources are better able to make their voices heard in the political system. But scholars of political participation have largely focused on the tangible costs of mobilizing ordinary citizens to political action. The results presented in chapters 4 and 5 suggest that the participatory advantage of the resource rich is due not simply to the fact that they are better able to pay the costs of opinion expression, but to their similar advantage in the process of opinion formation. So no matter how much we change the costs of opinion expression through various political reforms—for example, by making it easier for citizens to cast votes in elections through absentee ballots or by mail—it is important to recognize that the very process by which people become engaged with the world of politics could exclude a segment of the public from measures of opinion.

It could be that the *don't know* responses examined here merely reflect weak opinions on the part of particular citizens. But the systematic patterns of nonresponse uncovered in this book indicate that something more is at work. It is not only that certain individuals are silenced. Instead, particular types of interests are muted. Thus, to ensure political equality, at the most basic level we must ensure that people are able to make meaningful links between their personal concerns and the world of politics. We must do more than simply mobilize the politically silent to action. In order truly to foster equality in participation—be it an opinion poll or writing one's member of Congress—we need to ensure that when citizens do speak, they speak with their interests in mind. As issues become more complex and cognitively challenging, such a goal becomes increasingly difficult to achieve.

The effects of exclusion bias become more significant when we move from an examination of distortions in the process of opinion formation to those in the course of opinion expression. As chapter 3 demonstrates, the fact that some individuals in the present day conceal racially conservative sentiment behind a *don't know* response means that collective measures of opinion on those issues miss a significant base of opposition to government policies designed to ensure racial equality.

These findings, while strong, are a product of the present social and political environment surrounding policies designed to ensure racial equality. In the 1970s, unlike the present day, the *don't know* response was not a refuge for individuals who opposed policies designed to ensure racial equality but did not want to express such sentiments in the context of the survey interview. At that earlier time, when the norms concerning the correctness of school integration were not fully crystallized, and before busing came to dominate how ordinary citizens viewed integration, the *don't know* response seems to have been an expression of genuine uncertainty and ambivalence at the attitude formation stage. The projected sentiment of the question-abstainers was identical to that of the question-answerers. This finding is not simply a product of the rhetoric surrounding school integration. An identical pattern of bias was demonstrated in the realm of fair employment. In sum, the results presented in chapter 3 underscore the importance of attending to the larger political and social context surrounding an issue and, more importantly, accounting for the evolution of that context and its effect on respondents' reactions to the survey interview. As the issue of race became more socially complex, a significant bias in opinion developed as well.

Opinion Polls: A Guide for the Critical Consumer .

Given the lessons of this book, what can producers and consumers of polls do to uncover and account for exclusion bias? One possibility would be for pollsters to design survey items and interviewing practices that discourage respondents from offering *don't know* responses. As discussed in chapter 1, the proportion of nonresponses to survey questions is clearly affected by the format of the questions. Items that explicitly offer respondents the *don't know* option produce much higher rates of nonresponse. Perhaps, then, the solution is to turn the survey researcher's old saw around. Instead of encouraging citizens to take the *don't know* option when they are unsure of their opinion (Converse and Presser 1986), we should be discouraging them from doing so.

But such a strategy creates problems of its own. A *don't know* response, after all, tells us something about the respondent's views— namely, that providing an answer is difficult from a cognitive standpoint, a social standpoint, or both. Pressuring citizens to give answers to all survey questions might increase the quality of information collected in some cases, but it could also exacerbate the problems identified in this book. After all, a citizen who is uncomfortable providing an answer to a socially difficult question will not easily collapse and say precisely what is on his or her mind, simply because of pressure to give an answer. More likely he or she will again try to abstain or—if he or she does give an answer—it is unlikely to be a fully truthful response. Consider, for example, the 1989 Virginia governor's race, a contest pitting a black Democrat, Douglas Wilder, against a white Republican, Marshall Coleman. In pre-election polls conducted in October, probing respondents who were not willing to declare support for either of the two candidates only exacerbated the reporting of support for Wilder—the socially desirable answer (Finkel, Guterbock, and Borg 1991).

Similarly, respondents who have a difficult time linking their predispositions to a particular political controversy will not suddenly find their political voice when pressured to give an answer. The gap between their underlying wants, needs, beliefs, and desires and the stakes of that controversy runs deeper than the surface. Given the complexities of the political world, the opinions of some respondents are more firmly grounded in their interests than others.

A better solution, I think, is to try to gain a greater understanding of what the *don't know* response is telling us about public opinion. Using the tools described in this book, we can examine those respondents who decline to answer a particular question. In this way, we can identify the precise character of the information we loose by ignoring nonrespondents.

The typology of issue hardness presented in figure 6.1 can help us identify those cases where a relatively high rate of question abstention could conceal certain types of opinions—those sentiments that run counter to particular social norms. On these issues, opinion polls might provide a poor guide for future public response. For example, polls concerning the Equal Rights amendment (ERA) in the mid-1970s showed majority support for the amendment, but typically 14–18 percent of the respondents said they had no opinion on the matter (Mansbridge 1986). These nonrespondents could have been genuinely uncertain or ambivalent, but it is also possible that some held their tongue rather than give an answer that could be construed as sexist. From this perspective, the failure of the ERA to attain passage in the late 1970s and early 1980s would not be surprising. Furthermore, questions concerning cognitively difficult issue areas that engender high rates of *no opinion* responses could miss underlying sentiment, or "latent opinion" (Key 1961). The early years of the Vietnam War provide an example of such a case. But other instances of the obscurement of latent opinion behind *don't know* responses are possible. For example, questions concerning specific economy policies could be difficult for some individuals to answer in the short run. But once their long-term effects on the economy become clear, a clear sentiment might develop. This is not to say that we should abandon polls as a way to measure the public will. The work in this book, however, suggests that we should cast a cautious eye on the enterprise of survey research.

Reading Opinion Polls

Not all opinion polls should be regarded with equal suspicion. Consider the case of public opinion concerning spending on education. This issue area is easy in both a cognitive and a social sense. It has been ingrained in the political culture over such a long period of time that respondents can answer questions on this topic with negligible cognitive costs. Furthermore, the social costs associated with expressing support or opposition to increased funding are minimal. Accordingly, it is not surprising that questions concerning school funding yield low *don't know* rates—on average about 2 percent.[2] There might be reason to question how citizens would trade off school spending against higher taxes, but in the case of school funding, we can take polls at their face.

The key to identifying areas of potential bias is to look for survey questions on cognitively or socially difficult topics, where the number of people who do not offer responses is unusually large relative to the other items in the survey.[3] It is important here to compare *don't know* response rates *within* a given survey. Rates of question abstention vary across polls depending on whether given survey organizations encourage or discourage *no opinion* responses. Furthermore, many of the polls carried out for media and politicians are conducted using only responses of registered voters or "likely" voters—the most engaged and

[2] The questions used to compute this rate were collected using the Public Opinion Online service at Lexis-Nexis. A search was conducted using the Boolean operator statement "spending and (school or education) and not (private or religious) and not (candidate or democrat or republican)" in the period from January 2000 to September 15, 2002. The "and not" statements were used to exclude questions about school vouchers and the stands of political candidates.

[3] As an example, consider the social welfare policy issue questions from 1996 examined in chapter 4. These items were likely candidates for the finding of cognitive bias for two reasons. First, as discussed in that chapter, social welfare policy is a cognitively difficult issue for those tending toward the liberal side of the political spectrum. Second, the abstention rate on those questions was high relative to other questions about economic priorities. On other, less cognitively complex questions, *don't know* rates were lower. For example, when asked about whether spending should be increased, be decreased, or be kept the same, on specific government programs—such as "spending on solving the problem of the homeless" and "financial aid to college students"—only 1 percent of the sample did not offer a response. While these spending priority questions are asked using a different question format from the social welfare policy questions, it is not simply the format that accounts for the high *don't know* rate on those questions. In 1996 respondents were asked about their views on the causes of crime using the same seven-point scale format as the social welfare policy items. Specifically, they were asked, "Some people say that the best way to reduce crime is to address the social problems that cause crime, like bad schools, poverty and joblessness. Suppose these people are at one end of a scale, at point 1. Other people say the best way to reduce crime is to make sure that criminals are caught, convicted and punished. Suppose these people are at the other end, at point 7. And, of course, some other people have opinions somewhere in between at points 2, 3, 4, 5, or 6. Where would you place yourself on this scale, or haven't you thought much about this?" On this question, fewer than 4 percent of respondents failed to offer a response.

involved segment of the electorate. In these polls, many of the citizens who would ordinarily gravitate to the *don't know* response at the opinion formation stage have been purged from the sample of poll respondents.[4]

Of course, even with a high *don't know* rate, the presence of bias is not assured. But such questions should raise warning flags. For example, consider opinion concerning the proper means to stimulate a weak economy. In September 2001, Princeton Survey Research Associates conducted a poll for *Newsweek* asking, "Which of the following [programs], if any, would you personally favor to try to stimulate the economy and avoid a long recession?" When asked about a program that was relatively easy in a cognitive sense, "Major new government spending for security and infrastructure improvements, and to help New York City," only 3 percent of respondents abstained. However, when asked about a more complex program, "Cutting capital gains taxes on profits from the sale of real estate, stocks and other investments," 14 percent of the respondents did not offer a response. Given the lessons in this book, the informed consumer should regard the second question—a more cognitively complex topic—with some suspicion.[5]

In addition, a vigilant consumer of polls should carefully interpret questions concerning socially difficult issues. Throughout the last two decades of the twentieth century, for instance, popular portrayals of homosexuals in American society changed greatly. Social norms concerning discussion of issues of homosexuality showed a corresponding change. This is not to say that all individuals felt compelled to keep antihomosexual views to themselves. But almost certainly, for a portion of the public, questions concerning gay rights became highly sensitive topics. Like questions concerning policies designed to ensure racial equality, we should therefore be suspicious of questions with high rates of question abstention. In May 2000, a poll conducted by International Communications Research (ICR) for the Associated Press poll asked one-half of its 1,012 national adult sample, "In general, do you think gays and lesbians should or should not be allowed to be legally married?" The poll showed that a majority of American opposed the practice. But given the lessons of this book, the rates of question abstention suggest that underlying opposition might be even higher: 11 percent of respondents said they did not know where they stood, and

---

[4] Though, as the 1989 New York Mayoral race demonstrates, using samples of registered voters does not prevent bias arising from *don't knows* at the opinion expression stage.

[5] These poll results were obtained from the Polling.com website (www.pollingreport.com/index.html), accessed October 15, 2002.

another 3 percent outright refused to answer the question.[6] The other half of the sample on that same survey was asked, "In general, do you think gays and lesbians should or should not be allowed to form a domestic partnership that would give the same-sex couple the same rights and benefits as opposite-sex marriage?" While a plurality of respondents opposed the measure, 11 percent claimed to have no opinion, and another 3 percent balked at providing any response.[7] Given the emerging social difficulty of the issue, it could be that polls are not capturing the full extent of anti–gay marriage sentiment.

Public Opinion Polling and Representation in the United States

This discussion of the problems involved with measuring public opinion leads back to where I started this book, namely, the broader questions of representation and equality in participation. Tying an understanding of individual political cognition to an understanding of the larger political environment enables us to understand how public opinion develops over time in reaction to changes in the political

---

[6] The exact breakdown of opinion was 51 percent *should not*, 34 percent *should*, 11 percent *don't know*, 3 percent *refused*. Compared with other questions from this organization, this is a relatively high *don't know* rate. For example in October 2001, a national adult sample was asked, "One of the responses to the terrorist attacks (on the World Trade Center and the Pentagon on September 11, 2001) has been the move to place armed air marshals aboard commercial airplane flights. Do you favor or oppose having armed air marshals aboard commercial airplane flights?" Only 3 percent of the sample said they didn't know or refused to answer the question. (These data were taken from the Public Opinion Online service at Lexis-Nexis; the *don't know* responses and refusals are reported as a single category).

[7] The precise breakdown of opinion was 46 percent *should not*, 41 percent *should*, 11 percent *don't know*, 3 percent *refused*. These high rates of question abstention were consistent with polls concerning gay marriage conducted by other organizations at that time. A Fox News/Opinion Dynamics national poll of registered voters in January 2000 asked, "There has been a lot of discussion recently about whether gay couples should be granted either marriage or its equivalent in terms of legal rights. Do you believe gays and lesbians should be: allowed to get legally married, allowed a legal domestic partnership similar to but not called marriage, or should there be no legal recognition given to gay and lesbian relationships?" A plurality was opposed to any legal recognition, but 10 percent of respondents said they were *not sure* where they stood. Finally, a March 2000 *Newsweek* poll conducted by Princeton Survey Research Associates using a national adult sample asked, "Do you think there should or should not be legally sanctioned gay marriages?" Nine percent of the respondents said they did not know where they stood. All told, then, across similar questions from different polling organizations, 9 to 14 percent of citizens choose a *don't know* response, even though none of the organizations explicitly offered such an option.

world. Here, my work in many ways reinforces and builds upon the lessons of Zaller. In *The Nature and Origins of Mass Opinion* (1992), Zaller demonstrated that changes in elite discourse might alter the salience that individuals give to different predispositions. Over time, if the balance of the mix of elite messages found in the political world shifts, such a process can alter the shape of public opinion. Such processes may explain the shift I find in bias on opinion concerning the Vietnam War. But I demonstrate that changes in the political world can change the shape of opinion not simply by altering the individual distribution of those opinion ingredients underlying opinions, but also by altering the costs to the respondents of freely speaking their minds. As the norms governing social interaction within a society change, respondents' ability to say what is on their minds also changes. Thus, when the social norms surrounding an issue evolve, the apparent distribution of opinion on that issue may change, regardless of the types of opinion ingredients people hold.

An examination of the collective effects of opinion distortions at the stages of both opinion formation and opinion expression can inform and modify our conclusions regarding opinion change over time. For example, Page and Shapiro (1992) demonstrate that Americans' collective preferences concerning economic matters have exhibited remarkable stability from the beginning of the New Deal programs of the 1930s until the present day. Given the stability in the larger political context on questions of social welfare policy, such steadiness is not surprising. However, the findings from chapter 4 suggest that this stability might obscure a larger problem. The mere measurement of the opinions of individuals introduces a bias into public opinion by inadvertently silencing some individuals predisposed to support the policies of the welfare state. Thus, public opinion on economic policies may be stable, but it suffers from an equally stable conservative exclusion bias.

On other questions, the findings of those who study public opinion may be even more troubling. Page and Shapiro (1992, 67) note that an examination of collective opinion on social issues over the last fifty years reveals a number of "exceptionally large" opinion changes. And most of these changes "involved movement in a liberalizing, more tolerant, or more egalitarian direction." Page and Shapiro attribute this change to the collective public's reaction to new and relevant information—changes in the way that people form attitudes. The analyses presented here suggest that some of this movement may instead be the result of alterations in what people feel is appropriate to voice publicly—changes in the way that people express attitudes. This is not to say that all of the change observed by Page and Shapiro can be attributed to changes in social norms. However, some issues, like race, are extremely tricky and complex; they involve difficult mixes of general principles and particular applications. Given the centrality of racial issues in the modern political system, it seems that it would behoove us to disentangle in public opinion the changes that arise because people are forming different attitudes, and those that arise because people are less willing to express their judgments in the survey interview. The former represents real political change in the types of beliefs that individuals hold. The latter might represent a change only in what people say in the low-cost/low-benefit environment of the survey interview, not how they are willing to act in the political world once the potential costs and benefits of action and inaction become salient.

Some might argue that this change is in and of itself an important one. Perhaps elites are aware that the public will echo the discussions taking place in larger society. Thus elites might try to strategically shape the public debate so as to suppress certain opinions and make others easier to express (Page and Shapiro 1992). For example, the African American leadership has labored to make the public expression of antiracial sentiments unacceptable (Mendelberg 2001). For these leaders, the lesson of chapter 3 might be a happy one: a poll result that shows that people feel constrained to voice racially liberal sentiment could be a good thing. But other conclusions could be drawn as well. As the consideration of racial and other socially sensitive issues moves from the abstract environment of the survey interview to the world of political action, the same leaders may be surprised by unfavorable popular reactions to new public policies.[8] Specifically, if the process of opinion expression creates systematic gaps between what the people think and what they say in the survey interview, the mass public may act in ways that cannot be predicted by opinions polls. The history of failure in pre-election polling in biracial elections suggests that polls on sensitive issues may indeed be flawed. It may be better for elites to identify sources of opposition to unpopular policies on controversial issues than to hear a comforting but misleading silence from the mass public.

The biases uncovered in this book are not mere technical findings of interest only to a narrow audience. Rather, because these biases have the potential to exclude particular sentiment from opinion polls, the very collection of opinions through polls serves inadvertently to disenfranchise individuals of a particular ideological or political type. Even if we think that it is acceptable to exclude certain segments of the mass population from public opinion, the findings of this book

---

[8] Of course, other elites might try to encourage racially conservative opinions.

cause trouble for the representational relations in the current era. Biased polls may damage the link between representatives and their constituents if elites use opinion polls in any way to collect information about mass preferences.

There may, however, be hopeful results in the findings of this book as well. In *The Semisovereign People*, E. E. Schattschneider (1960) pointed to the importance of political entrepreneurs in expanding the scope of political conflict past a narrow range of interests, particularly on questions of economic equality. Political entrepreneurs who seek potential supporters for the policies they advocate may find that opinion polls paint an overly pessimistic portrait of such latent support. With investment in political education and mobilization, perhaps ordinary citizens could better connect their interests to current political controversies. To use the language of Bartels (1990), perhaps political entrepreneurs could lead citizens to their "enlightened preferences" (see also Fishkin 1991). Such citizens could comprise a strong base of support for new policies, thereby changing the direction of government. Issue areas where large segments of the mass public appear uninterested or disengaged might prove fertile ground for the expansion of political conflict.

Final Thoughts

The term "public opinion" encompasses many different constructs. Public opinion can refer to support for prominent political leaders. It can also encompass the importance that people assign to the different concerns of government—the public agenda. But when commentators speak of public opinion, they often mean the direction of public sentiment on the issues of the day. It is this conception that has occupied this book. I have chosen to focus my analysis on three broad issue areas—race, social welfare policy, and war—at important moments in American history. Through such analysis, I show that the potential for bias in polls is pervasive.

The presence of bias in opinion polls in a broad variety of issue topics works against the rosy picture painted by scholars in the egalitarian tradition, from Gallup in the 1930s to Page and Shapiro and Verba in the present day. More generally, then, this book points to the need to pay closer attention to the micro foundations of collective public opinion. As Converse (1990, 378) argues, the reason that collective public opinion appears "rational" is that "aggregation drives out noise, and noise is what most vividly roars to attention with the total disaggregation of the sample survey." Similarly, as demonstrated above, the very process of deciding to answer survey questions drives out certain types of individuals with particular opinions. Put another way, the aggregate public may be "rational," but it is a public that speaks with a biased voice.

The bias found in this book is only the tip of the iceberg. Examining the missing sentiments of the *don't know* respondents is an important task. However, the decision to answer particular questions is only one part of the survey response process. Biases of a similar nature surely arise through the opinions citizens actually express in the survey interview. It is likely that the concerns that lead to item nonresponse would also lead to an increased level of noise in their opinions. Respondents who feel conflicted about presenting a racist public face may choose a *don't know* response, as I suggest here. On the other hand, they may also choose to express greater support for policies designed to ensure racial equality than their underlying predilections would lead them to support. Respondents who would benefit from policies designed to increase the scope of the social welfare state but are led to ambivalence and uncertainty by the current political climate may abstain from survey questions, as I suggest. However, these same individuals may also speak with less clarity when they do offer opinions on these same questions. In short, the analyses presented in this book provide a floor for the levels of bias in opinion. How high the ceiling goes remains to be determined.

Constructing more clever question wordings cannot solve the problems uncovered here. Instead, we need to think harder about what kinds of interests we lose in opinion polling, and how we can account for such interests. Future public opinion research should not *just* focus on rejuvenating our view of the "rationality" of the American public. In addition, researchers should seek to identify the causes of variation in uncertainty and ambivalence in individual preference formation, the social factors at work in the process of attitude expression and—most importantly—the consequences of this variation for public opinion. By acknowledging the vast differences in the way that individuals form and express political opinions, instead of looking for ways to rehabilitate our picture of the mass public, we will be forced to turn to the less pleasant, but equally critical, task of redressing the inequalities in the voice of different segments of the mass public.

But before I conclude, I wish to take a different course and offer a final defense of opinions polls. The analyses reported in this book should not be taken as an indictment of the survey enterprise. Opinion polls are certainly not perfect, but they are quantified information about public preferences. Therefore, in combination with traditional forms of participation, opinion polls may play a valuable role in the American political system by giving us a window onto the shape of the will of the people.

This is not to say that we should take opinion polls at their face. Before we accept polls, we need to recognize and account for their limitations as sources of information. Some individuals are unable to draw clear links from their underlying predilections to the closed-ended options available to them on opinion surveys. Other individuals misrepresent their political preferences in the environment of the survey interview. But the message to take from this book is not that we cannot gain valid information from polls. Instead, the results in these analyses highlight the importance of paying attention to and accounting for the types of biases that taint measures of public opinion.

To poll effectively, we need to pay close attention to the context of an issue and consider how the social climate might affect the opinion distribution on that issue. However, we can do more than think about this critical issue. In this book, I have demonstrated the use of techniques that allow us not only to speculate on the presence of biases in opinion formation and expression to measure and, more importantly, to account for such bias. With a more critical and discerning eye toward the larger political and social environment, then, we may measure public opinion more effectively and move toward an understanding of public sentiment on key issues facing the nation.

APPENDIX TO CHAPTER 3

To EASE THE interpretation of the analyses presented in this book, I presented the results in a way that required little detailed knowledge of statistics or data analysis. In these appendices, I present more detailed discussion for the interested reader.

A Note about the Treatment of Missing Data in the Analyses

In all the analyses in chapter 3 (as well as those in chapters 4 and 5), I include a number of control variables to ensure that any selection bias estimated is not simply an artifact of omitting explanatory variables common to both the selection and outcome equations.[1] Including these variables not only decreases the parsimony of the results, but also introduces other potentially serious problems to the analyses. Because we do not have complete information about all the characteristics of all the respondents, some cases are lost because of listwise deletion of the missing data. In many instances, the listwise deletion of cases in analysis can lead to biased parameter estimates (see King et al. 2001; Little and Rubin 1987). The question of bias is especially relevant problem here because as the number of variables used in the analysis increases, the percentage of cases that "go missing" increases as well. Thus, introducing a large number of control variables also increases the potential for biased coefficient estimates.

To allay these concerns, I ran a series of robustness tests in which I used the demographic characteristics of the respondents (and some political engagement measures) to see if my results changed when I used more limited model specifications, where fewer cases were listwise deleted. The percentage of listwise deleted cases ranged from 1 percent to 12 percent. In all the analyses presented in chapters 3, 4, and 5, the analyses were robust to the model respecification.[2] Thus, the inclusive modeling strategy described in chapter 3 does not introduce bias into my coefficient estimates.

[1] The selection equation predicts the decision to offer a response to a given item; the outcome equation predicts the direction of the response.
[2] Some of these results are presented in Berinsky (2000). The others are available from the author upon request.

It should also be noted that the differences found between the predicted positions of question-answerers and question-abstainers do not
vary greatly based on the specific model used to forecast opinion.
While models with more variables sharpen the predicted differences
between question-answers and question-abstainers, the basic thrust of
the results is robust to model respecification.

Bivariate Probit Selection Model

The bivariate probit selection accounts for selection bias in the case of
an outcome equation with a binary dependent variable and is intended
to analyze data that have been censored—that is, data for which we
do not have information about the dependent variable of interest for
some respondents, but we do have some information about the attributes of the nonrespondents (Breen 1996; Greene 1997). This model
combines information about the untruncated successes and failures
(the outcome equation) with information about the untruncated observations (those excluded by the selection equation) in a MLE switching
model. The model can be represented as a bivariate probit with one of
the quadrants collapsed over those individuals who are selected out
of the outcome equation. The log-likelihood of this model is, following
Greene (1995):

$$
\begin{aligned}
Ln\ L(\beta_1,\beta_2,\rho) &= \Sigma_{y_2=1,y_1=1} \ln\ \Phi_2\ (\beta_1'x_{i1},\beta_2'x_{i2},\rho) \\
&+ \Sigma_{y_2=1,y_1=0} \ln\ \Phi_2\ (-\beta_1'x_{i1},\beta_2'x_{i2},-\rho) \\
&+ \Sigma_{y_2=0} \ln\ \Phi_2\ (-\beta_2'x_{i2})
\end{aligned}
$$

Where: $Y_{i1} \sim f_{bern}\ (y_{1i} | \pi_{1i})$, π_{1i} defined by the underlying probability term

   $Y_{i1}^* = \beta x_{i1} + u_{1i}$ is the outcome process,

   $Y_{i2} \sim f_{bern}(y_{2i} | \pi_{2i})$, π_{2i} defined by the underlying probability term

   $Y_{i2}^* = \beta x_{i2} + u_{i2}$, is the selection process

   $y_{1i} = 0$ and $y_{2i} = 1$ is an untruncated failure,

   $y_{1i} = 1$ and $y_{2i} = 1$ is an untruncated success,

   $y_{2i} = 0$ is a truncated observation.

$\Phi_2\ (\beta_1'x_1, \beta_2'x_2, \rho)$ is the cumulative bivariate normal function defined
by $\beta_1'x_1, \beta_2'x_2$ and ρ; and u_{1i} and u_{2i} are bivariate normally distributed
iid, with $\sigma_{u1,u2} = \rho$.

Coding of Variables for Analysis in Chapter 3

These coding protocols apply to the variables used in the analyses for the 1990–1994 NES data presented in tables A3.1–A3.4.

Age: Age of respondent, in years, divided by 100

Hispanic: Dummy indicating whether the respondent is Hispanic (0 = non-Hispanic; 1 = Hispanic)

Male: Dummy indicating the gender of the respondent (0 = female; 1 = male)

Homeowner: Dummy indicating whether the respondent owns their home (0 = no; 1 = yes)

Education: Five-category NES education variable measuring highest level of education (0 = grade school, 1 = advanced degree)

Income variables: A series of eight dummy variables indicating the respondents reported income, or if respondent's income was not ascertained. The omitted category is an income of $25,000–$34,999.

Region variables: A series of four dummy variables indicating the respondent's census region of residence (North-East, North-Central, West, and South). The omitted category is respondents who live in the Northeast.

Grew up in South: 0 = did not grow up in the South, 1 = did grow up in the South

Religion variables: A series of five dummy variables indicating the respondent's religion (Protestant, Catholic, Jewish, other religion, and no religion). The omitted category is respondents who are Protestant.

Occupation variables: A series of eight dummy variables indicating the respondent's occupation, according to classifications developed by Hout, Brooks, and Manza (1995) (professional, manager, white-collar, self-employed, skilled worker, unskilled or semiskilled homemaker, and other). The omitted category is respondents who are unskilled or semiskilled.

Number of school-age children: The natural log of the number of children in the household ages 6–17 (+1)

Party identification: Five-category partisanship variable. This variable is simply the NES seven-category partisanship variable with the independent leaners collapsed with the weak partisans (see Keith et al. 1992 for justification). The results do not change if the full seven-category scale is used (–1 = strong Republican; –0.5 = weak Republican/leaning Republican; 0 = pure Independent; 0.5 = weak Democrat/leaning Democrat; 1 = strong Democrat).

Liberal: Dummy (variable) indicating self-identification as "extremely liberal," "liberal," or "slightly liberal" on the NES seven-point ideology scale (0 = not liberal; 1 = liberal)

Conservative: Dummy indicating self-identification as "extremely conservative," "conservative," or "slightly conservative" on the NES seven-point ideology scale (0 = not conservative; 1 = conservative)

Moderate: Dummy indicating self-identification as "moderate; middle of the road" on the NES seven-point ideology scale (0 = not moderate; 1 = moderate)

No ideology: Dummy indicating respondents who *don't know* or "haven't thought much about" where they place on the NES seven-point ideology scale (0 = claim ideology; 1 = claim no ideology)

Equality: Six-item NES Equality scale. Respondents are assigned their mean score across all the individual Equality items as long as they answer half or more of those items (0 = low support for equality; 1 = high support for equality)

Racial resentment: Six-item NES Racial Resentment scale. Respondents are assigned their mean score across all the individual Racial Resentment items as long as they answer half or more of those items (0 = low support for racial resentment; 1 = high support for racial resentment)

Moral conservatism: Four-item NES Moral Conservatism scale. Respondents are assigned their mean score across all the individual Moral Conservatism items as long as they answer half or more of those items (0 = low support for moral conservatism; 1 = high support for moral conservatism)

Religious importance: Four-category variable that gauges the degree of guidance religion provides in the respondent's everyday life (0 = not important; 1 = provides a great deal of guidance)

Political information: An additive scale of the NES variables used to measure knowledge of politics. The exact number of items used to construct the scale varies by year. The scale construction follows the general guidance of Zaller (1992) and includes factual items as well as the interviewer's assessment of the respondent's knowledge of politics. The results do not change if only the factual items are used to construct the scale (0 = low; 1 = high).

Discuss politics: Eight-category variable measuring the number of days in the past week in which the respondent discussed politics with their friends and family, recoded to the 0–1 intervals (0 = never discuss politics; 1 = discuss politics every day)

Number of calls: The natural log of the number of face-to-face and telephone calls made to the respondent's home to obtain the interview.

Refusal conversion: Dummy variable indicating whether the interviewer attempted to convert a respondent who initially refused to participate in the NES (0 = no; 1 = yes)

Persuasion letter: Dummy variable indicating whether a persuasion letter was sent to the respondent (0 = no; 1 = yes)

These coding protocols apply to the variables used in the analyses for the 1989 New York City mayoral election data presented in table A3.5.

Age: Age of respondent, in years, divided by 100

Black: Dummy indicating the race of the respondent. Excludes black Hispanics (0 = nonblack; 1 = black).

Hispanic (white and other): Dummy indicating whether the respondent is Hispanic. Excludes black Hispanics (0 = non-Hispanic; 1 = Hispanic).

Black Hispanic: Dummy indicating whether the respondent is a black Hispanic (0 = nonblack Hispanic; 1 = black Hispanic)

Female: 0 = male, 1 = female

Education: Six-category NES education variable measuring highest level of education (0 = grade school; 1 = advanced degree)

Income variables: A series of seven dummy variables indicating the respondent's reported income, or if the respondent's income was not ascertained. The omitted category is an income of $30,000–$49,999.

Religion variables: A series of five dummy variables indicating the religion in which the respondent was brought up (Protestant, Catholic, Jewish, other religion, and refused to identify religion). The omitted category is respondents who are Protestants.

Republican: Dummy indicating if the respondent is registered with the Republican Party (0 = not registered as a Republican; 1 = registered as a Republican)

Democrat: Dummy indicating if the respondent is registered with the Democratic Party. This category of party identification is the omitted category in the analyses (0 = not registered as a Democrat; 1 = registered as a Democrat).

Independent: Dummy indicating if the respondent is registered as an independent (0 = not registered as an independent; 1 = registered as an independent)

Other party identifier: Dummy indicating if the respondent is registered with a party other than the Democratic Party or the Republican Party (0 = not registered with another party; 1 = registered with another party)

Liberal: Dummy indicating self-identification as "very liberal" or "liberal" on a five-point ideology scale (0 = not liberal; 1 = liberal)

Conservative: Dummy indicating self-identification as "very conservative" or "conservative" on a five-point ideology scale (0 = not conservative; 1 = conservative)

Moderate: Dummy indicating self-identification as "moderate" on a five-point ideology scale (0 = not moderate; 1 = moderate)

No ideology: Dummy indicating respondents who *don't know* their ideology or "don't think in those terms" and decline to place themselves on a five-point ideology scale (0 = claim ideology; 1 = claim no ideology)

Certainty of voting: Variable indicating how likely the respondent thinks it is that he or she will vote in the mayoral election. If the respondent thinks that he or she will "probably vote," "chances are 50/50," or "don't think they will vote," this variable is scored a "0." If the respondent is "certain to vote," the variable is scored a "1."

Voted in 1988: Dummy variable indicating whether the respondent voted in the 1988 presidential election (0 = no; 1 = yes)

These coding protocols apply to the variables used in the analyses for the 1972 NES data presented in tables A3.6–A3.7. Variables coded the same in 1972 as in 1990–1994 are not detailed.

Income variables: A series of five dummy variables indicating the respondent's reported income, or if the respondent's income was not ascertained. The omitted category is an income of $12,000–$24,999.

Region variables: The region variables are reconfigured here to capture in greater detail the differences between the South and the rest of the nation. As Schuman et al. (1997) discuss, the key regional difference through the 1970s was between the South and the rest of the nation. In the present day, these differences are minimal (as evidenced here by the consistently small effect of the region dummy variables in the 1990s analysis).

Metropolitan area: A series of five dummy variables indicating the size of the metropolitan area within which the respondent lives. Based on census bureau designations, the metropolitan areas are divided as follows: large cities, small cities, large suburbs, small suburbs, and rural areas.

Trust in government: Four-item Trust in Government scale. Respondents are assigned their mean score across the items as long as they answer half or more of those items. The items include the following: whether government wastes tax money; how much of the time the government in Washington can be trusted; whether the government is run by a few big interests or for the benefit of all the people; and how many people running for the government are a little crooked (0 = low trust in government; 1 = high trust in government).

Efficacy: Two-item NES Efficacy scale. Respondents are assigned their mean score across the two Efficacy items (politicians care about people like the respondent and the respondent believes he or she has a say in government), as long as they answer at least one of the items (0 = low efficacy; 1 = high efficacy).

Engagement: A scale of interest in the campaign and the performance of five campaign acts: (1) voting in the presidential election; (2) trying to convince other people they should vote for one of the parties or candidates; (3) attending political meetings; (4) doing work for one of the parties or candidates; and (5) wearing a button supporting one of the parties or candidates (0 = perform no acts; 1 = perform all acts).

TABLE A3.1
Support for School Integration, 1990

Variable	Outcome Equation	
	Independent Probit Coefficient (SE)	*Bivariate Probit Coefficient (SE)*
Constant	0.88 (0.85)	−0.00 (0.90)
Age	−0.07 (2.89)	0.66 (2.85)
Age^2	−0.84 (2.98)	−1.22 (3.03)
Hispanic	0.46 (0.28)*	0.35 (0.27)
Male	0.17 (0.16)	0.15 (0.15)
Homeowner	−0.29 (0.16)*	−0.27 (0.16)*
Education	0.09 (0.34)	0.23 (0.34)
Income: <$10,000	−0.09 (0.29)	−0.22 (0.27)
Income: $10,000–$14,999	−0.12 (0.28)	−0.20 (0.25)
Income: $15,000–$24,999	−0.03 (0.24)	−0.20 (0.24)
Income: $35,000–$49,999	−0.06 (0.22)	−0.12 (0.22)
Income: $50,000–$74,999	0.01 (0.26)	−0.08 (0.27)
Income: $75,000+	−0.22 (0.29)	−0.27 (0.27)
Income Not Ascertained	0.39 (0.31)	0.28 (0.31)
North-Central	−0.42 (0.21)**	−0.33 (0.22)
South	−0.03 (0.24)	0.07 (0.24)
West	0.02 (0.21)	0.07 (0.21)
Grew Up in South	0.04 (0.23)	0.12 (0.23)
No Religion	−0.09 (0.16)	0.01 (0.17)
Catholic	0.08 (0.17)	0.15 (0.16)
Jewish	−0.30 (0.50)	−0.29 (0.57)
Other Religion	0.38 (0.25)	0.33 (0.28)
Occupation: Professional	−0.14 (0.25)	−0.02 (0.26)
Occupation: Manager	−0.36 (0.32)	−0.36 (0.32)
Occupation: White Collar	0.00 (0.25)	0.01 (0.23)
Occupation: Self-Employed	−0.07 (0.29)	0.03 (0.29)
Occupation: Skilled Worker	−0.36 (0.29)	−0.24 (0.29)
Occupation: Homemaker	0.20 (0.28)	0.16 (0.26)
Occupation: Other	0.24 (0.28)	0.22 (0.27)
Number of School-Age Children	0.25 (0.15)*	0.24 (0.15)*
Racial Resentment	−1.47 (0.33)**	−1.28 (0.38)**

TABLE A3.1 (*cont'd*)
Support for School Integration, 1990

| | Outcome Equation | |
Variable	Independent Probit Coefficient (SE)	Bivariate Probit Coefficient (SE)
Equality	0.78 (0.43)*	0.69 (0.41)*
Trust in Government	0.59 (0.31)*	0.51 (0.30)*
Moral Conservatism	−0.72 (0.40)*	−0.53 (0.41)
Religious Importance	0.17 (0.21)	0.14 (0.19)
Party Identification	−0.04 (0.11)	−0.02 (0.10)
Liberal	0.16 (0.21)	0.13 (0.20)
Conservative	−0.46 (0.18)**	−0.40 (0.17)**
No Ideology	0.07 (0.20)	−0.08 (0.21)
	Selection Equation	
Constant		−0.38 (0.50)
Age		1.76 (1.82)
Age^2		−1.26 (1.92)
Hispanic		−0.09 (0.19)
Male		−0.02 (0.12)
Homeowner		−0.11 (0.12)
Education		0.17 (0.27)
Income: <$10,000		−0.33 (0.21)
Income: $10,000–$14,999		−0.22 (0.22)
Income: $15,000–$24,999		−0.46 (0.19)**
Income: $35,000–$49,999		−0.24 (0.19)
Income: $50,000–$74,999		−0.29 (0.21)
Income: $75,000+		−0.22 (0.24)
Income Not Ascertained		−0.15 (0.26)
North-Central		0.07 (0.15)
South		0.19 (0.18)
West		0.18 (0.16)
Grew Up in South		0.32 (0.17)*
No Religion		0.20 (0.12)*
Catholic		0.22 (0.13)*
Jewish		−0.29 (0.46)
Other Religion		−0.07 (0.17)
Occupation: Professional		0.25 (0.19)

TABLE A3.1 (*cont'd*)
Support for School Integration, 1990

	Selection Equation	
	---	---
Variable	*Independent Probit Coefficient (SE)*	*Bivariate Probit Coefficient (SE)*
Occupation: Manager		−0.23 (0.22)
Occupation: White Collar		0.05 (0.18)
Occupation: Self-Employed		0.27 (0.22)
Occupation: Skilled Worker		0.14 (0.22)
Occupation: Homemaker		−0.18 (0.21)
Occupation: Other		−0.08 (0.20)
Political Information		0.67 (0.35)*
Discuss Politics		0.37 (0.17)**
No Ideology		−0.37 (0.12)**
Number of School-Age Children		0.07 (0.12)
Refusal Conversion		0.59 (0.28)**
Persuasion Letter		0.22 (0.14)
Number of Calls		−0.10 (0.94)
	Correlation Parameter	
ρ		0.70 (0.37)*
N/Log Likelihood	471/−253.71	777/−728.98

* = $p < .10$; ** = $p < .05$.

TABLE A3.2
Support for School Integration, 1992

	Outcome Equation	
	---	---
Variable	*Independent Probit Coefficient (SE)*	*Bivariate Probit Coefficient (SE)*
Constant	1.51 (0.59)**	0.56 (0.53)
Age	−5.12 (1.63)**	−3.75 (1.46)**
Age^2	5.64 (1.63)**	4.37 (1.48)**
Hispanic	0.90 (0.20)**	0.70 (0.19)**
Male	−0.21 (0.10)**	−0.13 (0.09)
Homeowner	0.04 (0.11)	0.04 (0.09)
Education	0.25 (0.23)	0.12 (0.19)
Income: <$10,000	0.00 (0.17)	0.05 (0.15)
Income: $10,000–$14,999	0.05 (0.17)	0.14 (0.15)
Income: $15,000–$24,999	−0.15 (0.16)	−0.16 (0.13)
Income: $35,000–$49,999	−0.29 (0.15)*	−0.27 (0.13)**
Income: $50,000–$74,999	−0.24 (0.16)	−0.23 (0.13)*
Income: $75,000+	−0.16 (0.19)	−0.09 (0.16)
Income Not Ascertained	−0.18 (0.22)	−0.24 (0.19)
North-Central	−0.26 (0.13)**	−0.19 (0.11)*
South	−0.26 (0.15)*	−0.16 (0.13)
West	0.01 (0.14)	0.04 (0.12)
Grew Up in South	0.20 (0.15)	0.18 (0.13)
No Religion	0.04 (0.14)	−0.02 (0.12)
Catholic	0.02 (0.11)	0.01 (0.10)
Jewish	−0.13 (0.29)	0.04 (0.26)
Other Religion	0.01 (0.17)	−0.03 (0.14)
Occupation: Professional	−0.20 (0.17)	−0.08 (0.14)
Occupation: Manager	−0.11 (0.20)	−0.05 (0.18)
Occupation: White Collar	−0.12 (0.18)	−0.10 (0.15)
Occupation: Self-Employed	−0.14 (0.19)	−0.10 (0.17)
Occupation: Skilled Worker	0.34 (0.20)*	0.32 (0.18)*
Occupation: Homemaker	−0.19 (0.19)	−0.13 (0.16)
Occupation: Other	−0.28 (0.16)*	−0.25 (0.14)*
Number of School-Age Children	−0.84 (0.42)**	−0.71 (0.37)**
Racial Resentment	−2.11 (0.42)**	−1.54 (0.36)**

TABLE A3.2 *(cont'd)*
Support for School Integration, 1992

	Outcome Equation	
Variable	*Independent Probit Coefficient (SE)*	*Bivariate Probit Coefficient (SE)*
Equality	1.51 (0.28)**	1.16 (0.23)**
Trust in Government	1.11 (0.21)**	0.83 (0.18)**
Moral Conservatism	−0.83 (0.25)**	−0.64 (0.20)**
Religious Importance	0.24 (0.13)**	0.19 (0.11)**
Party Identification	0.18 (0.08)**	0.14 (0.06)**
Liberal	−0.04 (0.14)	−0.01 (0.11)
Conservative	0.11 (0.12)	0.12 (0.09)
No Ideology	0.07 (0.13)	−0.11 (0.11)
	Selection Equation	
Constant		0.35 (0.33)
Age		−0.38 (1.24)
Age^2		0.61 (1.26)
Hispanic		0.10 (0.14)
Male		0.01 (0.08)
Homeowner		−0.00 (0.08)
Education		−0.32 (0.17)*
Income: <$10,000		0.09 (0.13)
Income: $10,000–$14,999		0.16 (0.14)
Income: $15,000–$24,999		−0.09 (0.12)
Income: $35,000–$49,999		−0.13 (0.11)
Income: $50,000–$74,999		−0.11 (0.12)
Income: $75,000+		0.01 (0.15)
Income Not Ascertained		−0.26 (0.16)*
North-Central		−0.04 (0.10)
South		0.06 (0.12)
West		0.06 (0.11)
Grew Up in South		−0.02 (0.12)
No Religion		−0.11 (0.10)
Catholic		0.01 (0.09)
Jewish		0.14 (0.24)
Other Religion		−0.10 (0.12)

TABLE A3.2 (*cont'd*)
Support for School Integration, 1992

Variable	Selection Equation	
	Independent Probit Coefficient (SE)	*Bivariate Probit Coefficient (SE)*
Occupation: Professional		0.18 (0.13)
Occupation: Manager		0.06 (0.15)
Occupation: White Collar		0.06 (0.13)
Occupation: Self-Employed		0.10 (0.14)
Occupation: Skilled Worker		0.15 (0.15)
Occupation: Homemaker		0.09 (0.14)
Occupation: Other		−0.03 (0.12)
Political Information		0.38 (0.15)**
Discuss Politics		0.32 (0.10)**
No Ideology		−0.28 (0.08)**
Number of School-Age Children		−0.22 (0.30)
Refusal Conversion		0.08 (0.28)
Persuasion Letter		−0.01 (0.13)
Number of Calls		0.02 (0.05)
Correlation Parameter		
ρ		0.90 (0.11)**
N/Log Likelihood	1082/−585.83	1675/−1641.23

$* = p < .10; ** = p < .05.$

TABLE A3.3
Support for School Integration, 1994

Variable	Outcome Equation	
	Independent Probit Coefficient (SE)	Bivariate Probit Coefficient (SE)
Constant	1.29 (0.58)**	0.68 (0.94)
Age	−4.53 (1.80)**	−3.31 (2.43)
Age^2	3.37 (1.80)*	2.42 (2.19)
Hispanic	0.43 (0.18)**	0.42 (0.17)**
Male	−0.09 (0.11)	−0.07 (0.11)
Homeowner	0.06 (0.12)	0.02 (0.12)
Education	−0.31 (0.26)	−0.18 (0.30)
Income: <$10,000	0.25 (0.20)	0.21 (0.20)
Income: $10,000–$14,999	−0.02 (0.22)	−0.09 (0.23)
Income: $15,000–$24,999	0.31 (0.17)*	0.25 (0.18)
Income: $35,000–$49,999	−0.06 (0.16)	−0.07 (0.16)
Income: $50,000–$74,999	−0.04 (0.17)	−0.07 (0.17)
Income: $75,000+	0.27 (0.19)	0.23 (0.20)
Income Not Ascertained	−0.02 (0.22)	−0.06 (0.22)
North-Central	−0.11 (0.16)	−0.12 (0.17)
South	0.15 (0.18)	0.12 (0.19)
West	0.00 (0.17)	0.06 (0.18)
Grew Up in South	−0.24 (0.16)	−0.21 (0.16)
No Religion	0.14 (0.16)	0.13 (0.16)
Catholic	−0.01 (0.13)	0.03 (0.13)
Jewish	0.11 (0.31)	0.17 (0.32)
Other Religion	0.02 (0.16)	0.04 (0.16)
Occupation: Professional	0.34 (0.18)*	0.29 (0.19)
Occupation: Manager	0.23 (0.20)	0.18 (0.21)
Occupation: White Collar	0.21 (0.20)	0.09 (0.25)
Occupation: Self-Employed	−0.50 (0.27)*	−0.53 (0.27)*
Occupation: Skilled Worker	0.46 (0.22)**	0.41 (0.22)*
Occupation: Homemaker	0.20 (0.21)	0.18 (0.21)
Occupation: Other	0.33 (0.19)*	0.24 (0.23)
Number of School-Age Children	−0.21 (0.11)*	−0.18 (0.12)
Racial Resentment	−1.20 (0.26)**	−1.12 (0.29)**
Equality	1.04 (0.31)**	0.96 (0.34)**

TABLE A3.3 (*cont'd*)
Support for School Integration, 1994

	Outcome Equation	
Variable	*Independent Probit Coefficient (SE)*	*Bivariate Probit Coefficient (SE)*
Trust in Government	0.39 (0.24)*	0.35 (0.24)
Moral Conservatism	−0.47 (0.27)*	−0.44 (0.27)*
Religious Importance	0.19 (0.15)	0.18 (0.14)
Party Identification	0.24 (0.09)**	0.22 (0.09)**
Liberal	−0.17 (0.16)	−0.15 (0.16)
Conservative	−0.23 (0.13)**	−0.21 (0.13)
No Ideology	−0.01 (0.15)	−0.05 (0.15)
	Selection Equation	
Constant		−0.64 (0.36)*
Age		3.13 (1.31)**
Age^2		−2.47 (1.30)*
Hispanic		0.05 (0.14)
Male		0.05 (0.08)
Homeowner		−0.12 (0.09)
Education		0.33 (0.20)*
Income: <$10,000		−0.06 (0.16)
Income: $10,000–$14,999		−0.29 (0.16)*
Income: $15,000–$24,999		−0.17 (0.13)
Income: $35,000–$49,999		−0.09 (0.12)
Income: $50,000–$74,999		−0.13 (0.13)
Income: $75,000+		−0.08 (0.15)
Income Not Ascertained		−0.14 (0.17)
North-Central		−0.06 (0.12)
South		−0.07 (0.13)
West		0.20 (0.13)
Grew Up in South		0.01 (0.11)
No Religion		−0.02 (0.11)
Catholic		0.16 (0.09)*
Jewish		0.22 (0.25)
Other Religion		0.12 (0.13)

TABLE A3.3 (*cont'd*)
Support for School Integration 1994

	Selection Equation	
Variable	*Independent Probit Coefficient (SE)*	*Bivariate Probit Coefficient (SE)*
Occupation: Professional		−0.11 (0.14)
Occupation: Manager		−0.16 (0.15)
Occupation: White Collar		−0.39 (0.14)**
Occupation: Self-Employed		−0.28 (0.17)*
Occupation: Skilled Worker		−0.06 (0.17)
Occupation: Homemaker		−0.09 (0.16)
Occupation: Other		−0.27 (0.14)*
Political Information		0.14 (0.18)
Discuss Politics		0.38 (0.12)**
No Ideology		−0.09 (0.10)
Number of School-Age Children		0.07 (0.08)
Refusal Conversion		0.12 (0.13)
Persuasion Letter		−0.14 (0.16)
Number of Calls		0.01 (0.07)
	Correlation Parameter	
ρ		0.49 (0.55)
N/Log Likelihood	885/−480.61	1414/−1370.76

* $= p < .10$; ** $= p < .05$.

TABLE A3.4
Support for Fair Employment, 1992

	Outcome Equation	
Variable	Independent Probit Coefficient (SE)	Bivariate Probit Coefficient (SE)
Constant	1.14 (0.58)*	0.22 (0.63)
Age	−0.61 (1.61)	0.35 (1.57)
Age^2	−0.30 (1.59)	−0.92 (1.53)
Hispanic	0.28 (0.20)	0.21 (0.19)
Male	0.31 (0.10)**	0.30 (0.10)**
Homeowner	0.08 (0.10)	0.02 (0.10)
Education	0.23 (0.22)	0.41 (0.22)*
Income: <$10,000	0.26 (0.18)	0.31 (0.16)*
Income: $10,000–$14,999	0.30 (0.18)*	0.38 (0.16)**
Income: $15,000–$24,999	0.10 (0.16)	0.15 (0.15)
Income: $35,000–$49,999	0.08 (0.15)	0.11 (0.14)
Income: $50,000–$74,999	0.07 (0.15)	0.12 (0.14)
Income: $75,000+	0.14 (0.19)	0.21 (0.18)
Income Not Ascertained	0.11 (0.21)	0.12 (0.20)
North-Central	−0.13 (0.13)	−0.10 (0.12)
South	0.02 (0.15)	0.07 (0.14)
West	0.14 (0.14)	0.15 (0.13)
Grew Up in South	0.14 (0.15)	0.08 (0.14)
No Religion	−0.10 (0.14)	−0.09 (0.14)
Catholic	−0.00 (0.11)	−0.03 (0.10)
Jewish	0.31 (0.29)	0.45 (0.30)
Other Religion	−0.11 (0.16)	−0.11 (0.15)
Occupation: Professional	−0.21 (0.17)	−0.09 (0.17)
Occupation: Manager	−0.58 (0.19)**	−0.48 (0.18)**
Occupation: White Collar	−0.08 (0.18)	−0.04 (0.17)
Occupation: Self-Employed	−0.35 (0.18)*	−0.22 (0.17)
Occupation: Skilled Worker	−0.09 (0.20)	−0.01 (0.18)
Occupation: Homemaker	−0.02 (0.19)	0.07 (0.17)
Occupation: Other	−0.08 (0.17)	−0.07 (0.15)
Racial Resentment	−3.59 (0.42)**	−3.16 (0.48)**
Equality	1.47 (0.27)**	1.27 (0.27)**

TABLE A3.4 (*cont'd*)
Support for Fair Employment, 1992

	Outcome Equation	
Variable	*Independent Probit Coefficient (SE)*	*Bivariate Probit Coefficient (SE)*
Trust in Government	0.49 (0.21)**	0.42 (0.20)**
Moral Conservatism	−0.09 (0.24)	−0.06 (0.21)
Religious Importance	0.19 (0.13)	0.20 (0.12)*
Party Identification	0.06 (0.08)	0.06 (0.07)
Liberal	0.22 (0.13)	0.21 (0.12)*
Conservative	−0.02 (0.11)	−0.01 (0.10)
No Ideology	−0.21 (0.13)	−0.34 (0.13)**
	Selection Equation	
Constant		−0.80 (0.36)**
Age		1.75 (1.28)
Age^2		−1.15 (1.28)
Hispanic		0.02 (0.14)
Male		0.03 (0.08)
Homeowner		−0.15 (0.08)*
Education		0.40 (0.19)**
Income: <$10,000		0.23 (0.14)
Income: $10,000–$14,999		0.27 (0.14)*
Income: $15,000–$24,999		0.17 (0.12)
Income: $35,000–$49,999		0.05 (0.12)
Income: $50,000–$74,999		0.11 (0.12)
Income: $75,000+		0.25 (0.16)
Income Not Ascertained		0.10 (0.16)
North-Central		0.02 (0.10)
South		0.12 (0.13)
West		0.09 (0.11)
Grew Up in South		−0.17 (0.12)
No Religion		−0.01 (0.11)
Catholic		−0.04 (0.09)
Jewish		0.44 (0.32)

TABLE A3.4 (cont'd)
Support for Fair Employment, 1992

	Selection Equation	
Variable	Independent Probit Coefficient (SE)	Bivariate Probit Coefficient (SE)
Other Religion		−0.03 (0.13)
Occupation: Professional		0.21 (0.13)
Occupation: Manager		0.05 (0.15)
Occupation: White Collar		0.07 (0.13)
Occupation: Self-Employed		0.25 (0.15)*
Occupation: Skilled Worker		0.13 (0.16)
Occupation: Homemaker		0.22 (0.15)
Occupation: Other		−0.04 (0.13)
Political Information		0.56 (0.17)**
Discuss Politics		0.67 (0.12)**
No Ideology		−0.32 (0.09)**
Refusal Conversion		0.44 (0.30)
Persuasion Letter		−0.00 (0.15)
Number of Calls		0.05 (0.05)
	Correlation Parameter	
ρ		0.69 (0.20)**
N/Log Likelihood	1126/−601.35	1651/−1538.82

* = $p < .10$; ** = $p < .05$.

TABLE A3.5
New York City Mayoral Race, 1989: Support for Dinkins

	Outcome Equation	
Variable	*Independent Probit Coefficient (SE)*	*Bivariate Probit Coefficient (SE)*
Constant	−0.11 (0.21)	−0.10 (0.21)
Republican	−1.14 (0.10)**	−1.02 (0.10)**
Independent	−0.42 (0.12)**	−0.37 (0.12)**
Other Party Identifier	−0.25 (0.25)	−0.22 (0.23)
Liberal	0.53 (0.08)**	0.54 (0.08)**
Conservative	−0.36 (0.09)**	−0.30 (0.09)**
No Ideology	0.55 (0.25)**	0.18 (0.25)
Education	0.46 (0.16)**	0.41 (0.16)**
Age	−0.33 (0.23)	−0.59 (0.22)**
Catholic	−0.39 (0.11)**	−0.40 (0.11)**
Jewish	−0.27 (0.12)**	−0.35 (0.12)**
Other Religion	−0.12 (0.17)	−0.15 (0.16)
Refused to Identify Religion	−0.48 (0.30)	−0.56 (0.26)**
Income: <$8,000	0.35 (0.18)*	0.27 (0.17)
Income: $8,000–$11,999	0.42 (0.18)**	0.34 (0.18)*
Income: $12,000–$19,999	0.17 (0.14)	0.12 (0.14)
Income: $20,000–$29,999	0.16 (0.11)	0.13 (0.11)
Income: $50,000+	−0.09 (0.10)	−0.07 (0.09)
Income Not Ascertained	0.31 (0.15)**	0.07 (0.18)
Female	0.02 (0.07)	−0.01 (0.07)
Hispanic (White and Other)	0.79 (0.11)**	0.80 (0.11)**
	Selection Equation	
Constant		1.55 (0.27)**
Republican		0.44 (0.11)**
Independent		0.06 (0.14)
Other Party Identifier		0.09 (0.27)
Liberal		0.26 (0.10)**
Conservative		0.16 (0.10)
No Ideology		−0.59 (0.17)**
Education		0.04 (0.18)
Age		−1.10 (0.26)**

TABLE A3.5 (*cont'd*)
New York City Mayoral Race, 1989: Support for Dinkins

	Selection Equation	
Variable	*Independent Probit Coefficient (SE)*	*Bivariate Probit Coefficient (SE)*
Catholic		−0.13 (0.14)
Jewish		−0.14 (0.21)
Other Religion		−0.39 (0.14)**
Refused to Identify Religion		−0.28 (0.25)
Income: <$8,000		−0.14 (0.19)
Income: $8,000–$11,999		−0.16 (0.19)
Income: $12,000–$19,999		−0.19 (0.16)
Income: $20,000–$29,999		−0.10 (0.13)
Income: $50,000+		0.03 (0.12)
Income Not Ascertained		−0.65 (0.13)**
Female		−0.15 (0.08)*
Hispanic (White and Other)		0.43 (0.17)**
Certainty of Voting		0.28 (0.18)
Voted in 1988		−0.06 (0.13)
	Correlation Parameter	
ρ		0.81 (0.25)**
N/Log Likelihood	1566/−833.55	1841/−1512.47

* = $p < .10$; ** = $p < .05$.

TABLE A3.6
Support for School Integration, 1972

	Outcome Equation	
Variable	Independent Probit Coefficient (SE)	Bivariate Probit Coefficient (SE)
Constant	0.42 (0.29)	0.45 (0.32)
Age	−4.57 (1.25)**	−4.54 (1.38)**
Age^2	4.71 (1.34)**	4.70 (1.46)**
Male	0.03 (0.07)	0.03 (0.07)
Education	0.31 (0.17)*	0.31 (0.17)*
Income: <$4,000	0.01 (0.12)	0.01 (0.13)
Income: $4,000–$5,999	−0.04 (0.13)	−0.04 (0.13)
Income: $6,000–$11,999	−0.02 (0.09)	−0.02 (0.09)
Income: $25,000+	−0.11 (0.17)	−0.12 (0.20)
Income Not Ascertained	−0.11 (0.28)	−0.07 (0.42)
Large City	−0.26 (0.16)*	−0.26 (0.16)
Small City	−0.05 (0.10)	−0.05 (0.10)
Small Suburbs	−0.20 (0.09)**	−0.20 (0.09)**
Deep South	−0.49 (0.19)**	−0.51 (0.20)**
Peripheral South	−0.25 (0.14)*	−0.26 (0.16)*
Border States	−0.01 (0.13)	−0.01 (0.13)
West	0.04 (0.10)	0.04 (0.10)
Raised in South	−0.10 (0.15)	−0.10 (0.15)
No Religion	0.10 (0.20)	0.09 (0.22)
Catholic	0.09 (0.09)	0.10 (0.09)
Jewish	0.34 (0.27)	0.33 (0.29)
Other Religion	−0.02 (0.18)	−0.03 (0.19)
Number of Children	0.05 (0.07)	0.05 (0.08)
Trust in Government	0.27 (0.15)*	0.27 (0.15)*
Efficacy	0.17 (0.09)*	0.17 (0.10)*
Party Identification	0.02 (0.06)	0.02 (0.06)
Liberal	0.50 (0.11)**	0.50 (0.11)**
Conservative	−0.13 (0.10)	−0.13 (0.10)
No Ideology	0.03 (0.10)	0.06 (0.18)

TABLE A3.6 *(cont'd)*
Support for School Integration, 1972

| | Selection Equation | |
Variable	*Independent Probit Coefficient (SE)*	*Bivariate Probit Coefficient (SE)*
Constant		1.16 (0.31)**
Age		−1.03 (1.25)
Age²		0.82 (1.32)
Male		−0.09 (0.08)
Education		−0.20 (0.18)
Income: <$4,000		0.02 (0.13)
Income: $4,000–$5,999		−0.07 (0.13)
Income: $6,000–$11,999		−0.05 (0.10)
Income: $25,000+		0.36 (0.22)
Income Not Ascertained		−0.72 (0.22)**
Large City		−0.05 (0.18)
Small City		0.04 (0.11)
Small Suburbs		0.02 (0.10)
Deep South		0.29 (0.19)
Peripheral South		0.19 (0.15)
Border States		0.00 (0.13)
West		0.07 (0.12)
Raised in South		0.01 (0.15)
No Religion		0.21 (0.24)
Catholic		−0.07 (0.09)
Jewish		0.39 (0.38)
Other Religion		0.14 (0.23)
Number of Children		−0.07 (0.08)
Political Information		0.55 (0.22)**
Engagement		0.13 (0.21)
No Ideology		−0.31 (0.10)**
	Correlation Parameters	
ρ		−0.14 (0.88)
N/Log Likelihood	1382/−864.50	1666/−1591.65

$* = p < .10; ** = p < .05.$

TABLE A3.7
Support for Fair Employment, 1972

	Outcome Equation	
Variable	Independent Probit Coefficient (SE)	Bivariate Probit Coefficient (SE)
Constant	−0.20 (0.29)	−0.24 (0.30)
Age	−1.71 (1.18)	−1.84 (1.22)
Age^2	1.80 (1.24)	1.93 (1.29)
Male	0.11 (0.07)	0.11 (0.07)
Education	0.36 (0.16)**	0.38 (0.17)**
Income: <$4,000	0.09 (0.12)	0.10 (0.12)
Income: $4,000–$5,999	−0.08 (0.12)	−0.07 (0.13)
Income: $6,000–$11,999	−0.07 (0.09)	−0.07 (0.09)
Income: $25,000+	−0.20 (0.16)	−0.19 (0.17)
Income Not Ascertained	0.20 (0.26)	0.18 (0.26)
Large City	0.12 (0.15)	0.13 (0.15)
Small City	−0.10 (0.10)	−0.09 (0.10)
Small Suburbs	−0.01 (0.09)	−0.01 (0.09)
Deep South	−0.21 (0.19)	−0.20 (0.19)
Peripheral South	0.00 (0.14)	0.01 (0.15)
Border States	0.08 (0.13)	0.09 (0.13)
West	−0.11 (0.10)	−0.11 (0.10)
Raised in South	−0.03 (0.15)	−0.02 (0.15)
No Religion	0.25 (0.19)	0.27 (0.21)
Catholic	0.22 (0.09)**	0.22 (0.09)**
Jewish	0.51 (0.29)*	0.53 (0.30)*
Other Religion	0.13 (0.18)	0.14 (0.19)
Unemployed	0.09 (0.22)	0.10 (0.22)
Trust in Government	0.24 (0.15)	0.23 (0.15)
Efficacy	0.21 (0.09)**	0.21 (0.10)**
Party Identification	0.04 (0.06)	0.04 (0.06)
Liberal	0.49 (0.11)**	0.49 (0.11)**
Conservative	−0.14 (0.09)	−0.14 (0.09)
No Ideology	0.09 (0.10)	0.07 (0.12)

TABLE A3.7 (*cont'd*)
Support for Fair Employment, 1972

	Selection Equation	
Variable	*Independent Probit Coefficient (SE)*	*Bivariate Probit Coefficient (SE)*
Constant		0.72 (0.29)**
Age		−2.58 (1.21)**
Age^2		2.53 (1.29)**
Male		−0.03 (0.07)
Education		−0.06 (0.17)
Income: <$4,000		0.07 (0.12)
Income: $4,000–$5,999		0.10 (0.13)
Income: $6,000–$11,999		0.05 (0.09)
Income: $25,000+		0.14 (0.18)
Income Not Ascertained		−0.19 (0.23)
Large City		0.08 (0.17)
Small City		0.14 (0.10)
Small Suburbs		−0.05 (0.09)
Deep South		0.09 (0.18)
Peripheral South		0.02 (0.13)
Border States		0.15 (0.13)
West		0.05 (0.11)
Raised in South		0.22 (0.13)*
No Religion		0.31 (0.20)
Catholic		−0.01 (0.09)
Jewish		0.23 (0.34)
Other Religion		0.17 (0.22)
Unemployed		0.07 (0.24)
Political Information		1.28 (0.20)**
Engagement		0.14 (0.18)
No Ideology		−0.16 (0.09)*
	Correlation Parameters	
ρ		0.16 (0.37)
N/Log Likelihood	1362/−890.74	1761/−177.54

* = $p < .10$; ** = $p < .05$.

APPENDIX TO CHAPTER 4

THE HECKMAN selection model is used to analyze data that have been censored; that is, data for which we do not have information about the dependent variable of interest for some respondents, but we do have some information about the attributes of the nonrespondents (Heckman 1979; Achen 1986; Breen 1996; Brehm 1993; Greene 1997).[1]

Heckman's model assumes that the relationship of interest can be specified as a simple linear model of the form:

$$y_i = \beta' x_i + \varepsilon_i \tag{1}$$

We also assume that Y is observed if and only if a second, unobserved latent variable, Z^*, exceeds a particular threshold (here set to 0):[2]

$$z_i^* = \alpha' w_i + u_i; \tag{2}$$
$$z_i = \begin{cases} 1 \ if \ z_i^* > 0; \\ 0 \ \text{otherwise} \end{cases}$$

This selection mechanism may be modeled as a probit:

$$\Pr(z_i = 1) = \Phi(\alpha' w_i) \tag{3}$$

Finally, the Heckman model assumes that the errors u_i and ε_i are distributed bivariate normal:[3]

$$\begin{pmatrix} \varepsilon_i \\ u_i \end{pmatrix} \sim N \left[\begin{pmatrix} 0 \\ 0 \end{pmatrix}, \begin{pmatrix} \sigma^2 & \rho\sigma \\ \rho\sigma & 1 \end{pmatrix} \right] \tag{4}$$

These assumptions lead to the following model:

$$E(y_i | y_i \text{ observed}) = E(\beta' x_i + \varepsilon_i | \alpha' w_i + u_i > 0) \tag{5}$$
$$= \beta' x_i + \rho\sigma\lambda$$

---

[1] This state of affairs contrasts to a truncated sample, in which we have no information about non-respondents, because observations are missing for *both* endogenous and exogenous variables (Breen 1996; Brehm 1993; Greene 1997).

[2] This selection equation is an integral part of the model because Heckman's model is a model of incidental selection, in that selection into the sample of respondents depends on a selection mechanism that is based on the observed exogenous factors. This contrasts to models of explicit selection, such as the Tobit (Greene 1997), where appearance in the sample depends on values of the endogenous variables only.

[3] σ_ε is normalized to one because α and σ_ε are not separately identifiable in the probit.

Where λ is known as the "inverse Mills ratio," or the "hazard rate" and:

$$\lambda = \frac{\phi\,(\alpha'w_i)}{\Phi\,(\alpha'w_i)} \tag{6}$$

Equation 2 implies that ignoring the sample selection mechanism in effect omits a variable—the expected value of the error term of the outcome equation under censoring—from the outcome equation. Thus, the OLS coefficient estimates of any independent variable, β_k, will be unbiased if and only if $\rho = 0$, so that the second term drops out of the equation or if the correlation between the hazard rate and X_k is zero, such that the "omitted" hazard rate does not bias our estimate of β_k.

This model can be estimated using two-stage techniques (see Achen 1986; Breen 1996; Brehm 1993; Heckman 1979). Here, however, I estimate the model using maximum likelihood techniques. The log-likelihood of this model is, following Breen (1996):

$$\text{Ln } L = \sum_0 \text{Ln }(1 - \Phi\,(w_i\alpha)) + \sum_1 \text{Ln }\left(\frac{1}{\sqrt{2\pi\sigma_u^2}}\right) + \sum_1 \frac{1}{2\sigma_u^2}(y_i - x'_i\beta)^2 \tag{7}$$

$$+ \sum_1 \text{Ln } \Phi\left(\frac{w_i\alpha + \rho\left(\dfrac{y_i - x'_i\beta}{\sigma_u}\right)}{\sqrt{(1 - \rho)^2}}\right)$$

There are a number of controversies in the statistical literature regarding the Heckman model. First, though it is possible to identify the Heckman model through the nonlinearity of the selection equation, identifying the equation system in this manner is problematic in practice. Specifically, there is the possibility for high levels of colinearity between the hazard rate instrument and the variables in the outcome equation. The hazard rate is a nonlinear transformation of the independent variables in the selection equation because the hazard rate is estimated through the probit results of the selection equation. In practice, however, the hazard rate often approaches a linear form for much of the range of observable values, thereby inducing the threat of colinearity with the outcome equation (see Breen 1996). These concerns also arise in the MLE techniques used in chapter 4. I address this concern in my work by avoiding the use of nonlinearity to achieve identification (see text for details).

Second, estimating the Heckman requires assuming that the joint distribution of the selection and outcome equation errors is bivariate normal. This is true even though the Heckman model requires only that (1) the error for the selection equation be normal and (2) the conditional expectation of the outcome equation, given the selection equation error, be linear (Breen 1996). Some authors have questioned whether these assumptions are valid (see, for example, Goldberg 1983). A variety of semi- and nonparametric methods have, therefore, been developed to estimate the selection models (for a review, see Vella 1998). While these techniques have the advantage of greater generality, they are extremely complex and are generally limited in the types of models they can accommodate (Greene 1997). As Greene notes, the utility of semi- and nonparametric selection models remains unsettled. Thus, here I follow the conventions of the empirical literature and estimate the fully parametric Heckman model.

Coding of Variables for Analysis in Chapter 4

These coding protocols apply to the variables used in the analyses for the 1992 and 1996 NES data presented in tables A4.1–A4.2. Variables coded the same in chapter 4 as in chapter 3 are not listed.

> *Income variables*: A series of five dummy variables indicating the respondent's reported income, or if the respondent's income was not ascertained. The omitted category is an income of $50,000–$104,999 in 1996 and $40,000–$89,999 in 1992.
>
> *Value conflict:* One minus the absolute value of the difference in placement on the equality and limited government value scales. Mathematically, it is expressed as: $1 - |$(equality score-limited government score)$|$ (0 = low conflict; 1 = maximum conflict).

These coding protocols apply to the variables used in the analyses for the 1972 and 1976 NES data presented in table A4.3. Variables coded the same in chapter 4 as in chapter 3 are not listed.

> *Income variables*: A series of five dummy variables indicating the respondent's reported income, or if the respondent's income was not ascertained. The omitted category is an income of $12,000–$24,999.

TABLE A4.1
Social Welfare Policy Items, 1996

	Outcome Equation (Regression)		
Variable	Spending Coefficient (SE)	Guaranteed Jobs Coefficient (SE)	Redistribution Coefficient (SE)
Constant	3.23 (0.21)**	2.79 (0.23)**	2.68 (0.30)**
Education	−0.29 (0.17)*	−0.19 (0.19)	−0.24 (0.23)
Income: <$12,000	0.31 (0.12)**	0.37 (0.14)**	0.76 (0.17)**
Income: $12,000–$21,999	0.29 (0.12)**	0.22 (0.14)	0.63 (0.17)**
Income: $22,000–$49,999	−0.01 (0.09)	−0.01 (0.11)	0.43 (0.13)**
Income: $105,000+	0.21 (0.16)	0.02 (0.19)	−0.06 (0.22)
Income: Not Ascertained	0.06 (0.14)	0.27 (0.16)*	0.22 (0.19)
Unemployed	0.36 (0.23)	0.65 (0.27)**	0.11 (0.35)
Liberal	0.19 (0.11)*	−0.24 (0.13)*	0.01 (0.15)
Conservative	−0.01 (0.10)	−0.33 (0.11)**	−0.07 (0.13)
No Ideology	0.18 (0.12)	0.10 (0.13)	0.14 (0.18)
Party Identification	0.39 (0.07)**	0.39 (0.08)**	0.36 (0.09)**
Equality	1.43 (0.20)**	2.14 (0.22)**	2.21 (0.27)**
Limited Government	−1.02 (0.10)**	−0.78 (0.12)**	−0.98 (0.15)**
Value Conflict	0.48 (0.14)**	−0.04 (0.16)	0.00 (0.20)
	Selection Equation (Probit)		
Constant	0.33 (0.31)	0.95 (0.34)**	0.53 (0.27)**
Education	0.66 (0.24)**	0.26 (0.26)	0.48 (0.20)**
Income: <$12,000	0.15 (0.16)	−0.17 (0.18)	−0.07 (0.14)
Income: $12,000–$21,999	0.16 (0.16)	−0.14 (0.17)	−0.28 (0.14)**
Income: $22,000–$49,999	0.01 (0.13)	−0.09 (0.15)	−0.19 (0.11)*
Income: $105,000+	0.51 (0.42)	Not Applicable	0.03 (0.24)
Income: Not Ascertained	−0.19 (0.19)	−0.20 (0.20)	−0.24 (0.16)
Unemployed	−0.10 (0.29)	−0.14 (0.31)	−0.43 (0.24)*
Liberal	0.09 (0.15)	0.16 (0.18)	0.34 (0.13)**
Conservative	0.27 (0.14)*	0.18 (0.15)	0.06 (0.11)
No Ideology	−0.70 (0.12)**	−0.51 (0.14)**	−0.45 (0.11)**
Equality	0.03 (0.28)	0.08 (0.30)	−0.01 (0.23)
Limited Government	0.23 (0.14)*	0.02 (0.15)	0.50 (0.12)**
Value Conflict	−0.16 (0.21)	−0.22 (0.23)	−0.47 (0.18)**

TABLE A4.1 *(cont'd)*
Social Welfare Policy Items, 1996

	Selection Equation		
Variable	*Spending* Coefficient (SE)	*Guaranteed Jobs* Coefficient (SE)	*Redistribution* Coefficient (SE)
Information	0.79 (0.25)**	0.52 (0.27)*	0.60 (0.21)**
Discuss Politics	−0.02 (0.16)	0.45 (0.19)**	0.27 (0.14)*
Calls	0.13 (0.06)**	0.09 (0.07)	−0.09 (0.05)*
Interviewer Experience	0.00 (0.01)	0.02 (0.01)	0.00 (0.01)
	Correlation Parameter		
ρ	0.07 (0.13)	0.06 (0.15)	0.09 (0.16)
N/ Log Likelihood	1495/−2587.61	1495/−2826.88	1492/−2861.32

Note: Every respondent with a family income of greater than $105,000 answered the Guaranteed Jobs item. Those respondents were therefore excluded from the analysis.
    * = $p < .10$; ** = $p < .05$.

TABLE A4.2
Social Welfare Policy Items, 1992

	Outcome Equation (Regression)	
Variable	*Services vs. Spending* Coefficient (SE)	*Guaranteed Jobs* Coefficient (SE)
Constant	3.74 (0.20)**	2.83 (0.23)**
Education	−0.25 (0.16)*	−0.13 (0.18)
Income: <$10,000	0.46 (0.12)**	0.58 (0.14)**
Income: $10,000–$19,999	0.15 (0.11)	0.11 (0.12)
Income: $20,000–$39,999	0.01 (0.08)	0.16 (0.10)
Income: $90,000+	−0.15 (0.15)	−0.12 (0.18)
Income: Not Ascertained	0.09 (0.15)	0.18 (0.17)
Unemployed	−0.10 (0.16)	0.54 (0.18)**
Liberal	0.12 (0.10)	0.22 (0.12)*
Conservative	−0.20 (0.09)**	−0.17 (0.11)
No Ideology	0.02 (0.12)	0.12 (0.12)
Party Identification	0.28 (0.06)**	0.35 (0.07)**
Equality	1.11 (0.19)**	1.36 (0.22)**
Limited Government	−1.21 (0.10)**	−0.94 (0.12)**
Value Conflict	0.29 (0.14)**	0.29 (0.17)*

TABLE A4.2 (cont'd)
Social Welfare Policy Items, 1992

	Selection Equation (Probit)	
Variable	Services Vs. Spending Coefficient (SE)	Guaranteed Jobs Coefficient (SE)
Constant	0.42 (0.26)	0.85 (0.29)**
Education	0.68 (0.19)**	0.45 (0.20)**
Income: <$12,000	0.01 (0.13)	0.00 (0.14)
Income: $12,000–$21,999	−0.05 (0.12)	−0.01 (0.13)
Income: $22,000–$49,999	0.06 (0.10)	−0.06 (0.11)
Income: $105,000+	−0.01 (0.22)	0.11 (0.25)
Income: Not Ascertained	−0.11 (0.15)	−0.22 (0.16)
Unemployed	0.01 (0.16)	−0.07 (0.16)
Liberal	0.25 (0.13)**	0.27 (0.14)**
Conservative	0.23 (0.11)**	0.12 (0.12)
No Ideology	−0.68 (0.10)**	−0.43 (0.11)**
Equality	−0.01 (0.23)	−0.14 (0.26)
Limited Government	0.13 (0.13)	0.31 (0.15)**
Value Conflict	−0.29 (0.19)	−0.40 (0.20)**
Information	1.12 (0.23)**	0.57 (0.24)**
Discuss	0.28 (0.13)**	0.60 (0.16)**
Calls	−0.06 (0.05)	0.06 (0.06)
Interviewer Experience	0.00 (0.01)	0.00 (0.01)
	Correlation Parameter	
ρ	0.04 (0.11)	0.06 (0.12)
N/ Log Likelihood	2079/−3718	2078/−4123

$* = p < .10$; $** = p < .05$.

TABLE A4.3
Guaranteed Jobs, 1972–1976

Outcome Equation (Regression)		
Variable	*1972* *Coefficient (SE)*	*1976* *Coefficient (SE)*
Constant	3.40 (0.14)**	3.16 (0.16)**
Education	−0.06 (0.19)	0.13 (0.21)
Income: <$4,000	0.71 (0.15)**	1.15 (0.18)**
Income: $4,000–$5,999	0.49 (0.16)**	0.42 (0.15)**
Income: $6,000–$11,999	0.09 (0.11)	0.16 (0.12)
Income: $25,000+	−0.41 (0.21)*	−0.05 (0.21)
Income: Not Ascertained	−0.26 (0.31)	0.46 (0.22)**
Unemployed	0.19 (0.26)	0.45 (0.24)*
Liberal	0.74 (0.13)**	0.46 (0.14)**
Conservative	−0.40 (0.12)**	−0.55 (0.13)**
No Ideology	0.33 (0.14)**	0.47 (0.15)**
Party Identification	0.43 (0.08)**	0.49 (0.08)**
Selection Equation (Probit)		
Constant	0.63 (0.16)**	0.26 (0.15)*
Education	−0.18 (0.18)	0.13 (0.18)
Information	1.97 (0.24)**	2.06 (0.26)**
Income: <$4,000	−0.01 (0.13)	−0.22 (0.13)
Income: $4,000–$5,999	0.01 (0.15)	−0.09 (0.12)
Income: $6,000–$11,999	−0.07 (0.11)	−0.14 (0.10)
Income: $25,000+	−0.15 (0.22)	−0.02 (0.22)
Income: Not Ascertained	−0.32 (0.22)	−0.37 (0.16)**
Unemployed	0.45 (0.26)*	0.11 (0.20)
Liberal	−0.05 (0.14)	0.19 (0.14)
Conservative	−0.08 (0.12)	−0.04 (0.11)
No Ideology	−0.59 (0.11)**	−0.41 (0.10)**
Campaign Interest	0.33 (0.11)**	0.15 (0.11)
Correlation Parameter		
ρ	−0.01 (0.11)	−0.09 (0.11)
N/ Log Likelihood	2094/−4399.43	1864/−3782.19

$* = p < .10; ** = p < .05.$

APPENDIX TO CHAPTER 5

These coding protocols apply to the variables used in the analyses for the 1966 War in Vietnam Study.

Age: Age of respondent, in years

Black: Dummy indicating the race of the respondent (0 = non-black; 1 = black)

Male: Dummy indicating the gender of the respondent (0 = male; 1 = female)

Vietnam information level: Six-item information scale, tapping the respondent's level of knowledge about Vietnam. The scale includes questions about the capital of South Vietnam, the capital of North Vietnam, whether the United States is currently bombing North Vietnam, who the Viet Cong are, whether the South Vietnamese government is freely elected, and whether the United States Congress has declared war (0 = answered no questions correctly; 1 = answered all questions correctly).

Too soft on communist countries: Three-item scale indicating whether the respondent is hawkish or dovish toward Russia, China, and Cuba. Respondents are assigned their mean score across three items for which they indicate whether the United States has been "too soft," "just about right," or "too tough" on Russia, China, and Cuba. Higher scores indicate greater hawkishness (0 = too tough on countries; 1 = too soft on countries).

These coding protocols apply to the variables used in the analyses for the 1964 NES data. Variables used for the robustness analyses in other years were identical (except that the information scale followed Zaller [1992] and the income categories followed the quintiles detailed in the NES cumulative file codebook).

Age: Age of respondent, in years, divided by 100

Black: Dummy indicating the race of the respondent (0 = nonblack; 1 = black)

Male: Dummy indicating the gender of the respondent (0 = female; 1 = male)

Education: Five-category NES education variable measuring highest level of education (0 = grade school; 1 = college graduate or higher)

Income variables: A series of six dummy variables indicating the respondent's reported income, or if the respondent's income was not ascertained. The omitted category is an income of $5,000–$7,499.

Region variables: A series of four dummy variables indicating the respondent's census region of residence (North-East, North-Central, West, and South). The omitted category is respondents who live in the North-Central.

Religion variables: A series of five dummy variables indicating the respondent's religion (Protestant, Catholic, Jewish, other religion, and no religion). The omitted category is respondents who are Protestants. Respondents with no religion are also omitted.

Church attendance: Four-category variable indicating how often the respondent attends church (0 = never; 1 = regularly)

Party identification: Five-category partisanship variable (see appendix to chapter 3 for coding and justification)

Trust in government: Four-category NES Trust in Government scale. Respondents are assigned their mean score across all the individual limited government items as long as they answer half or more of those items (0 = low trust in government; 1 = high trust in government).

Efficacy: Two-item NES Efficacy scale. The items measure agreements with the statements "politicians care about people like me" and "I have a say in government." Respondents are assigned their mean score across the two efficacy items as long as they answer at least one of the items (0 = low efficacy; 1 = high efficacy).

Government responsiveness: Two-item Government Responsiveness scale. The items measure agreement with the statements, "Government pays attention to what people think" and "Elections make government pay attention to what the people think" (0 = respondent believes government is responsive "not much"; 1 = government is responsive "a good deal"). Respondents are assigned their mean score across the two responsiveness items if they answer at least one of the items.

Political information: Fifteen-item political information scale, tapping respondents' level of knowledge about prominent political figures and topics, following Zaller (1992) (0 = answered no questions correctly; 1 = answered all questions correctly)

Campaign interest: Measure tapping the respondent's level of interest in the 1964 political campaigns (0 = low interest; 1 = high interest)

Salience of major party presidential candidates: Sum of all "likes" and "dislikes" about both the Democratic and Republican presidential candidates. The NES accepted up to twenty mentions. I divided the scale by 20 to give it a similar range to the other variables included in the analysis (0 = no likes and/or dislikes mentioned; 1 = 20 likes and/or dislikes mentioned).

Selection Bias Tests

While I do not believe that respondents self-censored their views on Vietnam at the opinion expression stage, it is important to ensure that the Vietnam data are not contaminated by selection bias that could arise from other factors relating to nonresponse. In all the analyses presented in this chapter, I ran a series of tests to ensure that the probit analysis was not contaminated by selection bias. However, given the large number of questions analyzed in this chapter, it would be too cumbersome to present all the selection bias analyses here. In the tables that follow, therefore, I present only the coefficients for the variables of theoretic interest. The full model results are available from the author upon request. However, the projected opinion positions reported in the text of chapter 5 are robust to model respecification; no matter which variables are used to predict opinion, the results are virtually identical.

For the interested reader, I illustrate the robustness check using an example from the 1964 NES, which asks, "Do you think we did the right thing in getting into the fighting in Vietnam, or should we have stayed out?" The first column of table A5.1 presents the results of a simple probit with age, gender, and race as independent variables. The second column of that table presents the results of a fully specified bivariate probit selection model. In the first column, the analysis assumes no selection bias. In the fuller, more cumbersome model, a Wald test (as well as a likelihood ratio test of independent equations) allows us to reject the null hypothesis of selection bias with virtual certainty. The important point to note for my purposes is that while the coefficients on age, gender, and race differ between the two models, the predicted positions on Vietnam generated by the two models are almost identical.[1] The independent probit coefficients from table A5.1 generated a predicted level of support among question-answers of 39 percent and among question-abstainers of 43 percent. The bivariate probit generates a predicted level of support among question-answers of 38

---

[1] This is true even though some of the more limited models showed evidence of selection bias. For example, a selection bias model using the outcome equation presented in the first column of table A5.1 had a $\rho = 0.56$ with a standard error of 0.39. However, adding variables to the selection and outcome equations yielded the results presented in the second column—a $\rho = 0.01$ with a standard error of 0.73. As the predicted probability analysis presented here demonstrates, the more limited specification gives the same answer as the fuller specification. Similarly, for the 1966 analysis, a limited model of the question-answering process yielded a $\rho = 0.90$ with a standard error of 0.11—strong evidence of selection bias from both a substantive and a statistical standpoint. However, adding variables omitted from both equations in this limited specification greatly reduced the point estimate and precision of ρ ($\rho = 0.29$; standard error = 0.64). Thus, the apparent selection bias is merely an artifact of model misspecification.

TABLE A5.1
Agree That "We Should Have Stayed Out of Vietnam"
Selection Bias Analysis, 1964 NES

	Outcome Equation	
Variable	Independent Probit Coefficient (SE)	Bivariate Probit Coefficient (SE)
Constant	−0.83 (0.14)**	0.57 (0.75)
Age	1.43 (0.28)**	0.76 (0.52)
Black	0.39 (0.16)**	0.34 (0.25)
Male	−0.26 (0.09)**	−0.23 (0.13)*
Education		−0.06 (0.05)
Income: $0–$2,999		0.16 (0.19)
Income: $3,000–$4,999		0.14 (0.15)
Income: $7,500–$14,999		−0.16 (0.14)
Income: $15,000 +		−0.19 (0.20)
Income Not Ascertained		−0.29 (0.28)
North-East		0.18 (0.15)
South		−0.07 (0.13)
West		−0.40 (0.17)**
Catholic		−0.21 (0.13)
Jewish		0.02 (0.30)
Other Religion		−0.17 (0.29)
Church Attendance		−0.03 (0.14)
Party Identification		−0.08 (0.08)
Trust Government		−0.49 (0.21)**
Efficacy		−0.21 (0.14)
Government Responsiveness		−0.49 (0.19)**
Political Information		−0.08 (0.59)
Campaign Interest		−0.08 (0.19)

percent and among question-abstainers of 44 percent. These results are extremely close, indicating that using the more limited model to characterize predicted opinion is an acceptable strategy, provided that we can demonstrate that the analyses are not tainted by selection bias.[2]

[2] The differences that exist between the predicted probabilities are partially a property of differences in the characteristics of the sample. The bivariate probit analysis contains a great number of variables, thereby reducing the sample size because of listwise deletion of missing data. The way that the cases "go missing" yields a sample in the bivariate probit analysis of question-abstainers that is slightly more dovish and a sample of question-answerers that is slightly more hawkish, as compared to the separate probit analysis.

TABLE A5.1 (*cont'd*)
Agree that "We Should Have Stayed Out of Vietnam"
Selection Bias Analysis, 1964 NES

	Selection Equation	
Variable	*Independent Probit Coefficient (SE)*	*Bivariate Probit Coefficient (SE)*
Constant		−0.40 (0.20)**
Age		−0.97 (0.28)**
Black		−0.37 (0.14)**
Male		0.23 (0.08)**
Education		0.04 (0.04)
Income: $0–$2,999		−0.17 (0.13)
Income: $3,000–$4,999		0.10 (0.12)
Income: $7,500–$14,999		−0.20 (0.11)*
Income: $15,000 +		−0.05 (0.18)
Income Not Ascertained		−0.00 (0.22)
North-East		−0.14 (0.11)
South		−0.04 (0.10)
West		−0.20 (0.12)*
Catholic		0.05 (0.10)
Jewish		−0.16 (0.24)
Other Religion		−0.02 (0.21)
Church Attendance		0.06 (0.11)
Political Information		1.28 (0.18)**
Campaign Interest		0.26 (0.11)**
Salience of Presidential Candidates		0.05 (0.02)**
	Correlation Parameters	
ρ		0.01 (0.74)
N/Log likelihood	902/−583.18	1309/−1236.15

* = $p < .10$; ** = $p < .05$.

TABLE A5.2

War in Vietnam Study Analysis: Model Results

Variable	Item 1	Item 2	Item 3	Item 4	Item 5	Item 6	Item 7	Item 8
	Questions Relating to Escalation of War Effort							
	Opinion Direction (Coefficient with Standard Error in Parenthesis)							
Constant	−0.04 (0.20)	−0.22 (0.23)	0.62 (0.20)**	−0.01 (0.21)	0.37 (0.21)*	0.99 (0.22)**	1.00 (0.22)**	0.99 (0.21)**
Vietnam Information Level	−0.37 (0.14)**	−0.49 (0.17)**	−0.14 (0.14)	−0.32 (0.15)**	0.27 (0.15)*	−0.10 (0.15)	0.41 (0.16)**	−0.23 (0.14)
Too Soft on Communists	−0.49 (0.16)**	−1.21 (0.19)**	−0.63 (0.16)**	−0.88 (0.17)**	−0.81 (0.17)**	−0.58 (0.17)**	−0.56 (0.18)**	−0.94 (0.17)**
Black	0.46 (0.10)**	0.59 (0.11)**	0.10 (0.11)	0.48 (0.10)**	0.12 (0.11)	0.15 (0.11)	0.17 (0.12)	0.30 (0.11)**
Male	−0.34 (0.07)**	−0.43 (0.09)**	−0.35 (0.07)**	−0.41 (0.07)**	−0.41 (0.08)**	−0.57 (0.08)**	−0.45 (0.08)**	−0.35 (0.07)**
Age	0.00 (0.00)	0.00 (0.00)	−0.01 (0.00)**	0.01 (0.00)**	0.01 (0.00)**	−0.01 (0.00)**	−0.01 (0.00)**	0.00 (0.00)**
	Opinion Holding (Coefficient with Standard Error in Parenthesis)							
Constant	1.30 (0.31)**	2.12 (0.35)**	1.42 (0.28)**	1.17 (0.29)**	1.42 (0.28)**	1.27 (0.31)**	1.17 (0.31)**	0.96 (0.28)**
Vietnam Information Level	0.84 (0.23)**	0.58 (0.25)**	0.64 (0.20)**	1.32 (0.23)**	1.08 (0.21)**	1.13 (0.23)**	1.38 (0.24)**	0.97 (0.21)**
Too Soft on Communists	0.44 (0.25)*	0.40 (0.27)	0.53 (0.23)**	0.32 (0.24)	−0.11 (0.24)	0.07 (0.25)	0.09 (0.26)	0.47 (0.23)**
Black	0.24 (0.17)	−0.30 (0.15)*	−0.09 (0.14)	0.05 (0.15)	−0.09 (0.14)	0.13 (0.16)	0.21 (0.17)	0.15 (0.15)
Male	0.44 (0.12)**	0.78 (0.15)**	0.49 (0.11)**	0.44 (0.12)**	0.32 (0.11)**	0.33 (0.12)**	0.09 (0.12)	0.19 (0.11)*
Age	−0.01 (0.00)*	−0.01 (0.00)**	−0.01 (0.00)**	−0.01 (0.00)**	−0.01 (0.00)	0.00 (0.00)	−0.01 (0.00)*	−0.01 (0.00)**

Notes: Escalation Items:

1: Disapprove of 200,000 U.S. troops in South Vietnam?
2: Disapprove of bombing military targets in North Vietnam?
3: Disapprove of half a million troops in South Vietnam?
4: End involvement in Vietnam if involvement means fighting the Chinese Army?
5: End involvement in Vietnam if involvement means a ground war with China?
6: End involvement in Vietnam if involvement means atomic war with China?
7: End involvement in Vietnam if involvement means atomic war with Russia?
8: End involvement in Vietnam if involvement means total mobilization of U.S. Army?

TABLE A5.2 (cont'd)
War in Vietnam Study Analysis: Model Results

| | | Opinion Direction (Coefficient with Standard Error in Parenthesis) | | | | | | |
Effort	Item 9	Item 10	Item 11	Item 12	Item 13	Item 14	Item 15	Item 16
Constant	0.72 (0.21)**	-0.04 (0.21)	0.99 (0.23)**	0.36 (0.21)*	0.66 (0.22)**	-0.61 (0.25)**	2.46 (0.32)**	-0.14 (0.24)
Vietnam Information Level	-0.26 (0.14)*	0.69 (0.15)**	-0.69 (0.16)**	-0.94 (0.14)**	-0.99 (0.15)**	-0.54 (0.18)**	-1.06 (0.21)**	-0.67 (0.17)**
Too Soft on Communists	-0.86 (0.17)**	-0.64 (0.17)**	-0.32 (0.18)*	-0.64 (0.16)**	-0.78 (0.17)**	-0.45 (0.20)**	-0.76 (0.24)**	-1.09 (0.19)**
Black	0.10 (0.11)	-0.10 (0.11)	-0.11 (0.11)	0.63 (0.11)**	0.46 (0.11)**	0.54 (0.11)**	-0.15 (0.15)	0.47 (0.11)**
Male	-0.09 (0.07)	0.06 (0.08)	-0.27 (0.08)**	-0.28 (0.07)**	-0.03 (0.08)	0.03 (0.09)	-0.23 (0.10)*	-0.02 (0.09)
Age	0.01 (0.00)**	0.01 (0.00)**	0.01 (0.00)**	0.00 (0.00)	0.00 (0.00)	0.00 (0.00)	0.00 (0.00)	0.00 (0.00)
		Opinion Holding (Coefficient with Standard Error in Parenthesis)						
Constant	1.72 (0.28)**	1.51 (0.26)**	1.38 (0.29)**	1.86 (0.33)**	1.10 (0.27)**	1.12 (0.28)**	2.07 (0.38)**	0.78 (0.35)**
Vietnam Information Level	1.45 (0.21)**	1.17 (0.19)**	1.31 (0.22)**	0.62 (0.24)**	1.02 (0.20)**	1.19 (0.21)**	1.10 (0.30)**	0.90 (0.27)**
Too Soft on Communists	-0.29 (0.23)	-0.28 (0.22)	0.03 (0.24)	0.15 (0.27)	0.32 (0.23)	0.63 (0.23)**	0.04 (0.32)	0.83 (0.29)**
Black	-0.29 (0.12)**	-0.31 (0.12)**	0.00 (0.14)	-0.31 (0.15)**	-0.02 (0.14)	-0.07 (0.14)	-0.28 (0.17)	-0.10 (0.17)
Male	0.41 (0.10)**	0.33 (0.10)**	0.26 (0.11)**	0.30 (0.12)*	0.35 (0.10)**	0.46 (0.11)**	0.46 (0.15)**	0.07 (0.14)
Age	-0.01 (0.00)**	-0.01 (0.00)**	-0.01 (0.00)**	-0.01 (0.00)*	-0.01 (0.00)*	-0.01 (0.00)**	-0.01 (0.00)*	0.00 (0.00)

Notes: De-escalation Items:

9: To end fighting, form South Vietnam government in which Viet Cong takes part?

10: To end fighting, hold elections in South Vietnam even if Viet Cong may win?

11: To end fighting, a truce with each side holding the territory it now has?

12: To end fighting, troop withdrawal and let South Vietnam work it out?

13: End fighting, if it means Viet Cong eventually controlling South Vietnam?

14: End fighting, if it means loss of independence for Laos and Thailand?

15: Approve American negotiations with Viet Cong, if they are willing?

16: Approve if President Johnson withdrew troops letting communists rule?

$* = p < .10; ** = p < .05.$

TABLE A5.3
Vietnam Analysis, 1964–1972 NES

Opinion Direction: It Was a Mistake to Get Involved in Vietnam				
Variable	*1964*	*1966*	*1968*	*1970*	*1972*
Constant	−0.83 (0.14)**	−0.67 (0.13)**	−0.17–0.11	−0.46 (0.11)**	−0.12–0.08
Age	1.43 (0.28)**	1.09 (0.27)**	1.42 (0.23)**	1.74 (0.23)**	1.27 (0.16)**
Black	0.39 (0.16)**	0.27 (0.15)*	0.24 (0.13)*	0.57 (0.14)**	0.53 (0.10)**
Male	−0.26 (0.09)**	−0.24 (0.08)**	−0.34 (0.07)**	−0.15 (0.08)*	−0.11 (0.06)**
N	902	928	1273	1193	2304
Log-Likelihood	−583.18	−608.97	−806.95	−752.64	−1420.07

Opinion Holding				
Variable	*1964*	*1966*	*1968*	*1970*	*1972*
Constant	0.67 (0.11)**	1.05 (0.13)**	1.19 (0.12)**	1.06 (0.12)**	1.52 (0.10)**
Age	−0.91 (0.22)**	−1.18 (0.24)**	−0.70 (0.24)**	−0.66 (0.22)**	−0.68 (0.20)**
Black	−0.48 (0.11)**	−0.40 (0.12)**	−0.19 (0.12)	−0.05 (0.13)	0.14 (0.13)
Male	0.32 (0.07)**	0.46 (0.08)**	0.34 (0.08)**	0.35 (0.08)**	0.35 (0.08)**
N	1426	1258	1525	1473	2530
Log-Likelihood	−908.44	−690.49	−669.19	−701.61	−742.64

* = $p < .10$; ** = $p < .05$.

REFERENCES

Achen, Christopher. 1978. "Measuring Representation." *American Journal of Political Science* 22:475–510.

———. 1986. *The Statistical Analysis of Quasi-Experiments.* Berkeley: University of California Press.

Aldrich, John H. 1993. "Rational Choice and Turnout." *American Journal of Political Science* 37:246–278.

Almond, Gabriel A. 1960. *The American People and Foreign Policy.* New York: Praegar.

Althaus, Scott. 1998. "Information Effects in Collective Preferences." *American Political Science Review* 92:545–558.

Alvarez, R. Michael. 1998. *Information and Elections.* Ann Arbor: University of Michigan Press.

Alvarez, R. Michael, and John Brehm. 1995. "American Ambivalence towards Abortion Policy: A Heteroskedastic Probit Method for Assessing Conflicting Values." *American Journal of Political Science* 39:1055–1082.

———. 1996. "Uncertainty and Ambivalence in the Ecology of Race." Paper presented at the Annual Conference of the American Political Science Association, San Francisco.

———. "Are Americans Ambivalent toward Racial Policies?" *American Journal of Political Science* 41:345–375.

———. 2002. *Hard Choices, Easy Answers: Values, Information, and American Public Opinion.* Princeton: Princeton University Press.

Anderson, Barbara A., Brian D. Silver, and Paul R. Abramson. 1988. "The Effects of Race of the Interviewer on Race-related Attitudes of Black Respondents in SRC/CPS National Election Studies." *Public Opinion Quarterly* 52:289–324.

Arian, Asher, et al. 1990. *Changing New York City Politics.* New York: Routledge.

Arnold, Douglas. 1990. *The Logic of Congressional Action.* New Haven: Yale University Press.

Bachrach, Peter and Morton S. Baratz. 1962. "Two Faces of Power." *American Political Science Review* 56:947–952.

———. 1963. "Decisions and Nondecisions: An Analytical Framework." *American Political Science Review* 57:632–642.

Bartels, Larry M. 1990. "Public Opinion and Political Interests." Paper presented at the Annual Meeting of the Midwest Political Science Association, Chicago.

———. 1996. "Uninformed Votes: Information Effects in Presidential Elections." *American Journal of Political Science* 40:194–230.

———. 1998. "Democracy with Attitudes." Princeton University, ms.

Bauer, Raymond A., Ithiel de Sola Pool, and Lewis Anthony Dexter. 1963. *American Business and Public Policy: The Politics of Foreign Trade.* New York: Atherton Press.

Beatty, Paul, and Douglas Herrmann. 2002. "To Answer or Not to Answer: Decision Processes Related to Survey Item Nonresponse." In *Survey Nonresponse*, ed. Robert M. Groves et al. New York: John Wiley & Sons.

Bennett, Stephen E., and David Resnick. 1990. "The Implications of Non-Voting for Democracy in the United States." *American Journal of Political Science* 34:771–802.

Berinsky, Adam J. 1999. "The Two Faces of Public Opinion." *American Journal of Political Science* 43:1209–1230.

———. 2000. "The Search for the Voice of the People: Public Opinion Polling and Political Representation in America." PhD. diss., University of Michigan.

———. 2002a. "Political Context and the Survey Response: The Dynamics of Racial Policy Opinion." *Journal of Politics* 64:567–584.

———. 2002b. "Silent Voices: Social Welfare Policy Opinions and Equality in America." *American Journal of Political Science* 46:276–287.

———. 2003. "Can We Talk? Self-Presentation and the Survey Response." Working paper. Princeton University.

Bernstein, Robert A. 1989. *Elections, Representation, and Congressional Voting Behavior: The Myth of Constituency Control.* Englewood Cliffs, NJ: Prentice-Hall.

Bizer, George Y., et al. 2000. "Need for Cognition and Need to Evaluate in the 1998 National Election Survey Pilot Study." *NES Pilot Study Report.* Ann Arbor: Center for Political Studies.

Blauner, Bob. 1989. *Black Lives, White Lives: Three Decades of Race Relations in America.* Berkeley: University of California Press.

Blumer, Herbert. 1948. "Public Opinion and Public Opinion Polling." *American Sociological Review* 13:542–554.

Bogart, Leo. 1967. "No Opinion, Don't Know, and Maybe No Answer." *Public Opinion Quarterly* 31:331–345.

Breen, Richard. 1996. *Regression Models: Censored, Sample Selected, or Truncated Data.* Sage University Paper Series on Quantitative Applications in the Social Sciences, 07–111. Thousand Oaks, CA: Sage.

Brehm, John. 1993. *The Phantom Respondents: Opinion Surveys and Political Representation.* Ann Arbor: University of Michigan Press.

Brown, Penelope, and Stephen C. Levinson. 1987. *Politeness: Some Universals in Language Usage.* Cambridge: Cambridge University Press.

Cacioppo, John, and Richard Petty. 1982. "The Need for Cognition." *Journal of Personality and Social Psychology* 42:116–131.

Carmines, Edward G., and James A. Stimson. 1980. "The Two Faces of Issue Voting." *American Political Science Review* 79:78–91.

———. 1989. *Issue Evolution.* Princeton: Princeton University Press.

Carney, James, and John F. Dickerson. 2000. "Behind the Rhetoric: Polling for the Perfect Pitch." *Time,* October 9.

Cavanagh, Thomas E., ed. 1983. *Race and Political Strategy: A JCPS Roundtable.* Washington, DC: Joint Center for Political Studies.

Chong, Dennis. 1993. "How People Think, Reason, and Feel about Rights and Liberties." *American Journal of Political Science* 37:867–899.

———. 1996. "Creating Common Frames of Reference on Political Issues." In *Political Persuasion and Attitude Change*, ed. Diana C. Mutz, Paul M. Sniderman, and Richard A. Brody. Ann Arbor: University of Michigan Press.

Clymer, Adam. 1989. "Election Day Shows What the Opinion Polls Can't Do." *New York Times*, November 12.

Converse, Jean M., and Stanley Presser. 1986. *Survey Questions: Handcrafting the Standardized Questionnaire*. Beverly Hills: Sage Publications.

Converse, Jean M., and Howard Schuman. 1974. *Conversations at Random: Survey Research as Interviewers See It*. New York: John Wiley & Sons.

Converse, Philip E. 1970. "Attitudes and Non-Attitudes: Continuation of a Dialog." In *The Quantitative Analysis of Social Problems*, ed. Edward R. Tufte. Reading, MA: Addison-Wesley.

Crespi, Irving. 1989. *Public Opinion, Polls, and Democracy*. Boulder: Westview.

Dahl, Robert. 1956. *A Preface to Democratic Theory*. Chicago: University of Chicago Press.

Davis, Darren W. 1997. "The Direction of Race of Interviewer Effects among African-Americans: Donning the Black Mask." *American Journal of Political Science* 41:309–322.

Dovidio, John F., and Russell H. Fazio. 1992. "New Technologies for the Direct and Indirect Assessment of Attitudes." In *Questions about Questions: Inquiries into the Cognitive Bases of Surveys*, ed. Judith M. Tanur. New York: Russell Sage Foundation.

Dubin, Jeffrey A., and Douglas Rivers. 1989/90. "Selection Bias in Linear Regression, Logit and Probit Models." *Sociological Methods and Research* 18, 2& 3:360–390.

Dunton, Bridget C., and Russell Fazio. 1997. "An Individual Difference Measure of Motivation to Control Prejudiced Reactions." *Personality and Social Psychology Bulletin* 23:316–326.

Erikson, Robert S. 1978. "Constituency Opinion and Congressional Behavior: A Reexamination of the Miller-Stokes Representation Data." *American Journal of Political Science* 22:511–535.

Fazio, R., J. Jackson, B. Dunton, and C. Williams. 1995. "Variability in Automatic Activation as an Unobtrusive Measure of Racial Attitudes—A Bona Fide Pipeline?" *Journal of Personality and Social Psychology* 69:1013–1027.

Feldman, Stanley. 1989. "Measuring Issue Preferences: The Problem of Response Stability." *Political Analysis* 1:25–60.

Feldman, Stanley, and John Zaller. 1992. "The Political Culture of Ambivalence." *American Journal of Political Science* 36:268–307.

Fenno, Richard. 1978. *Home Style: House Members in Their Districts*. Boston: Little, Brown.

Finkel, Steven E., Thomas M. Guterbock, and Marian J. Borg. 1991. "Race-of-Interviewer Effects in a Preelection Poll: Virginia 1989." *Public Opinion Quarterly* 55:313–330.

Fiorina, Morris. 1981. *Retrospective Voting in American National Elections*. New Haven: Yale University Press.

Fischoff, Baruch. 1991. "Value Elicitation: Is There Anything in There?" *American Psychologist* 46:835–847.

Fishkin, James S. 1991. *Democracy and Deliberation: New Directions for Democratic Reform*. New Haven: Yale University Press.

Flemming, Gregory, and Kimberly Parker. 1998. "Race and Reluctant Respondents: Possible Consequences of Non-Response for Pre-Election Surveys." Paper presented at the Annual Meeting of the American Association for Public Opinion Research.

Foyle, Douglas C. 1999. *Counting the Public In: Presidents, Public Opinion, and Foreign Policy*. New York: Columbia University Press.

Frankovic, Kathleen A. 1992. "Technology and the Changing Landscape of Media Polls." In *Media Polls in American Politics*, ed. Thomas E. Mann and Gary R. Orren. Washington, DC: The Brookings Institution.

Gallup, George, and Saul Forbes Rae. 1940. *The Pulse of Democracy: The Public-Opinion Poll and How It Works*. New York: Simon and Schuster.

Gartner, Scott Sigmund, and Gary M. Segura. 2000. "Race, Opinion, and Casualties in the Vietnam War." *The Journal of Politics* 62:115–146.

Gaventa, John. 1980. *Power and Powerlessness*. Chicago: University of Illinois Press.

Geer, John G. 1996. *From Tea Leaves to Opinion Polls: A Theory of Democratic Leadership*. New York: Columbia University Press.

Gilens, Martin, Paul M. Sniderman, and James H. Kuklinski. 1998. "Affirmative Action and the Politics of Realignment." *British Journal of Political Science* 28:159–183.

Ginsberg, Benjamin. 1986. *The Captive Public: How Mass Opinion Promotes State Power*. New York: Basic Books.

Goldberg, Samuel. 1983. *Probability in Social Science*. Cambridge: Birkhauser Boston.

Green, Donald P., and Jonathan A. Cowden. 1992. "Who Protests: Self-Interest and White Opposition to Busing." *The Journal of Politics* 54:471–496.

Green, Donald P. 1996. "Book Review: Private Truths, Public Lies: The Social Consequences of Preference Falsification." *Public Opinion Quarterly* 60:335–338.

Green, Joshua. 2002. "The Other War Room: President Bush Doesn't Believe in Polling—Just Ask His Pollsters." *The Washington Monthly*. April.

Greene, William H. 1995. *LIMDEP Version 7.0 User's Manual*. New York: Econometric Software.

———. 1997. *Econometric Analysis, Third Edition*. New York: Macmillian.

Grice, Paul. 1975. "Logic and Conversation." in *Syntax and Semantics, 3: Speech Acts*, ed. Peter Cole and Jerry L. Morgan. New York: Academic Press.

Hall, Mimi. 2001. "New White House, New 'War Room' for Strategizing." *USA Today*, July 5.

Hansen, John Mark. 1998. "Individuals, Institutions, and Public Preferences over Public Finance." *American Political Science Review* 92:513–531.

Harris, John F. 2000. "Policy and Politics by the Numbers." *Washington Post*, December 31.

Heckman, James J. 1979. "Sample Selection Bias as a Specification Error." *Econometrica*. 47:153–161.

Herbst, Susan. 1993. *Numbered Voices: How Opinion Polling Has Shaped American Politics*. Chicago: University of Chicago Press.

———. 1998. *Reading Public Opinion: How Political Actors View the Democratic Process*. Chicago: University of Chicago Press.

Herzog, Don. 1998. *Poisoning the Minds of the Lower Order*. Princeton: Princeton University Press.

Hippler, Hans J., and Norbert Schwarz. 1989. " 'No Opinion'-Filters: A Cognitive Prospective." *International Journal of Public Opinion Research* 1:1.

Hochschild, Jennifer L. 1981. *What's Fair? American Beliefs about Distributive Justice*. Cambridge: Harvard University Press.

———. 1984. *The New American Dilemma: Liberal Democracy and School Desegregation*. New Haven: Yale University Press.

Hochschild, Jennifer L., and Bridgett Scott. 1998. "Governance and Reform of Public Education in the United States." *Public Opinion Quarterly* 62:79–120.

Holsti, Ole R. 1996. *Public Opinion and American Foreign Policy*. Ann Arbor: University of Michigan Press.

Hout, Michael, Clem Brooks, and Jeff Manza. 1995. "The Democratic Class Struggle in the United States: 1948–1992." *American Sociological Review* 60:805–828.

Huckfeldt, Robert, and John Sprague. 1995. *Citizens, Politics, and Social Communication: Information and Influence in a Presidential Campaign*. New York: Cambridge University Press.

Huddy, Leonie, et al. 1997. "The Effect of Interviewer Gender on the Survey Response." *Political Behavior* 19:197–220.

Hurley, Norman. 1997. "Do People Really Feel What They Tell Us in Surveys: Toward Unobtrusive Measures of Racial Attitudes." Paper presented at the 1997 Annual Conference of the American Political Science Association, Washington, DC.

Hurwitz, Jon, and Mark Peffley. 1987. "How Are Foreign Policy Attitudes Structured? A Hierarchical Model." *American Political Science Review* 81:1099–1120.

Hyman, Herbert H. 1954. *Interviewing in Social Research*. Chicago: University of Chicago Press.

Iyengar, Shanto, and Donald Kinder. 1987. *News That Matters: Television and American Opinion*. Chicago: University of Chicago Press.

Jackman, Mary R. 1978. "General and Applied Tolerance: Does Education Increase Commitment to Racial Integration?" *American Journal of Political Science* 22:302–324.

Jackson, John E. 1993. "Attitudes, No Opinions, and Guesses." *Political Analysis* 6:39–60.

Jacobs, Lawrence R., and Robert Y. Shapiro. 2000. *Politicians Don't Pander: Political Manipulation and the Loss of Democratic Responsiveness*. Chicago: University of Chicago Press.

Jacoby, William G. 2000. "Issue Framing and Public Opinion on Government Spending." *American Journal of Political Science* 44:750–767.

Johanson, G. A., C. J. Gips, and C. E. Rich. 1993. " 'If You Can't Say Something Nice': A Variation on the Social Desirability Response Set." *Evaluation Review* 17:116–122.

Kalton, Graham. 1983. *Introduction to Survey Sampling*. Beverly Hills: Sage Publications.

Keith, Bruce E., et al. 1992. *The Myth of the Independent Voter*. Berkeley: University of California Press.

Key, V. O. 1961. *Public Opinion and American Democracy*. New York: Alfred Knopf.

———. 1966. *The Responsible Electorate: Rationality in Presidential Voting 1936–1960*. Cambridge: Harvard University Press.

Kinder, Donald R. 1998. "Opinion and Action in the Realm of Politics." In *Handbook of Social Psychology*, fourth edition, ed. Daniel Gilbert, Susan Fiske, and Gardner Lindsey. Boston: McGraw Hill.

Kinder, Donald R., and Thomas E. Nelson. 1998. "Democratic Debates and Real Opinions." In *The Dynamics of Issue Framing: Elite Discourse and the Formation of Public Opinion*, ed. Nayda Terkildsen and F. Schnell. Cambridge: Cambridge University Press.

Kinder, Donald R., and Lynn M. Sanders. 1996. *Divided by Color: Racial Politics and Democratic Ideals*. Chicago: Chicago University Press.

King, Gary, et al. 2001. "Analyzing Incomplete Political Science Data: An Alternative Algorithm for Multiple Imputation." *American Political Science Review* 95:49–69.

King, Gary, Michael Tomz, and Jason Wittenberg. 2000. "Making The Most of Statistical Analyses: Improving Interpretation and Presentation." *American Journal of Political Science* 44:347–361.

Kingdon, John W. 1973. *Congressmen's Voting Decisions*. New York: Harper & Row.

Kohut, Andrew. 1999. Interview by author, February 26.

Krosnick, Jon A. 1991. "Response Strategies for Coping with the Cognitive Demands of Attitude Measurement in Surveys." *Applied Cognitive Psychology* 5:213–236.

———. 2002. "The Causes of No-Opinion Responses to Attitude Measures in Surveys: They Are Rarely What They Appear to Be." In *Survey Nonresponse*, ed. Robert M. Groves et al. New York: John Wiley & Sons.

Krysan, Maria. 1998. "Privacy and the Expression of White Racial Attitudes." *Public Opinion Quarterly* 62:506–544.

Kuklinski, James H., and Michael D. Cobb. 1998. "When White Southerners Converse about Race." In *Perception and Prejudice*, ed. Jon Hurwitz and Mark Peffley. New Haven: Yale University Press.

Kuran, Timur. 1995. *Private Truths, Public Lies: The Social Consequences of Preference Falsification*. Cambridge: Harvard University Press.

Ladd, Everett Carll, and John Benson. 1992. "The Growth of News Polls in American Politics." In *Media Polls in American Politics*, ed. Thomas E. Mann and Gary R. Orren. Washington, D.C.: The Brookings Institution.

Ladd, Everett Carll, and Seymour Martin Lipset. 1980. "Public Opinion and Public Policy." In *The United States in the 1980's*, ed. Peter Duignan and Alvin Rabushka. Stanford: Hoover Institution.

Lane, Robert E. 1962. *Political Ideology: Why the Common Man Believes What He Does*. New York: Free Press.

Levinson, Stephen C. 1983. *Pragmatics*. New York: Cambridge University Press.

Lippmann, Walter. 1922. *Public Opinion*. New York: Harcourt, Brace.

———. 1925. *The Phantom Public*. New York: Harcourt, Brace.

Little, Roderick, and Donald Rubin. 1987. *Statistical Analysis with Missing Data*. New York: John Wiley & Sons.

Lowell, A. Lawrence. 1926. "Public Opinion and Majority Government." In *Public Opinion and Popular Government*. New York: Longmans, Green.

Luevano, Patricia. 1994. "Response Rates in the National Election Studies, 1948–1992." National Elections Study Technical Report.

McClosky, Herbert, and Jon Zaller. 1984. *The American Ethos: Public Attitudes toward Capitalism and Democracy*. Cambridge: Harvard University Press.

McConahay, John B. 1986. "Modern Racism, Ambivalence and the Modern Racism Scale." In *Prejudice, Discrimination, and Racism: Theory and Research*, ed. John F. Dovidio and Samuel L. Gaertner. Orlando: Academic Press.

McConnell, Scott. 1990. "The Making of the Mayor 1989." *Commentary* 48: 29–38.

Macpherson, C. B. 1977. *The Life and Times of Liberal Democracy*. Oxford: Oxford University Press.

Maddala, G. S. 1983. *Limited-Dependent and Qualitative Variables in Econometrics*. Cambridge: Cambridge University Press.

Mansbridge, Jane. 1986. *Why We Lost the ERA*. Chicago: University of Chicago Press.

Mendelberg, Tali. 2001. *The Race Card: Campaign Strategy, Implicit Messages, and the Norm of Equality*. Princeton: Princeton University Press.

Merritt, Anna J., and Richard L. Merritt. 1970. *Public Opinion in Occupied Germany: The OMGUS Surveys, 1945–1949*. Urbana: University of Illinois Press.

Mill, John Stuart. 1861. *Considerations on Representative Government*. London: Parker, Son, and Bourn.

Miller, Warren E., and Donald E. Stokes. 1963." Constituency Influence in Congress." *American Political Science Review* 57:45–56.

Modigliani, Andre. 1972. "Hawks and Doves, Isolation and Political Distrust: An Analysis of Public Opinion on Military Policy." *American Political Science Review* 56:960–978.

Moore, David W. 1992. *The Superpollsters: How They Measure and Manipulate Public Opinion in America*. New York: Four Walls Eight Windows.

Morris, Dick. 1997. *Behind the Oval Office: Winning the Presidency in the Nineties*. New York: Random House.

Mueller, John E. 1973. *War, Presidents, and Public Opinion*. New York: Wiley.

Mutz, Diana C. 1998. *Impersonal Influence: How Perceptions of Mass Collectives Affect Political Attitudes*. New York: Cambridge University Press.

Page, Benjamin I., and Robert Y. Shapiro. 1992. *The Rational Public: Fifty Years of Trends in American Policy Preferences*. Chicago: University of Chicago Press.

Pettigrew, Thomas F., and Denise A. Alston. 1988. *Tom Bradley's Campaigns for Governor: The Dilemma of Race and Political Strategies*. Washington, DC: Joint Center for Political Studies.

Reeves, Keith. 1997. *Voting Hopes or Fears? White Voters, Black Candidates and Racial Politics in America*. New York: Oxford University Press.

Richards, Clay. 1989. "Polls Didn't Anticipate Big Turnout by Whites." *Newsday*, November 9, p. 19.

Rodgers, Harrell R., Jr. 1974. "The Supreme Court and School Desegregation: Twenty Years Later." *Political Science Quarterly* 89:751–776.

Roper, Burns W. 1983. "Some Things That Concern Me." *Public Opinion Quarterly* 47:303–309.

Rosenberg, Milton J., Sidney Verba, and Philip E. Converse. 1970. *Vietnam and the Silent Majority*. New York: Harper & Row.

Rosenstone, Steven J., and John Mark Hansen. 1993. *Mobilization, Participation, and Democracy in America*. New York: MacMillian.

Rosenthal, Andrew. 1989. "The 1989 Elections: Predicting the Outcome; Broad Disparities in Votes and Polls Raising Questions." *New York Times*, November 9.

Sanders, Lynn M. 1999. "Democratic Politics and Survey Research." *Philosophy of the Social Sciences* 29:248–280.

Schattschneider, E. E. 1960. *The Semisovereign People: A Realist's View of Democracy in America*. Fort Worth: Harcourt Brace Jovanovich.

Schuman, Howard. 1972. "Two Sources of Antiwar Sentiment in America." *American Journal of Sociology* 78:513–536.

Schuman, Howard, and Jean M. Converse. 1971. "The Effect of Black and White Interviewers on Black Responses." *Public Opinion Quarterly* 35:44–68.

Schuman, Howard, et al. 1997. *Racial Attitudes in America: Trends and Interpretations*. Revised edition. Cambridge: Harvard University Press.

Schwarz, Norbert. 1996. *Cognition and Communication: Judgmental Biases, Research Methods, and the Logic of Conversation*. Mahwah, NJ: L. Erlbaum Associates.

Shapiro, Robert Y., and John T. Young. 1989. "Public Opinion and the Welfare State: The United States in Comparative Perspective." *Political Science Quarterly* 104:59–89.

Singer, Eleanor, Dawn R. Von Thurn, and Esther R. Miller. 1995. "Confidentiality Assurances and Response: A Quantitative Review of the Experimental Literature." *Public Opinion Quarterly* 59:66–77.

Slovic, Paul. 1995. "The Construction of Preference." *American Psychologist* 50:364–371.

Snyder, Mark. 1983. "The Influence of Individuals on Situations: Implications for Understanding the Links between Personality and Social Behavior." *Journal of Personality* 51:497–516.

———. 1987. *Public Appearances/Private Realities: The Psychology of Self-Monitoring*. New York: W. H. Freeman.

Sobel, Richard. 2001. *The Impact of Public Opinion on U.S. Foreign Policy since Vietnam*. New York: Oxford University Press.

Stimson James A., Michael B. MacKuen, and Robert S. Erikson. 1995. "Dynamic Representation." *American Political Science Review* 89:543–565.

Suchman, Lucy, and Brigitte Jordan. 1990. "Interactional Troubles in Face-to-Face Survey Interviews." *Journal of the American Statistical Association* 85:232–253.

———. 1992. "Validity and the Collaborative Construction of Meaning in Face-to-Face Surveys." In *Questions about Questions: Inquiries into the Cognitive Bases of Surveys*, ed. Judith M. Tanur. New York: Russell Sage Foundation.

Sudman, Seymour, Norman M. Bradburn, and Norbert Schwarz. 1996. *Thinking about Answers: The Application of Cognitive Processes to Survey Methodology*. San Francisco: Jossey-Bass Publishers.

Swim, J. K., et al. 1995. "Sexism and Racism: Old Fashioned and Modern Prejudices." *Journal of Personality and Social Psychology* 68:199–214.

Terkildsen, Nayda. 1993. "When White Voters Evaluate Black Candidates: The Processing Implications of Candidate Skin Color, Prejudice, and Self-Monitoring." *American Journal of Political Science* 37:1032–1053.

Tetlock, Philip E. 1986. "Value Pluralism Model of Ideological Reasoning." *Journal of Personality and Social Psychology* 50:819–827.

Tilly, Charles. 1983. "Speaking Your Mind Without Elections, Surveys, or Social Movements." *Public Opinion Quarterly* 47:461–478.

Tourangeau, Roger, and Kenneth Rasinski. 1988. "Cognitive Processes Underlying Context Effects in Attitude Measurement." *Psychological Bulletin* 103:299–314.

Tourangeau, Roger, Lance Rips, and Kenneth Rasinski. 2000. *The Psychology of Survey Response*. Cambridge: Cambridge University Press.

Tourangeau, Roger, and Tom W. Smith. 1996. "Asking Sensitive Questions: The Impact of Data Collection Mode, Question Format, and Question Context." *Public Opinion Quarterly* 60:275–304.

Traugott, Michael W., and Vincent Price. 1992. "Exit Polls in the 1989 Virginia Gubernatorial Race: Where Did They Go Wrong?" *Public Opinion Quarterly* 56:245–253.

Vella, Francis. 1998. Estimating Models with Sample Selection Bias: A Survey." *Journal of Human Resources* 33:127–169.

Verba, Sidney. 1996. "The Citizen as Respondent: Sample Surveys and American Democracy." *American Political Science Review* 90:1–7.

Verba, Sidney, et al. 1967. "Public Opinion and the War in Vietnam." *American Political Science Review* 61:317–333.

Verba, Sidney, and Norman H. Nie. 1972. *Participation in America: Political Democracy and Social Equality*. New York: Harper & Row.

Verba, Sidney, and Gary R. Orren. 1985. *Equality in America: The View from the Top*. Cambridge: Harvard University Press.

Verba, Sidney, et al. 1993. "Citizen Activity: Who Participates? What Do They Say?" *The American Political Science Review* 87:303–318.

Verba, Sidney, Kay Lehman Schlozman, and Henry E. Brady. 1995. *Voice and Equality: Civic Voluntarism in American Politics*. Cambridge: Harvard University Press.

Warren, Kenneth F. 2001. *In Defense of Public Opinion Polling*. Boulder: Westview Press.

Waterbury, Lester E. 1953. "Opinion Surveys in Civil Litigation." *Public Opinion Quarterly* 17:71–90.

Wolfinger, Raymond E., and Steven J. Rosenstone. 1980. *Who Votes*. New Haven: Yale University Press.

Ying, Yu-Wen. 1989. "Nonresponse on the Center for Epidemiological Studies Depression Scale in Chinese Americans." *The International Journal of Social Psychiatry* 35:156–163.

Zaller, John. 1990. "Experimental Tests of the Question-Answering Model of the Mass Survey Response." NES Pilot Study Report.

———. 1992. *The Nature and Origins of Mass Opinion*. Cambridge: Cambridge University Press.

Zaller, John, and Stanley Feldman. 1992. "A Simple Theory of the Survey Response." *American Journal of Political Science* 36:579–616.

Zaroulis, Nancy, and Gerald Sullivan. 1984. *Who Spoke Up?: American Protest against the War in Vietnam*. Garden City, NY: Doubleday.

INDEX